THE
FUNCTIONS
OF
CITIES

FRAN P. HOSKEN

SCHENKMAN PUBLISHING COMPANY
Cambridge, Massachusetts

Schenkman Books are distributed by
GENERAL LEARNING PRESS
250 James Street
Morristown, New Jersey 07960

SCHENKMAN PUBLISHING COMPANY, INC.
Cambridge, Massachusetts 02138

Library of Congress Catalog Card Number: 72-91414

Printed in the United States of America

iv

CONTENTS

v

PREFACE

This book is an attempt to deal with the practical problems of cities in a realistic, firsthand, and new way. Change is the predominant reality of today's cities, while the process of becoming never stops. Therefore these discussions of urban functions and problems take an entirely pragmatic approach. They are based on a series of taped interviews, most of which are also available in taped form.

As a journalist in urban affairs, nationally and internationally, with an academic background in architecture and city planning, I have become aware that cities today change much faster than academic research can follow; frequently carefully collected data are obsolete before they even reach the computer. That is, the future is made every day in the cities by the people, by their actions, and by political decisions in entirely pragmatic ways.

The gap between the academic, research-oriented education, and the real world is ever widening, while teaching about cities is becoming more removed from reality. This book tries to bridge the gap and fill the need to teach about cities in a new and direct way. In my own teaching, I have consistently introduced firsthand journalistic techniques to my students by going out into the city to learn to observe and talk to the people; by visiting the institutions and organizations discussed; by arranging interviews with the administrators and representatives involved. This book is designed to support such a direct approach to teaching about the functions of cities and their institutional framework.

Each of the discussions with a specialist in his field is an attempt to broaden the base from a one-sided, academic view, based on research, to a pragmatic, live discussion of relevant experiences and problems in the city. All the participants have had many years of practical experience in their fields. The topics were chosen to give an overview of the complexity of the urban situation and to serve as a pragmatic introduction to further study. Bibliographies of each topic are supplied.

The introduction to each discussion was carefully prepared to introduce each topic, and the questions were outlined, but the discussion itself was entirely unrehearsed. I am grateful to the contributors for their excellent cooperation in this project and for reading and editing their discussions.

The interviews were taped in the spring of 1970, except for the discussion with Mr. Edward Logue, which was made in November of that year.

The interviews with Mr. Alan Altshuler and Mr. Richard Westebbe were taped in early 1972. All the discussions were updated in early 1972, just prior to delivery of the manuscript to the publishers, in order to make them as relevant and topical as possible.

To students who want to truly learn about cities, I suggest that there is nothing more useful than to work for a city newspaper; to see, hear, smell, and feel the city as it really is, and to observe the people, actions, and problems firsthand, to get "involved." No carefully researched purified book can teach what a city really is or what you can learn on the spot or from interviews with those who make the city scene.

To read carefully every day one or more city newspapers, including the editorial page, is a *sine qua non* for any student of urban affairs. It is the best education that you can buy at any price, with the *New York Times* certainly as first choice. There are many magazines with excellent, extensive research facilities, which publish all kinds of statistics that are more up to date than most books. A clipping file arranged by subject matter and updated continuously is a most useful tool for any student of urban affairs.

For long-range analysis of urban problems, anthologies of urban topics that have recently been published are helpful, especially since any one author can no longer cover the subject of urban affairs, which is becoming more and more specialized. One caveat: the urban field is swamped with publications, while few have anything new to offer, and none have any real solutions. For there are no solutions to the problems of urban life and cities—only a process of change that can and must be guided pragmatically, and that is responsive only to great political pressure and strong leadership.

Cities the world over are becoming very much the same, and the same urban problems in different degrees beset all cities. The beautiful old historic cities of Europe still manage to preserve much of their character by careful protection of their historic buildings and monuments. But their metropolitan areas, where most growth is taking place, are becoming much the same everywhere. Transportation holds the same dilemmas, though sometimes different vehicles are involved; the distance to work is as unreasonable in New York as it is in New Delhi, Tokyo, Buenos Aires, or London. Urban problems are similar everywhere, regardless of what political systems prevail. Buildings are becoming more and more alike, no matter how far north or south, what the geography, or whether the people are black, yellow, or white. Pollution also is quite international by now and is rapidly becoming a foremost concern in developing countries, where exhaust fumes of buses and motorcycles, if not cars, increasingly poison the air.

Two of the discussions are concerned with cities in developing countries, where social and economic problems are at this stage quite overwhelming and virtually defy control. To date, all official action has been quite unable to deal with squatter problems or to produce the jobs and economic base that their urban immigrants so desperately need.

Identifiable city form is disappearing in U.S. metropolitan areas that have become the new cities of today. In the absence of any enforced plans or controls, most metropolitan areas, which have shown their greatest growth these last twenty years, are dissolving into a huge, formless, polycentric mass of urbanization, which is similar from city to city throughout the United States, and covers ever more land with more pollution of every kind.

There are some answers, of course. New cities and the building of a new environment is a commitment for the future and the best hope for positive change, especially in the United States. In many other industrialized countries, new town building is well under way. The final chapter, on new towns, is the sum of my own worldwide experience in the field and is an attempt to translate my observations into a relevant, pragmatic approach to building new communities in the United States. This is a task that still lies before us, one that should open up entirely new directions and become one of the major challenges in the seventies and beyond. At the same time, this final chapter draws on the experiences and problems presented in the preceding discussions.

The lesson of the cities of the United States, clearly, is that the present deterioration of the urban environment and life is due to laissez-faire and greed, to ruthless competition, and public neglect. A city is a joint enterprise undertaken by many for all. The building of new cities and new towns requires planning for the public good; most of all, it requires controls, including self-control, so that all can share a better life and a decent environment.

Franziska P. Hosken
Lexington, Massachusetts
May, 1972

THE FUNCTIONS AND HISTORY OF CITIES

A discussion with HENRY A. MILLON
Professor of History of Architecture, Massachusetts Institute of Technology

INTRODUCTION

In his classic book, *The City in History*,[1] Lewis Mumford begins by asking: What is the city? How did it come into existence? What processes does it further? What functions does it perform? What purposes does it fulfill? These are precisely the questions we want to ask here.

Cities are both the result and cause of specialization. The shift from a rural to an urban way of life is characterized by an increasing differentiation of activities and by dividing into separate, increasingly specialized functions the many actions that constitute urban life. In turn, the form of the cities in their urban design and architecture expresses the functions and institutions of cities, as well as the values and activities of the urban citizens.

Historically, cities were built in strategic locations for the exchange of goods: at trade-route intersections, at harbors, at the mouths of rivers, and at river crossings. All major cities of the United States, from New York to San Francisco, in fact, all cities of the east and west coast and the cities of the great lakes region originated that way. Most of the great historic cities in Europe and cities all over the world began and developed because of their geography: from London and Paris to Vienna, Stockholm, and Istanbul, to Bombay, Hong Kong, and Singapore.

The city traditionally has been the local and regional market place and was built around a central square. Most Mediterranean cities in Italy, and also many old central European towns, have an open market place in their center, usually adjoining or in front of the cathedral or a major church. Spanish cities and their South American counterparts are organized around one or several large open squares used for markets and civic functions. The fact that our shopping centers are now all being built outside the cities, to be used only by people who have cars, has seriously affected the economic vitality of cities.

[1] Lewis Mumford, *The City in History* (New York: Harcourt, Brace and World, 1961).

With better transportation and communication, cities have become more and more specialized economically. London, New York, and Zürich are the financial and banking centers of the world; Paris is known for fashions, while Detroit is the world center for cars. Lausanne and Geneva are famous for their excellent watches and for producing fine scientific and optical instruments. Buying and selling, that is, trade, has been the foremost function of cities throughout history.

Transportation is intimately tied to the economic function of cities, as trade centers and as developers of specialized industry. The movement of people and goods is one of the basic needs of the city which determines its economic success as well as its development and form. Good transportation, for instance, rivers and harbors, is a determining factor in the initial location of a city and its entire physical development. Transportation problems and complaints about traffic congestion, crowding, and noise in cities go back to antiquity. Even in ancient Rome, rules had to be made against proliferating chariot traffic and carts that clogged the streets.

Cities from antiquity on were no larger than people could comfortably walk. The number of people who lived in any one city was limited by available transportation. Therefore, there was some social coherence; people met in the streets regularly and got to know each other through common pursuits. With the Industrial Revolution, many more people were needed to work for industry in factories, which were of course located in the cities, preferably close to some transportation. The railroad station became a new center of town, and trolley lines rapidly expanded the size of the city.

But the arrival of cars has utterly changed urban life and urban form. Highways today are destroying the fabric of cities and are accelerating the collapse of the communal functions of urban life. Yet traffic problems are increasing everywhere. Despite all kinds of mechanization and technology, transportation is a major problem of all urban inhabitants today as in the past.

The city traditionally was the home for its citizens. But housing today has become one of the most neglected functions of cities in the United States, with the result that more and more people are continually leaving the cities for the suburbs because of the lack of decent, attractive places to live that they can afford. Yet cities are communities for people, and when many people move out, something is very wrong.

Most of the urban housing in the United States was built after the Industrial Revolution, in response to business and industrial needs, and it was inhabited first by European immigrants. It was speculatively built for quick profits and often lacked the most basic sanitary provisions, as well as community facilities or recreation space of any kind. Unfortunately, much of this housing still exists, as the vast slums of all U.S. cities testify: from Harlem and Roxbury to the Chicago South Side. Most of this housing is now inhabited by blacks and minorities. Despite urban renewal, we have not even started to replan and rebuild these overcrowded, obsolete, deteriorating areas.

Defense and protection of a country has been one of the historic functions of cities and the reason why many cities were originally built. Many European cities began as Roman camps to protect the imperial borders, such as Vienna, Cologne, and many other cities along the Danube and the Rhine.

The medieval city was surrounded by a high wall and impenetrable fortifications of all kinds. These were both useful and needed at a time when roving bands pillaged the countryside, and plundering was the chief goal of war. Some cities around the world still have left standing some of their fortifications: Carcasonne in France, for instance, and several Italian cities, such as Lucca, Sienna, and San Giminiano. Many cities in Europe derive their shape from the original medieval cities; in others one can still discern street patterns that go back to Roman times.

Many of these cities were built around a castle or palace for protection. Thus the governmental and protective functions were central and highly visible. The secular and religious administrative functions were handled by the princes of the state and church, who occupied palaces in the center of town.

The cathedral, the house of God, symbolizing the religious function, surpassed in importance every other building in many historic cities and towns. That is, the religious function served as physical organizer of most European cities. Long before that, in antiquity, the Acropolis, the "high city" or "city of the gods," was the focus and center of many Greek cities. In ancient Rome, the Forum, or market place, together with the temples, was the social and physical center of town. At present, the modern office skyscraper dominates the image of the city, taking the physical place of the cathedrals of medieval times.

Cultural and recreational facilities have historically been part of every city, with parks and green areas and public open spaces designed for the use and enjoyment of people. Festivals and fairs, parades, and celebrations of all kinds have always attracted people to cities everywhere and have contributed to the sense of community of the urban citizens. Games and sport competitions have been identified with certain cities since Olympia in ancient Greece.

The city always has been the center of education and the location for universities. Many cities have become famous due to their universities, such as Padua and Bologna in the Renaissance, and later the German university cities. Oxford and Cambridge gave their names to their universities, and, in turn, university-cities within the city grew in Paris, Edinburgh, Vienna, and many other European towns. In turn, the city *itself* is the provider of education and information: through its many artifacts and symbols—from traffic lights to advertisements, from fire plugs to phone booths and street signs of all kinds—

the urban environment continually teaches and communicates with every citizen.

Existing functions of cities continually change and new ones emerge, while traditional ones disappear: all this change is expressed in the changing city form. The functions of cities must serve the citizens and the urban community. As their needs change, so does the city's form.

DISCUSSION

F.P.H.   Mr. Millon, I think we agree that, historically, cities are communities for people and their many different pursuits. But I fear the concept of the city, as a place that offers face-to-face contact, where all kinds of people can meet and mingle, has been lost, especially since the introduction of cars.

The present lack of "community," of any social or even physical coherence, destroys the meaning of the city. Cities have become too large. What do you think is happening to cities today, and how is their historic concept distorted by our present-day use?

H.A.M.   I am not sure that your analysis of the destruction of the city is an accurate one. It seems to me you are giving voice to a traditional lament that has existed since biblical times. You are blaming the current dissatisfaction with the city on technological advances and transportation.

The city as a center of evil, as the place of the machine, in opposition to the garden—the Garden of Eden—has a long history. One might look, for instance, at Leo Marx's *The Machine in the Garden*,[2] or Morton and Lucia White's *The Intellectual Versus the City*,[3] as two examples that define the antipathy of some people for the city. It should be clear that there have always existed many diverse views about the nature of the city.

The city depends first of all upon the economic well-being of the region. Our traditional definition of the city as something which is the center of an urban area probably needs to be changed and should include all that is normally called the sprawl around the city.

F.P.H.   You mean that our historic concept of the limited city, which was really created by the city wall, is gone. Instead the metropolitan area is becoming our new city of today.

H.A.M.   I think that is true. But it is also incorrect to imagine the historic city as a sharply contained and walled city. It is partly true if you are

---

[2] Leo Marx, *The Machine in the Garden* (New York: Oxford Press, 1964).

[3] Morton and Lucia White, *The Intellectual Versus the City* (Cambridge, Mass.: Harvard University Press and the MIT Press, 1962).

selective in the examples you choose. But it is also possible to select others that demonstrate sprawl even in ancient and medieval times and also in the Renaissance.

The key issue is always our viewpoint: The city is the result of what man thinks it is, rather than any other set of circumstances.

F.P.H.   Perhaps you can say that people are conscious of their environment in different ways. Throughout history people have been proud of their own cities. They had a sense of belonging and allegiance, a sense of community. In turn, the rulers of a city secured their place in history as a result of the improvements they made in their city, what they built to make it a better place to live. It was always the ambition of each king, prince, or ruler of a city to build an important new building, a church, market, palace, or monument.

H.A.M.   I think there are two issues here. One of them you quite rightly point to is the ruler and his relation to cities. Historically, one of the functions of a ruler, and, indeed, it was only a ruler who could do this, was the founding of cities. Great kings were known by the cities they founded. In other words, it was a royal prerogative to found cities. This also translated itself into the actions that a ruler made within existing cities, which were not only for the pride of the city, but had clear political ends.

If we look at Mr. Mumford's questions, what functions does the city perform or what function does a new building perform, we have to agree that building was done for political reasons, to win the approbation of the populace. The alterations or gifts to the city of Rome by Roman emperors, clearly, were political moves.

The way towns have been built in the recent past also seems to indicate political motives. First, there are political reasons for the location of the towns as well as for decisions about distributing land among their citizens. Both were influenced by the desire to strengthen the rule over a particular area by the king who founded the new town.

F.P.H.   But I think there was also a motivation on the part of the citizen. A citizen was proud of "his city" and had a sense of belonging. For instance, it was a great distinction to be a citizen of Rome, and only distinguished people received Roman citizenship. To be a citizen of Vienna was very desirable as opposed to living elsewhere in the Austrian Empire. And, certainly, every Frenchman wanted to be a Parisian, because Paris was without a doubt in his mind the center of the world.

At the same time, the people who lived in a certain town would defend it as "the best town," especially against inhabitants of another town. In turn, they took pride in their own house and neighborhood, or the parish to which they belonged. In many cases, people and their families lived in the same houses and neighborhoods for generations.

H.A.M.   That is the other part. I was thinking first of the role of the ruler. The second part is this issue of how an individual relates to the city where he lives. There are also people today who are proud to be Romans, or Parisians, or Bostonians, or New Yorkers. One only needs to read *The New Yorker* magazine or examine the traditional New Yorker's view of the world in order to see how proud the New Yorker is of his city. It is legendary what Bostonians feel about Boston, and Elizabeth Hardwick[4] in her book has shown how Bostonians have come to feel the way they do.

It seems to me that Athens was criticized in its day, as well as praised, and so was Rome. Cities still compete with one another for prizes. We only need to think about the competition for World's Fairs or for the Olympic Games. Clearly cities have pride. That pride shows also in the athletic teams which the cities have. I think we tend to overly exalt the view that a citizen had of his relationship with the city in the past. It may not be so very unlike the view that, for instance, a citizen of Boston has today about the qualities of Boston or its athletic teams.

F.P.H.   Yet today we ruthlessly tear down even some very beautiful historic buildings and monuments, simply to give way to commercial development. This happens in every city in the United States. People here seem quite oblivious of the architectural values of the past which surround them in the buildings of their cities. We are not taking care of our own architectural inheritance.

At the National Conference on Architectural Review Landmarks and Historic Districts held recently in Boston, some methods were defined of how to preserve historic buildings and areas. We also finally have some legislation to preserve historic buildings and districts. Not only the National Trust for Historic Preservation has numerous programs in this area, but HUD, the Department of Housing and Urban Development, is actively interested in historic rehabilitation, in terms of making funds available for that purpose.

Preservation is of interest not only to us but to our children. Perhaps we could discuss the methods of how to safeguard this part of our heritage.

H.A.M.   That is an interesting question. There are two viewpoints. One says the past does not have the right to deny to the present the development of its possibilities. And there is the viewpoint that William Morris stated, that the

[4] Elizabeth Hardwick, *"Boston: A View of My Own"* (New York: Noonday, 1962), pp. 145-149.

present does not have the right to deny to the future the appreciation of the past. Both, it seems to me, make some sense.

The history of the preservation movement throughout the world has been a dialogue between these two positions: the position of progress and the position of conservation. This dialogue goes on in the political arena, as well as in the intellectual arena. There is no clear view and no consistent view about what must be preserved and what ought to be destroyed to make way for something new. Our views about conservation are always changing and must be allowed to be reviewed. Because of the two points of view about conservation, there is a constant discussion.

There are those who argue that historic buildings, in fact, all old buildings, can continue to perform creditably in today's changed circumstances. As example they show that high quality floor space (after rehabilitation and renovation of the old building shells) turns out to cost much less than space in new construction. This is a clear issue for rehabilitation of both residential and office buildings. The second point is the importance of continuity with the past, reinforcing those qualities which continue to be important today.

By our selectivity in destroying or not destroying buildings, we reinforce certain aspects of past values. This action essentially reflects our critical view of the past; it is constantly changing and must be under constant discussion.

F.P.H.　In this connection, one of the important issues of the Boston Urban Renewal effort has been the emphasis on renewal of historic buildings. I think a very thorough survey was made of the historic market area around Faneuil Hall. Of course, Faneuil Hall itself is one of the most interesting historic buildings of Boston. The whole area was surveyed for buildings that should be preserved and renewed from inside out. In each case, the historic exterior is preserved and rehabilitated. Modern services are put into the buildings, such as elevators, plumbing, wiring, and so on.

Another example is the Quincy Market, which will be renewed inside by a commercial developer, while HUD is funding the exterior renovation, under the Urban Renewal program. This is a very interesting departure from the old method of simply tearing down and building something else in its place. Considering Boston's outstanding historic architectural heritage, this is particularly important.

H.A.M.　Yes, that is a splendid example of a more enlightened view than has existed in the past. The Quincy Market's superb granite building would grace any urban environment. The two rows of buildings on the north and the south of the Market, both built by Mayor Josiah Quincy, will also be restored, and this is where I have to voice a reservation about rigidly historic renovations.

From the early nineteenth century when they were constructed, the two rows of commercial buildings have continuously changed. There have been additional stories put on and dormers added. Changes have been made on the exteriors of all the buildings. These alterations have always seemed to be a marvelous demonstration of the way buildings are adapted to changing needs. But the renovation of the buildings will return them to their original 1830 character and will no longer show changes made over time, demonstrating how these buildings are a part of a living area. It seems to me that is a mistake.

Still another example is Boston's City Hall. To remove Scollay Square was a political and social decision. The argument was that the old Scollay Square area had to be torn down to build a new Government Center. The building of the new Government Center with a new monumental City Hall was based on the view that Boston needed this great new symbol. In the City government's terms, the Scollay Square area was a blot on the face of Boston. It was overlooked that in 1860 a great new symbol had been built in the old City Hall. But that symbol was not able to sustain itself. The constantly changing value of symbols is most important, and we should have an open and continuing dialogue about the changing role and value of buildings in the urban environment.

F.P.H.   I think what you say is very important. The city is a process. The whole way the city is built is a continuous process and is recorded in the city's form. We should not arbitrarily pick out one building and restore it to its original shape and form. A city bears witness to the continuous change of all its functions by its physical form. In its changing form, the city expresses the changing functions of urban life.

We should discuss here also the fact that the majority of people don't take an interest in their urban environment and cities. They want to get away from the cities and live dispersed among greenery and trees.

The city's original purpose, to my mind, is community and communication; it is to meet other people, to get together with many different people and have variety. Face-to-face contact cannot be replaced with electronic communication. The city as environment should favor this by its design or the arrangement of the buildings. There should be squares and areas where people can meet informally; where they can come together without an invitation; where they can engage in all kinds of informal activities, in marketing and shopping, in just plan fun, like parades and meetings and shows.

All the traditional functions of the city are being dispersed throughout the metropolitan area. We are destroying the city as community of and for people. I think the community function is still most important for cities. But we give it no room in the way we live and in the way our urban environment is organized and built.

H.A.M.   I think the idea of a city as community goes back to a time when the city was relatively small. As some cities grew, they tried to preserve this sense of community by adding more communities to the city. Particularly in the smaller cities, it has been possible to maintain some sense of community within the larger city.

F.P.H.   But cities traditionally adopted their surrounding communities. This was a continuous process which has stopped. Now we find the city is a politically bordered area, surrounded by suburbs that proclaim quite different values.

H.A.M.   Well, I am not sure about that. There is a very long and strong tradition in this country of people owning a piece of property, a house with a garden. That tradition goes back to England and the view of man as an independent individual on his own property.

The nineteenth century city that developed in the United States prior to the trolley railway system had to have great density. It is probably not a result of a conscious choice to have continuous-row housing, but it was a necessity due to the numbers of people who had to live near their places of work. When the trolley came, you could get away from the city and have your own piece of ground and your own house. Everyone who could moved out.

I think it is too simple for us to say that there was a coherent idea of what a city was in the seventeenth, eighteenth, and early nineteenth centuries and that that idea has been destroyed. It is, on the other hand, very likely that the idea of the garden city was limited in the past by the distance that people could walk in the absence of transportation.

F.P.H.   Walking in a city should not only be a pleasant recreational activity, but on foot one can see the urban environment in quite a different and more intimate way. However, some cities are entirely built for cars. If you try to walk in Los Angeles, for instance, not only are you likely to be the only person on the street, but it may happen that a police car comes along to ask if there is something wrong as it is too unusual, in some sections of town, to find anyone walking.

In turn, if you talk to young people in many of the suburbs, their complaint is that there is no place to go, there is nothing to do. They hang around in front of drug stores or ice cream parlors and become a nuisance for the rest of the people, simply because there is nowhere for them to go to meet their friends informally.

I think a city should provide places to meet because people have not lost their need to meet one another and to get together.

H.A.M.   There are two issues here. One of them is that there *is* no place to go in the cities. That is specifically a physical problem, an architectural problem that requires some action on the part of the city. Take, for example, Boston's City Hall Plaza. Along the edges of the Plaza are few places where one can stop. Along the arcaded side is a series of stores into which you go in order to buy something, but none of them are *places to be.* The same is true of the whole City Hall Plaza. With a little bit of attention the space might have been made into a series of places for people *to be* instead of non-places as they are now. I am concerned not only about public places, but about all open spaces and places where commercial activities are carried on. We are not providing spaces for people. But this is only part of it. Where I think you and I probably disagree is that in some sense Los Angeles, I think, may really be the model city of the future. We are making a grave error to assume that the tightly knit city of the past should continue in the future. It was tightly knit because of the absence of transportation. Los Angeles may indeed be the dispersed city of the future.

F.P.H.   In the past, "grand master plans" were prepared to guide the development of cities. The famous saying, "make no little plans," goes back to the Chicago plan by Burnham. All cities seem to have some form, except Los Angeles. Philadelphia and Washington were originally built according to a master plan. The redevelopment of Philadelphia that is taking place now is going back to that original Philadelphia plan. Many people go abroad just to see the cities of Europe, because they are beautiful and attractive places to be. Most of these cities are built according to a definite plan.

Los Angeles has no plan at all. It grows according to where commercial enterprises locate, and this is wherever it happens to be most profitable for each business. In fact, this is the way most metropolitan areas of United States cities grow today. Change is one of the realities of cities today. I see the functions of cities continuously changing through time, and I am not at all sure about the future. What do you believe the future holds for cities.

H.A.M.   Mrs. Moholy-Nagy's[5] book on city form documents fully what interests me here. She distinguishes between different types of cities. She talks at length about the "merchant *ad hoc* city". It seems to me that Los

[5] Sibyl Moholy-Nagy, *Matrix of Man* (New York, Washington, London: Frederick A. Praeger, 1968).

Angeles is a marvelous example of an *ad hoc* city. I would imagine that in the future we shall see a great deal more development of the *ad hoc* type, in other words cities with no overall planned development.

I think what is being done in Philadelphia is a disaster. The Washington Plan for the development of Pennsylvania Avenue and the National Square are also disastrous because those both represent overall planning schemes which are particularly desiccated. It seems to me, questions of *ad hoc* development are most important. It means that, rather than reviewing a development in relation to some large master plan for the future of a whole city, that we should see it always in terms of present need. In this way, the form of cities is not based on an idea several hundred years old, nor on one that we imagine will occur, but is constantly changing and responding to present needs.

F.P.H.   You really are saying that the traditional functions of the city should accommodate themselves constantly to changing needs, regardless of any preconceived notions or plans. Demographers have predicted that our population will be 300 million by the year 2000. These people will have to live somewhere. Most of them will come into the metropolitan areas because this is where most jobs will be. The question is, where and how will they settle and live? What kind of communities will be built? For instance, it has been predicted that New York will about double the size of its metropolitan population. What kind of quality of life will be the result of this uncontrolled *ad hoc* development? What will be the resulting environmental pollution? To my mind, this is a fundamental question.

H.A.M.   If we look, for example, at what might happen to New York or to Boston or to Los Angeles, the most important factor is to what degree these cities can be expanded. There are cities that have limited land, and New York or New Orleans are good examples. In those cities the land will have to become more and more intensely used.

Where a city has a chance of expanding, for instance, Los Angeles, you expect the expansion to continue and to maintain low density as long as it is possible.

The effect on people must also be considered in terms of what the governmental planning decisions are, because they are essentially representatives of the people. If the present is any indication, I imagine that in the future the city government and the planning agencies will become much more responsive to people's changing needs. The city will have to be operating on a much more *ad hoc* basis, willing to change rapidly and more easily than in the past. This means new kinds of buildings that are more capable of change and new kinds of systems within the city that will allow major changes to be made and more easily and more effectively in response to the needs and desires of citizens.

F.P.H.   I think the essential fact is for cities to change according to people's needs.
Thank you, Mr. Millon.

BIBLIOGRAPHY

Millon, Henry A., and Frazer, Alfred. *Key Monuments of the History of Architecture.* New York: Harry N. Abrams, Inc. No date.
Beautifully illustrated architectural history.

BOOKS

Churchill, Henry S. *The City is the People.* New York: W. W. Norton and Company, 1962. Paperback.
A classic, defining man's relationship to cities.
Giedion, Sigfried. *Space, Time and Architecture.* Cambridge, Mass.: Harvard University Press, 1967.
The most important book about the development of our urban environment written by the foremost architectural historian.
———. *Mechanization Takes Command.* New York: W.W. Norton and Company, 1961. Paperback.
A follow-up to *Space, Time and Architecture,* emphasizing mechanical inventions.
Handlin, Oscar, and Burchard, John, eds. *The Historian and the City.* Cambridge, Mass.: The MIT Press and Harvard University Press, 1963.
A historian's view of cities.
Hardwick, Elizabeth. *"Boston": A View of My Own.* New York: Noonday, 1962.
Hosken, Fran P. *The Language of Cities,* 2nd ed., Cambridge, Mass.: Schenkman Publishing Co., 1972. Paperback.
A visual analysis of urban functions.
Marx, Leo. *The Machine in the Garden.* New York: Oxford University Press, 1964.
Moholy-Nagy, Sibyl. *Matrix of Man: An Illustrated History of Urban Environment.* New York: Frederick A. Praeger, 1968.
Mumford, Lewis. *The City in History.* New York: Harcourt, Brace and World, 1961.
The most important history of cities, from antiquity to the present.
———. *Techniques and Civilization.* New York: Harcourt, Brace and World, Harbinger Book, 1963. Paperback.
———. *The Urban Prospect.* New York: Harcourt, Brace and World, 1968.
Rasmussen, Steen Eiler. *Towns and Buildings.* Cambridge, Mass.: MIT Press, 1969. Paperback.
A visual analysis of the urban environment.

White, Morton and Lucia. *The Intellectual Versus the City.* Cambridge, Mass.:
    The MIT Press and Harvard University Press, 1962.
    A most important book defining urban attitudes.
Whitehill, Walter Muir. *Boston: A Topographical History.* Cambridge, Mass.:
    The Belknap Press of Harvard University Press, 1963.
    The best history of Boston.

                                ARTICLES

"New Blood for the Heart of Olde Boston," *Boston Sunday Herald,* June 7,
    1970, Magazine section, p. 4.

2

URBAN ECONOMICS

A discussion with ALEXANDER GANZ
Boston Redevelopment Authority and Department of Urban
Studies and Planning, Massachusetts Institute of Technology

INTRODUCTION

Economics, as many economists attest, is an art and not an exact science. While scientific research and accurate statistics are a *sine qua non*, economists cannot forecast results with complete assurance. Because economic predictions are subject to all kinds of human influences, from unfounded rumors and political pressures to irrational fears, they can only represent educated guesses of the future.

Economic policies are based on political decisions; hence they should not be left to specialists. The economic policies that are made in Washington and by governments all over the world directly affect the pocketbooks of all citizens. These policies control the rate of unemployment and inflation and the creation of jobs. They set the taxes in every area, they influence the stock market and how much each one of us pays for a home or for rent.

Economic policies of the government also greatly influence what happens in cities. Government decisions of how and where public funds are spent influence the quality of life of every urban citizen. Economic decisions determine how federal money is used—that is your taxes and mine—for city services, for education and social programs, or for armaments and flying to the moon.

Our urban economy now is mainly concerned with services. As the economy of a country or region develops, it shifts from an agricultural economy to an industrial economy, and finally to a service economy. That is, more jobs are opening up in the growing service sector of the economy as more people live in urban areas.

Industrial production, by using new management techniques and automation, employs fewer people, while the service sector becomes more sophisticated and proliferates. Many typical service jobs, for instance computer programming or television repair, did not exist thirty years ago.

An urban, service-dominated economy depends heavily on skills, and skilled employment requires training. Hence, the paradox of unemployment and the city Sunday papers each week proclaiming in want ads the need for skilled personnel. Many of the city inhabitants lack the skills required for employment in many of the sophisticated urban service jobs. Job training, even though now heavily supported by governmental funds and programs, is still unable to coordinate the unemployed seeking work with the demand for help. This dislocation is strongest in the service sector, which dominates the urban economy.

The urban economy can thus be defined as a service economy. Urban economics can also be defined as being concerned with all those decisions and policies that influence cities. The urban economy affects all the people who live in an urban environment, who make their living producing goods and services rather than growing crops on the land.

Since nearly 80 per cent of the U. S. population now lives in urban areas where most goods and services are produced on which people depend, it is clear that what happens in our cities and metropolitan areas has a decisive influence on the economic well-being of everyone. For one thing, the cities produce most of the taxes that are used by the federal government. Therefore, the federal economic policies and programs for cities are of major importance to the whole country.

Unfortunately, the present economic policies of Washington are seriously threatening the economic viability of cities. More and more cities are rapidly approaching economic collapse. Their services, such as schools, transportation, garbage removal, and police protection, are deteriorating due to mounting financial deficits and the inability to produce enough local taxes, mainly through the property tax, for local expenditures. Most of the tax revenue produced in cities by business and industry is sent to Washington, and too little is returned.

Inflation and recent federal policies to control inflation are greatly contributing to the cities' financial difficulties. Inflation is a major problem that has periodically hit all modern industrial societies. Like all large-scale economic problems, inflation is hard to control through policy.

Generally, inflation is created when money is plentiful and goods and services are scarce. According to the law of supply and demand, this increases the cost of goods and services and decreases the value of money. As a result, prices go up.

The reason for our present inflation is our inflated defense and war spending. The statistics of the late 1960's confirm the correlation between the rise in the cost of living with the escalation of defense-and-war spending. Defense-and-war spending do not produce consumer goods. However, the wage earners employed in defense- and war-related industries compete in the market for consumer goods they don't produce.

The cities were hard hit by inflation, which escalated all their costs. When interest rates were drastically increased by the Nixon administration, cities, which heavily depend on borrowing, were badly hit again. Finally, unemployment, which is a result of the economic policies of the administration, affects the cities most of all, as the least skilled people who have the greatest difficulties finding jobs mostly live in cities.

At present, the debt service of every city is growing, while tax income is decreasing and welfare payments continue to increase due to growing unemployment. As a result, cities have to reduce services, which further increases urban unemployment, while the quality of life and the environment deteriorate. More and more cities are facing bankruptcy, and some cities have had to close their schools before the end of the school year, as they had no more funds.

The recent partial controls, price and wage freezes, have not helped the cities, as unemployment continues, and therefore welfare costs continue to grow—while all federal urban programs, on which cities depend, have been substantially reduced.

DISCUSSION

F.P.H.   Professor Ganz, since you are concerned with the economy of cities, how is inflation affecting cities? It seems to me that what is happening is very serious indeed.

A.G.   Cities are having an extraordinarily great difficulty in funding essential services such as schools, hospitals, water works, and other long-term projects. The municipal-bond market is drying up. Costs are accelerating faster than revenue.

F.P.H.   The cost of money also is increasing. The recent high interest rates set by the Federal Reserve Bank as a result of federal policies have greatly increased cities' debts.

A.G.   Cities all over the country are postponing the construction of essential public facilities and urgently needed public works. Urban redevelopment all over the country is being held up and postponed.

F.P.H.   But, in the final analysis, these projects are necessary and have to be built, and, if they are postponed, this does not really save anything at all.

We are simply piling up the debts and difficulties for future years. And we are generating social troubles as a result. Certainly, housing is one area that, it seems to me, has been hit very badly and most of all in the cities. Cities desperately lack housing, not only for the poor, but also for the middle-income groups.

A.G.   That is right. The urgent need for housing, especially for low-income families, is not being met, either by the private sector or the public sector. Federal funds are drying up. The private sector has found that it cannot build low-income housing at an interest rate of 8 or 9 per cent.

F.P.H.   The housing bill of 1968 estimated that in order to satisfy the needs of the growing population, that is, the people who were the war babies and who are forming families now, we should build at the rate of approximately 2.6 million housing units a year just to keep the current demands satisfied, with a sizeable percentage for low-income families. I understand that until quite recently we were building at only half that rate. That means we have accumulated a very large deficit. While recently housing has been booming, this is mainly in the middle- and upper-income groups or in mobile home construction. But there is little or no housing being built for low-income people in the cities.

A.G.   Our present economic and monetary policy is just not channeling a sufficient volume of funds to housing in the cities. In our economy at the present time, housing for low-income people—where the greatest demand is—does not have a sufficiently high priority. So we are accumulating a large volume of postponed needs and postponed advances in our living standards.

F.P.H.   We are living on borrowed time and money. Our national budget has the highest deficits in history, which increases inflation. The cities have not recovered from the recent high interest rates, which also affect all home owners. Even though interest rates have slightly decreased in 1971, they are still too high, and cities must borrow more and more to pay for past debts, while they cannot cope with current needs.

A.G.   Well, in our economy at the present time the biggest caller on available savings is the defense department. To this fact is added the big demand for manufacturers' plants and equipment. Very little is left and available for the less competitive sectors, especially municipal finance.

F.P.H.   One other result of the recent throttling down of the economy is the creation of unemployment. But unemployment hits most of all the inner cities, because the largest number of unskilled people live here. These are people who have recently come to the cities mainly from the South or in some cities from Puerto Rico to Mexico. They are unused to urban life and unskilled, while the urban service economy needs highly skilled workers. The result is that the cities have enormous welfare bills on top of all the additional services the immigrants need, while the cities' income is constantly shrinking.

A.G.   The large cities are performing a national task of absorbing and up-grading the largest migration of disadvantaged families in our nation's history, with insufficient help from the federal government. The cities as a conse-quence have a concentration of unemployment and poverty in deteriorating neighborhoods.

F.P.H.   Unemployment is now the highest in many years. But inner cities' unemployment is more than twice the national average, especially among the unskilled workers and young people. Unemployment has reached crisis pro-portions among black and Puerto Rican young men.

This situation creates a great deal of social unrest and must be met by urban programs or by some method of employing young people gainfully. The paradox is that there are so many jobs that need to be done in the urban public service sector that don't get done for lack of public funds. Or when funds are available skilled jobs cannot be filled by people who lack in educa-tion and skills which city schools fail to provide.

A.G.   What is happening is that expanding service-activity jobs available in the cities require greater skills than the newly immigrated workers have, whereas the manufacturing jobs that provided earlier generations a ladder of opportunities are now in the suburbs, out of reach.

F.P.H.   Many inner-city workers cannot afford a car to get to work, and there is insufficient public transportation. Industry has moved out of the cities because of the high city taxes; yet the people who used to be employed by these industries live in the cities for lack of housing they can afford in the suburbs. The people who work in the cities, the office and professional work-ers, mostly live outside the cities in the suburbs. This certainly contributes to the economic difficulties of the cities, because many of their prime taxpayers have been removed.

A.G.   Now, there are ways in which the situation of the cities could be improved. For example, if the federal government would absorb the cost of education and welfare, the cities would then be able to concentrate their scarce revenues on their other urgent needs for urban redevelopment, and for economic development, for services for their disadvantaged population, and for replacement of their obsolescent buildings and facilities.

F.P.H.   In most parts of the country, white suburbs surround increasingly black cities. Suburbs and cities don't cooperate; they have different tax systems, different administrative systems, and different service systems. City governments have suggested that the people who come to work from the suburbs, who use the facilities and services of the cities, should pay a payroll tax. I believe some cities have started that. Do you think that would help?

A.G.   This is precisely the kind of approach that is needed. The present tax base of the cities places them at a great disadvantage. The tax base is geared, for the most part, to their population role, but not geared to their income-generation role. Now, it happens that in our large cities their income-generation role is greater than their population role.

Our thirty largest cities presently house about half their metropolitan area's population, but they have some three-fourths of their metropolitan area's production of goods and services. Their public service requirements are geared more closely to their production-of-goods-and-services role rather than to their population role. Therefore, it would be more appropriate that a tax base also should be associated with their income-generation or goods-and-services-production role. The payroll tax or value-added tax would therefore greatly benefit the cities by relating the tax structure to the cities' much larger role in the metropolitan area economy, that is, to their role as generators of income and producers of goods and services.

F.P.H.   Metropolitan government has been cited as one answer for some of these problems. Should we combine the suburbs and cities into larger units? This has happened in certain service sectors already. For instance, water supply and transportation don't follow the political lines, but they follow the lines of need and demand.

A.G.   Metropolitan government is a long-term and perhaps a utopian solution of much merit, but one that is likely to take a generation or more to come about. In the meantime, there are immediate needs and potential solutions to the problems of the city that must be developed around the present institutional framework. The payroll tax or value-added tax, given the present institutional framework, could be an important measure that would immediately provide the city with an improved tax base.

F.P.H.   The tax the cities most depend on is the property tax. Yet the property tax has been termed a regressive tax. It means that, for instance, a business building is taxed according to its "assessed value," rather than on the income that the building produces. The property tax changes annually, based on the needs of the city; so you never know from one year to the next what you will have to pay.

In Boston, for instance, the property tax is particularly high. About ten years ago the property tax of Boston was under $100 per thousand dollars of assessed value. Now it is over $174 per thousand dollars and increasing annually at a rate over 10 per cent. At present Boston has the highest property tax of all major U. S. cities. One reason is that, due to the many institutions, Boston has the largest tax exempt land area. Many businesses are leaving Boston for the suburbs and metropolitan areas, where the property tax is lower. In turn, there is competition between different cities, which all want to attract tax-paying businesses to improve their own financial situation. The property tax, it seems to me, is to blame for many of the difficulties that the cities face today.

A.G.   That is correct. The property tax does not serve our largest cities well in general, and in the case of Boston, it serves the city of Boston rather badly. Because of lags in updating assessments and because of many tax-free institutions, the property-tax yield in the city of Boston and in other large cities does not grow as rapidly as their income-generating role and their goods-and-service-production role, whereas the call on public services *is* based proportionally on their income-generating role and goods-and-services-production role.

In the case of Boston, for example, it might be interesting to point out that, whereas Boston has only one-fourth of its metropolitan area's population, it makes up one-half of the generation of income and production of goods and services of the metropolitan area. Now, the services that Boston is called upon to provide are geared to this latter role, whereas the property-tax base rather badly reflects the recent decline in Boston's population.

So, here we have the basic fundamental contradiction. The city's tax base is reflecting one role, the slow-growing or declining population role; whereas its tax needs reflect its expanding role as a producer of goods and services and generator of income in the surrounding metropolitan area.

F.P.H.   Certainly, in Boston, I think, the situation of the city versus the surrounding suburbs is extreme. The city of Boston, I believe, has less than 650 thousand people now and is losing population. While the metropolitan area has something like 2½ million and is increasing in population rapidly. Boston is one of the oldest cities and has not adopted any surrounding areas for a long time. While in the past it was advantageous for surrounding communities to join the city, just the opposite is true now, and taxes are one reason.

The property tax has been called excessive and confiscatory with much justification. There have been all kinds of proposals to change the tax base of cities for many years. Yet I don't see any changes being made. Despite complaints, all the cities continue to rely on the property tax.

A.G.   I think that what we need is a basic educational campaign to persuade states to adopt value-added taxes or payroll taxes, which would be returned to the place of location of the economic activity. Such a change in tax structure would greatly benefit the cities and make them less dependent on other types of federal and state aid.

F.P.H.   At the present time the cities seem to be hard hit on every side by inflation, by the general curtailment of federal programs, by the high interest rates, by the increasing costs of city government. There have been numerous strikes by service workers' unions that have highlighted the situation, particulary in New York—for instance, the transportation worker strike and the garbage collectors' strike. In addition, police and firemen all want more pay. It seems to me that the cities just cannot cope any longer with their financial burden. What do you think of their economic future?

A.G.   Actually, I have just been completing a rather intensive study of the post-war development and future prospects of our thirty largest cities. I find that their recent evolution and future potential is good. Since the early 1960's, our large cities are no longer net losers of jobs. In addition, they have undergone rather fundamental changes in their economic structure and their economic role. While losing manufacturing jobs, they have been expanding their role as regional service activity centers. Productivity is expanding in the central cities, and the generation of income is growing substantially. The cities have a good economic potential.

F.P.H.   Though you sound hopeful about the future economic outlook, there is one problem in the cities that I would like to discuss. It seems that more and more housing is being abandoned by its owners. The cities are becoming involuntary heirs to all this tax-delinquent property. It seems to me that this is a very unhealthy situation when housing and other property can no longer make any tangible financial return, and the owners simply abandon their property. The low-income tenants in particular are the losers because more and more housing is removed from the market.

A.G.   The question you point to illustrates a fundamental diseconomy in the situation of the cities. On the one hand, the cities' economies for the production of goods and services are going relatively well and have a good potential. On the other hand, the cities do have very severe problems. They have the problem of obsolescence that you've just pointed to. They have the problem of unjust fiscal squeeze that we've been discussing. They also have a problem of poverty and concentration of unemployment in deteriorating neighborhoods. And they have a problem of poor transportation.

The unique observation can be made that the cities are experiencing both things at the same time: a moderately growing economy, with significant expansion in income and production of goods and services, coupled with a host of fundamental problems. But the hope for the future lies in the fact that the central-city economies are expanding. What cities need are new jobs, more federal and state revenue, and aid in replacing their obsolescent housing and public facilities.

F.P.H.   There has been much talk and promises about revenue sharing. However, this revenue sharing is interpreted as sharing federal taxes with the states, which in turn are supposed to share their added income with the cities. It has, however, been said by many urbanists and economists that this added income will never get to the cities but will be used elsewhere by the states. Do you think there is any hope for the cities to get their share of the federal government's revenue-sharing program?

A.G.   The federal revenue-sharing idea is an important one. What is needed is not only the implementation of the idea but an improvement in the design of sharing; one that would use a formula to funnel a greater share of the funds to the cities, a formula, for instance, that would take into account the larger role of the cities as producers of goods and services.

F.P.H.   One paradox that you pointed out previously is that the cities seem to do well in certain areas, particularly as office and administrative centers. There has been an enormous office building boom in New York City especially, but also in other cities. The CBD (Central Business District) seems to be doing well in most cities.

Yet the "gray areas," the older residential areas, between the central cities and the suburbs, are constantly deteriorating and getting much worse. You can see many streets with buildings boarded up. Stores are moving out and abandoning these areas, which look more and more desolate. People seem to just travel through these areas from the suburbs to the inner city and ignore their existence completely.

A.G.   What we really need are economic-development programs for the cities. One of the most optimistic of recent developments is that more than a dozen large cities all over the country have taken the initiative to design and implement economic-development programs. These programs vary from city to city, and they are all under-funded. But what is notable is that the cities have decided that now is the time to take the job into their own hands, and they are going about it with determination. They are focusing on expanding existing jobs, on creating new jobs, on increasing their fiscal base, and on pushing urban redevelopment. We ought to help these cities help themselves with additional revenues and other incentives from the state and federal government.

F.P.H.   You say that the cities have devised methods and ways to help themselves. The New York State Urban Development Corp. should be mentioned in this connection. It is a very interesting new organization, because it functions statewide, in all areas, including the cities. One of its functions is to help metropolitan areas regardless of political boundaries. Do you think that the states should participate more in the redevelopment of their cities, and, if so, how can they do it?

A.G.   The states have a big role, because, after all, it is the states which establish the revenue structures for all the cities. The states have been expanding their role in providing a broader range of services to their residents. The states have an increasing responsibility and can do much to funnel additional funds to the cities and encourage them to design and implement economic-development programs.

F.P.H.   Do you feel there is hope for the future of cities, despite the fact that the present looks very difficult?

A.G.   Yes, I am optimistic. The basis of my optimism is the fundamental economic strength of the cities, the important role they are playing, their ability to upgrade their economic structure and their job development in the last decade. I see this as a firm base for a possible turn-around. The cities need additional aid for their severe problems of obsolescent structures. They need help for their poverty population (which really is a national problem, but is in the lap of the cities) and with their unemployment and fiscal problems. The cities merit aid, and such aid will go to a going concern. Our cities are viable, and they are sure bets for the future.

F.P.H.   Thank you, Professor Ganz.

BIBLIOGRAPHY

BOOKS

Bair, Frederick H., Jr., (Virginia Curtis, Editor.) *Planning Cities: Selected Writings on Principles and Practice*. Chicago: American Society of Planning Officials, 1970.

Baker, John H. *Urban Politics in America*. New York: Charles Scribner's Sons, 1971.

Committee for Economic Development (CED), Distribution Division, 477 Madison Avenue, New York, N.Y. 10022.

CED publishes a series of pamphlets, many of them pertinent to the problems discussed. Write them for a bibliography and membership information.

Eldredge, H. Wentworth, ed. *Taming Megalopolis* (2 vol.). New York: Frederick A. Praeger, 1967.

An anthology containing a great variety of information.

Galbraith, John Kenneth. *The Affluent Society*. New York: The New American Library, Mentor Book, 1958. Paperback.

A classic and basic book, a must.

————. *The New Industrial State*. New York: Houghton Mifflin, 1967.

Galbraith's own concept of modern political economics.

Heller, Walter W. *New Dimensions of Political Economy*, Godkin Lectures at Harvard University, 1966. Cambridge, Mass.: Harvard University Press, 1966.

Discusses basic concept of revenue sharing ("Heller Plan").

Lindsay, John V. *The City*. New York: W. W. Norton & Co., 1970.

A most readable book of urban problems from a pragmatic point of view.

Loewenstein, Louis K. *Urban Studies: An Introductory Reader*. New York: The Free Press, 1971.

A basic and very informative reader.

Moynihan, Daniel P., ed. *Toward a National Urban Policy*. New York: Basic Books, Inc., 1970.

Netzer, Dick. *Economics and Urban Problems: Diagnoses and Prescriptions*. New York: Basic Books, Inc., 1970.

Perloff, Harvey S., and Lowdon, Wingo, Jr., eds. *Issues in Urban Economics*. Baltimore: The Johns Hopkins Press. 1968. Paperback.

Perloff, Harvey S., and Nathan, Richard P., eds. *Revenue Sharing and the City*. Baltimore: The Johns Hopkins Press, 1968. Paperback.

Samuelson, Paul. *Economics*. New York: McGraw-Hill, Inc., 1970.

The basic textbook of economics.

ARTICLE

Hosken, Fran P., "Inflation, Federal Cutbacks: Cities' Double Bill for War Spending," *St. Louis Post-Dispatch*, December 28, 1969.

3

HOUSING

A discussion with DENIS A. BLACKETT
President of Housing Innovations, Inc., of Boston

INTRODUCTION

Housing is a critical social issue in industrial urbanized countries all over the world. In developing countries, housing is also a political and economic problem of overriding magnitude, affecting the future of each country and its stability.

In the United States today, we face a critical housing shortage. The building of housing has not kept up with the needs for many years, especially those of low- and middle-income families. Recently, the demand for housing has increased, as the war babies have reached the family-forming stage and are entering the housing market. Simultaneously, inflation has escalated construction costs. The increase in interest rates, supported by the administration since 1969 in order to tighten the economy, has helped to increase the cost of housing. This has created more inflation, as everyone needs a house, regardless of price. Scarcity of money for mortgages has further reduced housing starts, so that in 1970 we were building only about half the housing that we needed. While housing starts have greatly increased in 1971, this increase has been mainly for upper-income groups. Mobile home production was for the first time included in the HUD (Department of Housing and Urban Development) statistics in the past two years, which has increased the count of housing starts, though mobile homes are excluded from cities by zoning regulations.

Demands for rent control have been made in every city, because people cannot find any shelter for what they can afford. In turn, housing in the cities is steadily deteriorating, while funds for housing and community programs are cut or withheld.

According to figures published by HUD, fewer than one family in five has enough income to buy a new house, and the housing situation, especially for people in the inner cities, is continuously and rapidly worsening.

The question is: How did we get to this sad state of affairs? In recent years we have built less housing per 1000 population than all other industrialized nations. Even Russia recently has built nearly twice as much housing proportionally than the United States.

The history of housing—that is, publicly supported housing—in the United States is relatively short and full of conflicts, controversy, and unkept promises from all sides. The first housing legislation to build housing for people who could not afford the market price was initiated in the late 1930's. However, these first public housing programs were really created to give people jobs during the depression. The banking loan and mortgage system was underwritten by the government because, as a result of the depression, large numbers of people were unable to continue to pay for their homes and banks were unable to get their money back.

When the war started in 1941, the budding public-housing program was converted into defense housing and war housing mainly for industrial workers. For instance, large publicly financed housing developments were built near shipyards or war plants.

After World War II, the Federal Housing Administration and the Veterans' Administration guaranteed mortgages in order to support home ownership as a means of creating stability and security. One unexpected result of the FHA legislation was that large numbers of middle-class people left the cities and settled in thousands of small houses in the suburbs. Thanks to the FHA, it became very profitable to build housing developments while land was still available around most cities. The G.I. loans after the war helped many people to acquire a home with a minimal down payment.

But the FHA legislation also helped to create ghettoes in the cities. Blacks and racial minorities were left behind in deteriorating housing in the inner cities, as housing in the suburbs, built entirely for the private market, was racially segregated or too expensive.

Public housing in the meantime became a discredited program. Often the housing projects were built to isolate and segregate the city's poor and minorities. Many public housing projects, which initially were created for the laudable purpose of clearing slums, soon became slums themselves. Congress, in order to build more housing, eliminated all the social services and community features that initially were part of the program.

The result was that such housing often became a trap for its inhabitants, who were unable to advance toward economic independence without help. The absence of any community features—social programs, counselling, or recreation—and the isolation of many public housing projects made them miserable, barren, and hopeless places to live. Most of all, there was just too little public housing in comparison with the need. The public housing projects, because of government regulations, look different and stand out from the surrounding city, which further marks and isolates their inhabitants.

The memorable Housing Bill of 1949 stated: "A decent home and suitable living environment is the right of every citizen." Now, more than twenty-two years later, we are further removed from this goal than ever before.

The Urban Renewal Program was also initiated in 1949 as it became apparent that housing was not the only thing wrong with cities. Cities, in order to be vital economic and social centers, needed to modernize, change, and renew large areas that had deteriorated; the building of housing was not enough.

Urban-renewal programs depend on local initiative and require a percentage of local financing. Under the urban-renewal legislation, cities may acquire large areas that have been declared blighted. Then, new land-use plans are made, often including changes of street patterns and renewal of the infrastructure and services. Finally, the land costs are written down, and parcels of land are sold among private redevelopers to the highest bidder with the best proposal for any given area.

One trouble with the urban-renewal program in many cities has been that while new profitable land development took place as far as the land-use and tax income were concerned, housing was often neglected. Frequently no adequate provisions were made for relocation of people who had to move as a result of redevelopment.

In fact, the urban-renewal program came to be called by many the "Negro Removal Program," as many cities used the program to push out minorities and the poor from potentially profitable areas. This land then was redeveloped for higher tax income to the city, while no or too little housing was built for the poor who were driven out.

The urban-renewal programs differ from city to city, depending on local commitment and initiative. Boston, after years of neglect and some very bad mistakes, such as the tearing down of the West End where a whole community was driven out, has developed since 1959 one of the best and most far-reaching urban-renewal programs in the United States. This includes the building of a great deal of housing.

DISCUSSION

F.P.H.   Mr. Blackett, you are currently involved in a housing program, the Infill Program, which was initiated by the Boston Redevelopment Authority. This is a very special kind of housing program, and it seems to me worth discussing here.

D.A.B.   Yes, the program does have several special aspects about it. First of all its name, Infill. The Infill Program is designed to fill in empty building lots where once houses stood. The area where we are working has mainly detached wood-frame houses. Over time, some of these houses have been abandoned and have become public hazards. As a result, they were torn down by the building department, and then the land was left unused by the city. It is on these vacant pieces of land that we are building new housing.

Another unusual feature about the Infill Program is that the housing is for very large low-income families. All of the housing will be turnkeyed, or sold, to the Boston Housing Authority. The average size of the housing unit is five bedrooms. This will be one of the first family projects to be built in Boston and one of very few in any city in the country in the last ten to fifteen years. It is probably the only scattered-site, large-family project in the country.

To build family housing on scattered sites avoids the problem of a large project where all the low-income families are identifiable. This has proven disastrous, for instance, in Columbia Point in Boston or Pruitt-Igoe in St. Louis. If the Infill housing is successful, it may provide a prototype for low-income family housing in cities throughout the country.

F.P.H.   I understand your firm, Housing Innovations, is building about a hundred units of this housing in the Dorchester area. You also mentioned that almost no public housing has been built in any city in the country for fifteen years. That is, no public housing has been built for families. There has been a certain amount of housing built for the elderly. However, the projects for the elderly separate old people from the rest of the community, and that is not to their advantage.

Infill Housing, as you mentioned, is built on scattered sites: there are never more than about six units in one area. Therefore the building of the housing does not disrupt the existing community and the new housing has a chance to upgrade the neighborhood by its newness.

D.A.B.   There is one question that we might discuss further: why public housing for families has not been built in the various inner-cities areas for more than ten years. Why was it built in the late thirties, forties, and early fifties, and not now? Looking at the tenants of the public housing units in the past, you find that they were what we could describe as the "deserving poor," or the upwardly-mobile working class. Certainly, during the depression there was no stigma attached to occupying public housing. In fact, it was felt to be a very good situation for a working-class family.

In the fifties I think the nature of the population in public housing changed. Because people began to be prosperous and make more money, many moved out of public housing. In part, they moved because of a substantial inmigration of lower-income groups into public housing projects. As this began to happen, housing projects, and particularly family housing projects, began to have a very bad reputation in the eyes of some city fathers. From that point on, that is, from the 1950's on, you will find that no more public housing for families was built in the inner cities of the United States.

F.P.H.   It is interesting to note that in the industrial democracies in North-ern Europe, the majority of all housing built is either subsidized or built outright by a public authority. Therefore this whole situation simply does not arise. The majority of people live in housing or houses subsidized by the government in one way or another. Nevertheless, private enterprise is profit-ably involved.

The actual building of housing is in the hands of private builders and developers. Private entrepreneurs do very well in these countries because they don't have to worry about selling their housing. They have a ready market, that is, the government. The developer or contractor is only concerned with the production of the housing and automatically disposes of every unit he can build. In turn, the government already has many people waiting for the housing. I think this is a very good system for the private developer. In Great Britain, up to 80 per cent of all housing built is publicly supported in one way or another.

We have a different kind of support in the United States, through the FHA, which really supports the banks via loan guarantees. As a matter of fact, the house owners also benefit, as they can deduct their property-tax payments and interest from their income tax. This amounts to a large subsidy for the middle class, as low-income people cannot afford to buy homes. So, there is the phenomenon of socialism for the middle class, or financial support by the government for middle-class housing. But we have private enterprise for the poor, who have to rent their housing; they cannot deduct any part of their rent from their income tax.

D.A.B.   Yes, with this addition, which I think really reflects a complicated situation. In England, most of the population, you said 80 per cent, lives in socialized housing. Actually I think you might find that the same thing is true here in the United States, except that the subsidies to the middle class are given in a much more subtle way; they don't appear as subsidies and are not thought of as subsidies. They are considered to be deserved or earned. The subsidies to the poor are given in a much different, more obvious way, so that there is a stigma attached to them.

In the United States, it does not seem that we regard all of our people equally. If we had a society where we felt that we were all one country, where the ethnic, black, and minority groups were not separated, we could develop a subsidy system that was evenly graded from poor to middle- or upper-middle class, where all people could obtain the benefits of adequate housing.

F.P.H.   The state of New York, I understand, tried out a new subsidy system under the Mitchell-Lama legislation, where people of all different income groups share the same housing complex. Tenants pay different rents, depending on their income, even if the apartments are the same. No one knows whose rents are subsidized. In this way desegregation was achieved both racially and economically.

Recently a rent supplementation program has been tried out by HUD in different areas in the country. It seems to me this is a far better way to deal with the housing situation. The family goes to the private market to get their own housing; however, a certain amount of the rent is paid by a government subsidy, usually directly to the landlord. Do you think this will work on a large scale?

D.A.B.   Certainly this is a much better way of trying to solve the problem. There also is the Housing Authority leasing program. Under this program, a private landlord can contract with the Housing Authority to lease a certain number of units to the Housing Authority for their own tenants. The Housing Authority pays the rent to the landlord and charges the tenants a lower rent, usually 20 to 25 per cent of their incomes. This can be done on a scattered-site basis throughout the community.

I would like to return to the point about Americans seeing each other as different kinds of people: middle class, lower class, black, white, Puerto Rican, etc. We would make a mistake, I believe, to think that any type of legislation, such as leased housing, or any particular program is going to change the very deep, inbred attitudes toward various groups of people in this country.

Suburban housing patterns indicate the length to which small communities will go to keep out people who are not of the same economic class; for instance, the large-lot or one-acre and two-acre zoning regulations serve this purpose. We must recognize this and be realistic, or we may institute the wrong housing programs for the wrong reasons. There is a great distrust among different classes or groups in this country.

F.P.H.   The federal "Open Housing Bill" was passed only a few years ago, after the murder of Martin Luther King. Up to that time in most communities—Massachusetts, which has had an open-housing law for a long time, excluded—it was perfectly legal to discriminate. "Open housing" makes it illegal for anyone anywhere in the country to discriminate in the sale or rental of housing. However, the housing patterns that have prevailed so long are established and are very difficult to change even with the open-housing legislation.

A National Committee against Discrimination in Housing was formed to enforce the open-housing legislation. It operates from New York, and after a long delay it was finally funded.

However, as you point out, the zoning legislation, through large-lot zoning, continues to practice economic discrimination in the suburbs. The zoning regulations prevent people, particularly black people and poor people, from moving into the suburbs, simply because it costs too much.

D.A.B.   Just recently the state of Massachusetts has attempted to rectify this problem somewhat by passing the so-called "anti-snob" legislation. It decrees that cities and towns must devote a certain portion of their total land area to low- and moderate-income housing. This will break the zoning regulations that require half-, one-, or two-acre zoning. Though I have not studied the bill in detail, I understand that it will take some time for the first test case. Therefore, a number of private developers are reluctant even now to go into the suburbs to build low- and moderate-income housing.

Secretary Romney of HUD has recently tried to put into the proposed housing legislation a kind of federal anti-snob legislation designed to break zoning in the suburbs where zoning is used to restrict the building of low- and moderate-income housing. However, President Nixon subsequently said that economic desegregation would not be enforced.

The point I want to make is that such legislation would fly in the face of a very strong desire on the part of the American people to live separately as far as class and race are concerned. I think we should watch these developments very carefully.

To enlarge on a point that you made earlier, the anti-discrimination clauses can be effective for middle-income minority ethnic groups toward providing housing where they were unable to live before. But this only gets at zoning legislation. We also must deal with the costs of housing, that is, subsidies, to allow the poor to be really integrated into the general pattern of housing in the United States.

F.P.H.   Other difficulties that contribute to the cost of housing are the antiquated methods of the production of housing. We still build houses one by one using craft union methods. This is slow, inefficient, and very expensive. As a result, housing prices are not competitive. The building codes compound the union regulations. There exist hardly any large housing manufacturers in the United States today.

In the European countries there was an enormous housing shortage after the war, due to the destruction. As a result, many countries had to support the creation of a national housing industry on a large scale. The industrialization of housing was supported by the governments. Recently, I have been abroad again to study some of the industrialized housing systems. Systems building is quite developed, though it could go much further. But it is now capable of producing large quantities of housing quickly and efficiently. Despite the developments of modern technology in all other areas of production in the United States, our housing industry is still stuck in the nineteenth century. The "Breakthrough" program of HUD has recently been trying to modernize the housing industry by introducing industrialization.

D.A.B.   Yes, but the reason why European countries were able to industrialize is not only their great need after the war, but also the fact that each country was a political unit. The United States is a federal democracy with fifty states, each with different regulations as far as building is concerned. Furthermore, each city and town has its own building regulations, which it guards very jealously. This has been the traditional way of running the country. The local building codes make it very difficult for a large manufacturer to come up with a building system that will work all over the country.

Inherent in building housing, which makes industrialization, although desirable, less effective, is the land on which the housing has to go. Each piece of land is unique and differs from site to site. Land costs vary and materially affect the total costs.

If we look at the whole delivery system of housing, we find that much more significant savings in cost can be accomplished by reducing interest rates. A 10 per cent reduction is the most that can be expected in construction costs through more efficient methods. I would say that the major gain to come from industrialization is the capacity of the industry to produce housing much faster. We find this in our own practice.

If you analyze the housing industry's inability to produce housing, you will find the reason for this is not its industrial capacity, but the problems we already talked about: lack of land, lack of mortgage money, zoning problems, and building code problems. These problems hold up projects for three or four years.

F.P.H.   The time it takes to get a project processed through the bureaucracy is one major obstacle in the production of housing. The Breakthrough program has been designed to streamline the production of housing also from the bureaucratic point of view.

The Breakthrough program, I should explain here, is a competition organized by HUD in which groups of producers combine many different qualifications: the design and production of housing; social, technical, and economic concerns; and also financing and developing. Breakthrough was started by Secretary Romney based on a program called "In Cities," which was initiated by the previous administration. Its purpose is to help to industrialize the production of housing, to produce more housing faster and more efficiently. The housing will not necessarily be less expensive for a start.

The housing bill of 1968 forecast that we shall need to produce about 2.6 million housing units a year for the next ten years in order to satisfy the demand. It was estimated that some 6,000 units a year of this should be

subsidized. In 1969 and 1970, we were building less than half of that estimate. This has created a great demand and pressure on housing production,
which recently has increased, as have building costs. But the building industry
is still not producing housing at the rate of 2.6 million units a year, let alone
dealing with the backlog. The Breakthrough program has been trying to pave
the way for more production. At the present time, Breakthrough is in trouble
in terms of funds, the same as many other federal housing programs.

D.A.B.   In the question of industrialized housing in terms of volume and
also in terms of cost, we must not be misled by the glamor of industrialization. Industrialization is terribly important, and it is true that our industry
does not have the capacity to produce at the rate that housing is needed. But
it is also true that we could produce considerably more housing with the same
number of workers without more industrialization if we could get around the
problems of building codes, bureaucracy, zoning regulations, and more.

One other important point we should always keep in mind is that housing
does not exist by itself, but in communities. When we are planning new
housing or when we are looking at existing housing in communities that are
deteriorating, we must look at the entire community: its facilities, its ability
to control its own destiny including the school system, the police, etc. We
cannot simply address ourselves to building new units or to rehabilitating
existing housing. Only by looking at the whole community can we understand the causes of decay and reverse them and build healthy new communities.

F.P.H.   You point at a most important factor, which also is the reason for
the failure of the public housing program: the absence of community facilities and social services, and the absence of tenant participation. Originally,
community centers and facilities, as well as social services, were designed into
the housing programs. Then Congress eliminated the social and community
aspects in order to spend more money just for buildings.

These community and social service features of all public housing were
removed quite early in the program. Consequently, housing became so many
storage boxes for people and did absolutely nothing to upgrade their lives or
help these disadvantaged people to become self-supporting, productive members of the community.

D.A.B.   Let me make a point about "community" in another, somewhat
different way. A low-income black community, for example, which cannot
control its schools so that the education for its children is adequate, which
cannot control its police, and which cannot get any response to any of its
needs will inevitably deteriorate.

F.P.H.   Schools, of course, are intimately related to housing patterns. I don't know of any inner city where schools are not in trouble now. We have heard a good deal about discrimination in schools. However, this is based, particularly in the northern cities, entirely on the segregated housing patterns.

Massachusetts, for instance, has a law requiring school integration in order to obtain state funds for schools. This is extremely difficult to achieve by present housing patterns. The need for busing to achieve integration in the schools is caused by segregated housing patterns. The suburbs all over the country have always used buses. However, it is not an ideal condition if small children have to go long distances by bus. There are better ways of achieving integration in schools. That is, there ought to be integrated housing, not only for different racial groups, but also for different income groups.

Earlier, we mentioned urban renewal as a means to upgrade the life in the cities and as a means to change the land-use pattern.

D.A.B.   The urban renewal program in the city of Boston has been successful in part in renewing residential areas. There has been a successful renewal of a black moderate-to-middle-income area in Washington Park. New housing has upgraded other residential areas.

Throughout its history, however, the urban-renewal program on the national level has been insensitive to relocation in the construction of new housing, and to user requirements. The program has focused its efforts and funds on downtown and commercial development. Even in Boston this is partly true, though Boston has one of the best urban-renewal programs in the country.

Not only in urban-renewal programs, but in all new housing for low- and moderate-income people, the developer and the builder of the housing often finds that his real client is the government, rather than the low-income and the moderate-income people who are to occupy the housing. This I think is unfortunate and something that we must avoid. We must design a system that makes the potential user the real client, rather than the government agency.

F.P.H.   Cities are by and for people. If there is no decent housing, people leave. Many middle-class people have moved out of the city because of the housing situation. The city has become a business center that is occupied only in daytime. Professionals, white-collar workers, and much of the middle class live in the suburbs, though most still work in the city, while the blue-collar workers and the minorities live in the city but frequently work in the industrial plants that have recently left the city.

As a result, commuting occupies an enormous amount of time and effort, which is an utter waste of economic strength. All this commuting is based on housing patterns and on the segregated urban life.

What do you see in the future for housing? Is there any hope to improve the housing situation, especially in the cities, but also in the growing metropolitan areas?

D.A.B.   Maybe I can separate that answer into two parts. In the short run, I am afraid I am rather pessimistic. I am pessimistic because I am not convinced of the federal government's commitment to solving the problems that we face in the inner city or in housing in general. It is also true in the short run that states like Massachusetts, New York, and New Jersey are making an effort on their own to try to cope with housing. But most of the states are not.

In the long run, I suppose, I am somewhat more optimistic, if only because I do not have the feeling that the professionals in the field, not simply the planners and architects or the developers, but also those who legislate, now understand in a much more profound way what the real problems are. There is legislation proposed which begins to deal with some of the real problems. The Urban Development Corporation of New York State proposes to do on a statewide basis what has been done only in cities before. This kind of bureaucratic breakthrough may in the long run prove more significant than some of the technological breakthroughs that we have been talking about. I see that there is a growing body of knowledgeable people who recognize what the housing problem really is—a very complex and difficult problem. I am hopeful that there will be some solutions forthcoming in the seventies.

F.P.H.   I am hopeful because I think some of our experience with housing, which we discussed here, can be positively applied in the building of new towns and new communities. Building new towns, we can start with entirely new housing patterns, with a new approach towards community functions and services, as well as community control.

Thank you, Mr. Blackett.

BIBLIOGRAPHY

BOOKS

Beyer, Glenn H. *Housing and Society.* New York: The Macmillan Company, 1965.

The Douglas Report. "More than Shelter: Social Needs in Low- and Moderate-Income Housing." Research Report # 8. Washington, D.C.: U.S. Government Printing Office, 1968.
   The most authoritative report on housing as a national problem.

Downs, Anthony. "Moving towards Realistic Housing Goals." In *Agenda for the Nation,* edited by Kermit Gordon, pp. 141-178. Washington, D.C.: The Brookings Institution, 1968.

Anthony Downs is one of the country's best informed housing experts, with practical experience.

Fried, Joseph P. *Housing Crisis USA.* New York: Frederick A. Praeger, 1971. A journalist's pragmatic account of housing problems.

Housing Yearbooks of the National Housing Conference, 1250 Connecticut Avenue, N.W., Washington, D.C. 20036

"The III Housed: A Compendium of Recent Writings and Reports on National Housing Policy." Published by Urban America, Inc., 1717 Massachusetts Avenue, N.W., Washington, D.C., 1968.

The Kaiser Report. "A Decent Home: The Report of the President's Committee on Urban Housing." Washington, D.C.: U.S. Government Printing Office, 1968. A "must" for everyone interested in housing.

McEntire, Davis. "Residence and Race." Final and Comprehensive Report to the Commission on Race and Housing. Berkeley: University of California Press, 1960.

Netzer, Dick. *Economics and Urban Problems: Diagnoses and Prescriptions.* New York: Basic Books, Inc., 1970.

Stegman, Michael, ed. *Housing and Economies: The American Dream.* Cambridge, Mass.: The MIT Press, 1971.

PERIODICALS

House and Home. Published by McGraw-Hill.

HUD Library: write for information on current programs and pamphlets including "Breakthrough Program." Department of Housing and Urban Development, Washington, D.C. 20410.

ARTICLES

Hosken, Fran P. "Boston's Public Housing." *Boston Herald-Traveler*, February 1, 1970, p. 12.

———. "Community Must be Heard in Planning of its Housing." *Boston Herald Traveler,* June 16, 1969, p. 14.

———. "How Can We Solve the Housing Shortage?" *Boston Sunday Herald Traveler Magazine,* February 9, 1969.

———. "How Tenants Decided to Own Their Homes." *Boston Sunday Herald Traveler,* February 20, 1972.

———. "Infill: Housing Boon for Boston." *Boston Sunday Herald Traveler Magazine,* Spring 1968.

———. "Suburbs Have an Obligation," *Boston Herald Traveler,* February 8, 1969, p. 4.

4

URBAN NEIGHBORHOODS

A discussion with Dr. DON SCHON
Visiting Professor of Urban Planning, M.I.T.; President, OSTI
(Organization for Social and Technical Innovations, Inc.), Newton

INTRODUCTION

One definition of an urban neighborhood is: "an area in the city distinguished by group values, to which a sense of community is added." An urban neighborhood frequently is expressed in its physical features—in the design, scale, and appearance of its buildings and streets.

The importance of the community ties of urban neighborhoods was recently highlighted when some federal highway and urban renewal programs uprooted and dislocated large numbers of people, who, as a result, not only lost their livelihood, but their friends, social ties, and stability. Up to that time, the social structure and cohesiveness of specific urban areas or neighborhoods was mostly ignored. The prevailing opinion was that a home or place to live was a sufficient basis for family stability.

Therefore, the public housing program addressed itself entirely to providing physical housing structures. The provisions for community facilities and programs, for social services and neighborhood centers, for recreation and education programs were cut out of the original housing legislation by Congress early in the program, in the mistaken belief that by putting the money into more buildings more people would be served. The result was that public housing projects did not become neighborhoods or communities, but simply storage boxes for people who had no roots and did not develop any interest or pride in their community or environment.

"Slum clearance," on the other hand, was the motto by which many genuine urban neighborhoods were destroyed. Only gradually, an understanding was formed for the very subtle human relationships of neighborhood and community ties, the sense of belonging and pride, of needing and being needed, which forms the bond of our urban structure.

Instead of tearing down areas that to many looked like slums, more careful investigation revealed that many of the buildings could be rehabilitated and preserved. Indeed, the social structure and community life that was housed in many of these areas was sound and full of vitality.

Rehabilitation programs and neighborhood-renewal programs were belatedly introduced in the middle 1950's after much damage had been done. Rehabilitation, the upgrading of urban neighborhoods from inside, requires broadly based community participation. Neighborhood meetings and community action became the strategies for neighborhood-renewal programs. In turn, this resulted in decentralizing money and power.

The requirement of a "workable program," which was part of the Urban Renewal legislation of HUD, demands, among other things, citizens' involvement. This means that citizens' groups, including the poor and minorities, must participate in planning and carrying out the programs.

Finally, the Model Cities Program is based from the start on neighborhood involvement and neighborhood renewal. It recognizes that an urban area is more than buildings, and that to restore a neighborhood you must start by upgrading the life of its people. Community action, self determination, and the political vitality of an urban neighborhood positively contribute to shaping model cities programs.

DISCUSSION

F.P.H.   Before discussing the Model Cities Program in any detail, what is your definition of an urban neighborhood, Dr. Schon?

D.S.   Well, the notion of a neighborhood in a city suggests, as you indicated, the idea of a cohesive subculture. But the answer to the question really depends on the reason for asking it.

For example, if you are interested in trying to identify sub-groups along the lines of the West End Urban Villagers that Herbert Gans[1] talks about in his book, you will be interested in ethnic homogeneity and the notion of people's membership in a single community. In that sense, the North End of Boston is an urban neighborhood. It hangs together as a social unit. But if you are interested in program and service-system design, then an urban neighborhood may have to be seen as the market or the catchment area for a given program. In that case, we may need to define it as a health district, or as a housing district within a city, or as an aggregate of a certain number of buildings of comparable kind.

Again, in a place like Columbia Point in Boston, a public housing project that was built on the trash-can theory, both tend to coincide. Some two to three thousand families are, for better or worse, on a spit of land isolated

<hr />

[1] Herbert J. Gans, *The Urban Villagers* (New York: The Free Press of Glencoe, 1962).

from the rest of the city. Political processes begin to develop that could have as their result a homogeneous or at least an identifiable kind of community. Services should be designed for this kind of group. F.P.H.   We have divided

F.P.H.   We have divided up cities in any number of different ways; from political boundaries and health districts to school districts and many kinds of service areas. But none of them seem to take the cohesiveness of the urban neighborhood into consideration. All these boundaries criss-cross each other and are superimposed on the social structure, which is the last thing that people really worry about. The question of the underlying social structure, it seems to me, is the most important single concern if we are really interested in people, if we are interested in making the city work.

D.S.   There is another dimension here, too, which is the political one. As you know, there is concern about community control, under the general heading of decentralization of government. The question is: What are the smallest manageable units of political power, considering that we are concerned about decentralizing services and decentralizing city government?

For a community group in Roxbury to take on political responsibility for a rather large area, it must cut across several diverse neighborhoods. Or a man like Herman Valez of Hunt's Point in the Bronx may succeed in developing a political power base over a heterogeneous group of white, black, and Puerto Rican residents. An urban neighborhood might turn out to be what a man like Herman Valez controls, as a basis for decentralizing government and services.

F.P.H.   One of the problems of the Urban Renewal program has been to identify an urban neighborhood, following the requirement of local participation that is stated in the program. To try to find and identify community leadership often is difficult, particularly in the black communities, where frequently nobody knows who really belongs to a given constituency. When it comes to getting neighborhood support for a program, it may happen that the group to which the urban renewal authority had addressed itself turns out to have no support from the majority of the people, even if it was a very vocal group.

D.S.   Your observation has a corollary. Because if the above condition occurs, then it may turn out that for a given purpose the definition of an urban neighborhood is a consequence of a political process: a process of conflict of various groups vying for power. It will be resolved in the end by a determination of who it is that really wields that power rather than, for example, a question of cultural unity or even the rational boundaries in terms of housing characteristics.

F.P.H.   Well, if we are interested in preserving the city as a viable organism, what should we do? Where should we look for boundaries, and how should we define an urban neighborhood?

D.S.   Most programs that I have been involved in, whether they have to do with health, housing, or whatever, have tended to founder on the political issues. They foundered because of underestimation of the difficulties of identifying political leadership, and because of internal community conflicts as well as conflicts between community and city. These conflicts arise the minute one tries to introduce any sort of new service into a center-city area.

But there is another problem, which is how large an area, or how complex an area can a service program really deal with effectively? This, in a sense, is the problem of the limits imposed by our own skills and the models of the practice that we have.

For example, if you identify any objective to which a development program might be directed, say in the area of childhood nutrition, the number of factors that need to be tackled and the number of variables that need to be controlled turn out to be very great. They turn out to go well beyond what one would ordinarily associate with nutrition. The issue may hinge on the size of the refrigerator in a public housing project. How much food can people store? Or, it may be directly related to the problem of disposable family income. Or it may have to do with the location of retail stores, or the transportation network that connects retail stores to the public housing project. That is only the very beginning of the complexity.

Someone who works effectively on the problem of nutrition is someone who is able to influence all of those related factors and influence them in a connective way. That is, you have to be able to do something about refrigerator volume, and at the same time you have to be able to influence store location and work with mothers on dietary knowledge. A whole network of services has to be influenced in order to do something about nutrition for small children. The agency that is able to do something about refrigerators is different from the agency that can do something about store location, which is different again from the group that can do something about educating mothers, and that is different from the agency that can do something about disposable family income.

Now the question is: For how large a group, for how many households, can effective network management of that kind be undertaken? My own feeling is that the limit of our current knowledge is in the order of two to three thousand families. From the point of view of problem-solving, the unit should not be larger than that.

A larger entity has to find ways of being divided into manageable units so that problems can be tackled in an integrated way.

F.P.H.   Recently we have had many demands for decentralization in urban school systems because people want some control over their children's education. New York has led the way and other cities have followed. Neighborhood parents want to decide what kind of school to have and what is taught. In fact, they want far greater control, including control over expenditures. In contrast, we have followed a systems approach to the city at large, one which is needed for dealing efficiently with a larger number of people.

We seem to use two methods that work against each other. One is to introduce better technology to deal with many people effectively. The other is to divide up the city into individual small neighborhoods that people can control themselves. How can we combine these two opposites?

D.S.   You put your finger on what I think is one of the central problems of method and policy in the city. The problem is insoluble if "decentralization" is taken as total decentralization. It is possible to think of decentralization in several dimensions. You can decentralize authority, the ability to decide. A community of ten thousand people acquires decision power over one element of its service systems, like a school in Harlem. You can also decentralize resources. For example, a neighborhood health center operates out of the community, although decisions about the center itself are made at a central office.

Given a specific service system there is a question of which functions are worth centralizing at what level of aggregation, and which functions should be decentralized. It would appear that there are appropriate scales of activity for different kinds of functions.

Let us take housing. Suppose you want to build a factory to produce prefabricated modules of low-income housing. A factory may require a minimal yearly volume of one thousand units. If you cannot produce the thousand units, it is not worth trying to build that factory. Suppose, on the other hand, you wanted to do something about the negative attitudes of craft unions toward low-income housing. Well, in order to do that you may need to be able to offer members of that union a guaranteed wage for a year. Again, in order to do that you may find that you need to produce ten thousand units per year in a large city like Detroit. Or suppose that your interest is in providing an incentive for manufacturers to make large capital investments in housing technology. Under those circumstances, you might find it necessary to guarantee an annual volume of thirty thousand per year.

Now, each of these quantities will dictate a different level of decentralization. Or, to put it another way, different administrative levels of the city serve as centers of activity for housing at each of these quantities depending upon their size.

The dilemma that you discussed is a function of the activities of a service system. Inquiry will show the relative merits of centralization and decentralization for each activity. But that is something that we have not done for every service system.

F.P.H.   In this sense, the city can be seen as a service system. However, the existing service system does not want to give up its power and allow the neighborhood to take over. One of the principal difficulties is that while ideally we can determine centralization or decentralization on a technical basis and decide what people need in terms of control, there remains the problem of the existing organizations. A central school system or a political system simply does not wish to be decentralized or give up power. This is very apparent in the Model Cities Program, for instance. When it comes to the point that a model cities community wishes to control its own schools, police, and other services—the federal program states that they should—the existing city structure does not want to give in, and you are facing a fight and a political dilemma.

D.S.   Well, that is a little oversimplified, I think. Model Cities has been a great laboratory for the whole set of issues centering around decentralization, around the management of service systems and community power. The expectation was, as I understand it, that the Model Cities Program would be an attempt to get at the problems of fragmentation in our service systems, which we discussed earlier. There is no agency responsible for coordination. The central task therefore would be to relate services in the community.

F.P.H.   You mean no single agency exists in Washington. For health services you have to go to HEW, for education you have to go to the Department of Education, for housing you have to go to HUD, etc., and none of the agencies communicates with each other.

D.S.   Right, and similar problems also exist at the city level, whether it is the city of Boston or the city of New York or Detroit, to take those three as examples. You can find analogs in the vertical fragmentation of cities that you also find at the national level. The expectation was that Model Cities would address itself to integration or "the establishment of linkages"—that was a favorite term—among these various agencies.

But the experience of the Model Cities planning process has been that the conflicts among agencies have taken a back seat to the conflicts of community groups and between community groups and cities. The major event of the Model Cities process has been the strong bid of some community groups for control, for power, and the equally strong resistance of mayors and city agency heads.

But Model Cities neighborhoods are by no means monolithic. They turn out to be composed of a variety of groups of different kinds. At any given time the majority of people in any neighborhood are not represented in any way at all in the political process of the neighborhood. They come to life only with major issues, a riot, for example, or the intrusion of a highway in the neighborhood. The groups that are frequently most vocal are fringe groups or small action groups that represent more involvement, more competence, and more sophistication.

There is a pattern to the development of these groups. The initial group composed of middle-class blacks, for example, may tend to be displaced over time by another younger group or one that is more militant. Conflicts will break out in the neighborhood between groups and within groups. The Model Cities process has to be regarded primarily as an exercise in the development of political competence and political identity on the part of neighborhoods. For anybody working for the city government, that kind of conflict, if it is not understood, can be a very frustrating process. It may turn out that the group the city begins to bargain with evaporates. It is often difficult to find a solid constituency with whom to continue the bargaining process, which Model Cities planning has turned out to be.

F.P.H. There is another factor to consider: urban neighborhoods are not static, by and large. They change while you are in the process of planning or while you are trying to decide what to do. This has happened certainly in city school districts where change is highly visible and many formerly white schools have become predominantly black. Schools in Massachusetts must be racially integrated according to state law in order to qualify for state support, especially if a new school is built. Often during the time the school is planned until it is completed the neighborhood changes and you end up with a black school, while you started out with a 50-50 black and white school. What is happening in cities at large is focused in the schools: neighborhoods are changing rapidly. People seem to continuously move in and out of many urban neighborhoods.

D.S. Neighborhoods vary in their degree of change. In center city areas, like the South End of Boston, for example, there is, as you say, enormous change, as blacks displace old whites, as Puerto Ricans in turn displace blacks.

There are, on the other hand, relatively stable areas in the center city. Parts of Roxbury would be an example. But they may be stable at a very low level of service and at a very low level of economic vitality, although that is not necessarily tied in with an impoverished life; it may be a very rich life indeed. This is a paradox.

I am thinking of a specific neighborhood that has a structure like this: first there is a layer of relatively well-to-do whites on a lake front. Behind them there is a layer of elderly whites and poor blue-collar, working-class whites. Behind them is a layer of middle-class blacks; behind them is a layer of working-class blacks; and behind them is a layer of welfare blacks, inmigrating from the South.

Now it seems to me what is going on in this neighborhood is that immigration of welfare blacks is pushing the black community up against the blue-collar white community which, among whites, is least prepared to receive the push. Great friction develops at that interface. The aims of this neighborhood can be expressed very differently by different members of the community. The lake-front people, for example, are worried about pollution of the lake. The blue-collar whites are worried about infringement of the blacks, whom they perceive as monolithic but who are from very different groups. The black blue-collar and middle-class groups are concerned about the deterioration of the neighborhood through invasion by welfare blacks.

Now, if the aim of the game is stabilization, one sort of strategy argues for an attempt to support the formation of a relatively cohesive political group, building on community organizations and working with all major service systems. Housing rehabilitation implies relocation of services and infusions of new capital into the area. A central program is now going on. The paradox is that, as the neighborhood improves, it becomes increasingly attractive to welfare clients. The very effort to build these service systems to improve the quality of the neighborhood has a tendency to exacerbate the problems those actions are designed to solve.

That kind of feedback relationship is built into all kinds of efforts to deal with urban problems. It derives from the fact that the systems with which we are dealing are not isolated systems; they are pieces of larger systems. This is an issue we have not solved.

F.P.H.   You point out two things. If the aim of the game is stability, we are trying to create neighborhood and community cohesion. In this connection, I think we should define right now what is the goal of all the urban renewal programs, model cities programs, and so on. Are they designed to create stability, to create a sense of belonging in people, to keep them in their neighborhood by improving the neighborhood, to make them satisfied with life as it is here and now? Or are we trying to create upward mobility, which frequently means outward mobility? I think most of the programs are not at all clear about what they want to accomplish.

On the other hand, you point out that one of the important areas where friction occurs is that of the availability of housing. At the present time we have an increasing housing shortage. The shortage of decent housing, especially for low-income people in urban neighborhoods, is going to get worse before it gets better. Therefore all the neighborhood problems and all the related urban problems are going to get much worse in the near future simply because of the competition for the physical housing, which is scarce.

D.S.   Yes, I think that is quite right. However, I have gotten past the point where I believe that clarity of objectives in these urban programs is possible in the sense you mean. What the programs turn out to be depends on the various actors involved. The actors are not going to go away. By the actors I mean people like heads of federal agencies, regional representatives of those agencies, mayors of cities, heads of city agencies like housing agencies, heads of neighborhood groups, political aspirants at the neighborhood level, residents of neighborhoods, and the like.

F.P.H.   Yes, I know all the actors. But what should we do with cities, play God?

D.S.   You cannot. Only very rarely is there a man in a position to play God, unless it is someone like Mellon in Pittsburgh. There are a number of operators, agencies or individuals, who behave as if they were self-annointed coordinators. But usually they are not accepted by others.

The central political fact is that there is no hierarchy, there is no control point capable of including and managing all of the elements. This means that the central process is one of maneuvering, negotiating, bargaining, brokering, and connecting. It is really quite useless to ask what would we do if we were in control of all the pieces. You must always work from some base which is only a part of a larger system.

So, for example, the head of an agency like HUD may look at the Model Cities Program and see in it an opportunity to demonstrate a new, more rational form of intergovernmental relations at the federal and local level, among federal agencies and between federal, regional, and city agencies. That may be his objective. The head of the city, a mayor, may see in the Model Cities Program an effort to make a visible contribution to the needs of people in a hard-hit area of the city, which can give him some leverage for the next election.

The political aspirant who is head of a community group in that neighborhood may see in Model Cities a piece of the action which, if he can get hold of it, he can use to build a political power base for himself in that neighborhood. Residents in the neighborhood may see in the Model Cities Program primarily a source of jobs—not jobs as the result of a planning program, but jobs stemming from the very process of planning and carrying out service delivery. Institutions like a city hospital, for example, may see in the Model Cities Program an opportunity or a challenge or a pressure to become connected to a population that they have tried to ignore for years. Each of the groups and agencies involved turns out to have quite different objectives. Their priorities are different and in the end the planning process turns out to be a bargaining process. The management of that bargaining process is really the activity that needs to be handled well, that needs to be learned, if the process that goes under the name of Model Cities is to work.

F.P.H.   Many people in coordinating positions in cities are increasingly frustrated. For instance, Paul Ylvisaker, who was Public Affairs Commissioner in New Jersey, had his hands very full trying to get something accomplished in urban neighborhoods. He took over just before the riots in Newark and only recently left. He sounded increasingly discouraged about the possibility of getting something done on the neighborhood level, because for every demand or group there was an equally strong opposite demand and group.

If we believe that people should control their own destiny we also should be able to find some kind of a structure or framework that makes this possible. Yet in talking to different urban officials and politicians, I hear it is more and more complicated to get things done, no matter what your outlook is and no matter what you want to accomplish. The goal or objective gets lost in the activity you are engaged in. You lose your direction in simply getting from here to there. The purpose is lost in the process. Of course, planning is a process and so is urban life. But on the other hand, if we get completely absorbed in the process, we shall never be able to accomplish anything, whatever its goal.

D.S.   The final goal depends again on the perspective with which you are looking at the problem. If you look at it from the planner's perspective, you have a different view from some of the other actors. My own opinion is that this notion of control over one's destiny is an illusion, a piece of ideology. Those of us who are optimists like Ylvisaker have learned in a very major way that it is an illusion.

What does control over one's destiny mean? Does it mean that a neighborhood organization should manage the delivery of services to itself? Does it mean that a neighborhood group should control economic activity in the neighborhood? Does it mean political decentralization? Or does it mean that the neighborhood becomes powerful as a voice in influencing activities, legislation, policies, agencies, and service delivery systems that affect the neighborhood?

Our experience has been that the effort to build neighborhood corporations that actually manage and directly control the delivery of services is very seldom successful. There are basically two sorts of circumstances. In one there is a pre-existing power base, or a strong person. In those circumstances the neighborhood corporation becomes a personal vehicle of that person, a servant of his desire to provide patronage and to build political power. By coincidence, it may provide some improvement in services for people in the community.

In other circumstances, there is no pre-existing power base, no strong organization—Louisville and Philadelphia are two examples that come to mind. The small neighborhoods in these cities are overwhelmed by "the process," as you put it, by the day-to-day effort to provide services. No organized or effective service delivery process was initiated nor any major political activity.

One of the most promising consequences of the whole Model Cities process has been the gradual building up of competence at the community level. Sophistication about what the issues are is generated and knowledge about how to enter into the political process or take part in political activities, where community interests lie, and how to make community voices heard. So I would argue that there is a lot of hope in the idea of the community influencing service systems through a base of increasing power. But there is very little to be gained from direct community management of these services.

F.P.H.   Earlier in our discussion we talked about housing. The physical environment, I believe, is going to be a growing source of difficulties in urban neighborhoods, because we simply have not kept up with building enough housing, particularly in central cities. Especially in the beginning of the Urban Renewal Program, much city housing was destroyed. Then through the non-profit sponsored and other middle-income programs such as the 221(d)3 program of HUD, some new housing in urban neighborhoods was built. But the greatest hope was attached to rehabilitation programs on the neighborhood level. A number of these programs were launched in many cities. For a while, rehabilitation was hailed as the answer to upgrading specific urban neighborhoods. It was also to be the vehicle to generate participation and revitalize the community.

But the housing rehabilitation programs turned out to be rather disappointing, because every time a house was rehabilitated the rent went up. Despite loans for rehabilitation, someone had to pay for the real costs in the end. Or, if the owner lived there, the house cost him more because he had to pay higher taxes. Or the families who had to move out while the buildings were rehabilitated never came back. Rehabilitation was not the salvation for the city neighborhoods, as many had expected, because the service component was missing. The Model Cities Program, based on this experience tries to include services and participation in terms of the community planning for itself from the start.

D.S.   That is a pretty legitimate critique of most rehabilitation efforts, although I think we have learned more about it now, especially not to expect too much. There have been some informal self-help efforts in neighborhood renewal that show some promise and should be supported.

F.P.H.   To sum up—What do you think of our urban future in terms of neighborhoods?

D.S.   We have learned in the last ten to twelve years that simplistic solutions do not work. And we have learned that ideologies built around "control of one's own destiny" can be very misleading. We need to develop what I would call learning systems that are capable of responding fast to the failures of these programs. Learning systems have some characteristics in common. They have to do with recognizing and building upon informal networks like the service networks related to nutrition that we discussed at first. They have to do with building on the capabilities of individuals and their informal efforts, like a self-help housing program. They have to do with supporting community confidence and supporting incipient political activity at the neighborhood level, with the management and distribution of information that allows people to exercise a kind of informal influence on city programs. This has been rare to date. We also have to learn about manipulation, maneuvering, and brokerage among the agency systems.

All of this means that urban planning becomes a very different sort of enterprise from the kind of idealized, hierarchical model that has dominated the planning field for quite some time.

F.P.H.   In fact, we have a great deal more to learn about urban neighborhoods and how they function, which is probably the best lesson of this discussion.

Thank you very much, Dr. Schon.

BIBLIOGRAPHY

BOOKS

Altshuler, Alan A. *Community Control: Pegasus, New York.* Racine, Wis.: Western Publishing Company, Inc., 1970.
A comprehensive discussion of community control, decentralization, and participation in city decisions and power distribution.
The Douglas Report. *More Than Shelter: Social Needs in Low- and Moderate-Income Housing.* Prepared for the consideration of the National Commission on Urban Problems, Research Report # 8. Washington, D.C.: U.S. Government Printing Office, 1968.

The best document on the U.S. housing problems in cities.

Downs, Anthony. *Urban Problems and Prospects.* Chicago: Markham Publishing Co., 1970.

A broad view of urban problems and future alternatives, seen from a realistic, pragmatic point of view.

Gans, Herbert J. *The Urban Villagers.* New York: The Free Press, 1962.

A classic, dissecting the social base of an urban neighborhood.

Glazer, Nathan, and Moynihan, Daniel. *Beyond the Melting Pot.* Cambridge, Mass.: The MIT Press, 1963.

A pragmatic evaluation of the melting pot theory.

Handlin, Oscar, ed. *Children of the Uprooted.* New York: George Braziller, 1966.

Inner-city immigrants and their future.

Implications of Social Change in the Macombs-Highbridge Community for Proposed Development Along the Harlem River. Cambridge, Mass.: OSTI: Organization for Social and Technical Innovations, Inc., 1967.

The Kaiser Report. *A Decent Home: The Report of the President's Committee on Urban Housing.* Washington, D.C.: U.S. Government Printing Office, 1968.

Keller, Suzanne. *The Urban Neighborhood: A Sociological Perspective.* New York: Random House, 1968. Paperback.

An analysis of urban neighborhoods by a noted sociologist.

The Kerner Report. *Report of the National Advisory Commission on Civil Disorders.* New York: E.P. Dutton and Co., Inc., 1968.

Keyes, Langley Carlton, Jr. *The Rehabilitation Planning Game.* Cambridge, Mass.: The MIT Press, 1969.

An evaluation of rehabilitation based on practical experience.

Mumford, Lewis. *The Urban Prospect.* New York: Harcourt, Brace & World, 1968.

Nash, William W. *Residential Rehabilitation: Private Profits and Public Purposes.* New York: McGraw-Hill Book Co., 1959.

Schrag, Peter. *Village School Downtown.* Boston: Beacon Press, 1967.

A devastating appraisal of the Boston school system.

5

TRANSPORTATION

A discussion with Dr. ALAN ALTSHULER
Secretary of Transporation and Construction
Commonwealth of Massachusetts

INTRODUCTION

Transportation is the lifeline of the city. As in the arteries of the human body, the life blood of the city, its activity, moves through its transportation corridors: the expressways, streets, pedestrian walks, the railroad, subway, bus, and trolley lines.

Good transportation facilities have influenced the location of most cities. Good harbors or major trade route intersections are the primary reasons for the founding of some of the greatest cities in the world; for instance, New York, San Francisco, Boston, Hong Kong, Singapore, Rio de Janeiro, Istanbul, and many other coastal cities were located because of their harbors. Chicago, St. Louis, Vienna, and many of the inland continental cities are situated at river crossings or on the paths of overland trade routes.

Recent innovations in transportation technology have drastically changed the life and form of cities. Throughout history, the size of a city was limited by the distance a man could comfortably walk or ride on horseback. In the twentieth century, mechanical transportation—trains, trolleys, subways, automobiles and buses—has spread cities out over many miles. This is a continuing world-wide trend.

Vertical transportation, that is elevators, make the use of highrise buildings possible. Without high speed elevators, it would be impossible to construct the vertical office cities that house much of business enterprise. This concentration of people and activities into a small area has totally changed urban life and city form. Los Angeles, by contrast, is a completely dispersed city that quite depends on highways and cars.

The automobile and truck, the individual transportation machines, have more drastically changed our way of life and our cities in a shorter time than almost anything else man has built. Our whole economy and culture is based on these vehicles with their ability to move people rapidly and to transport materials and goods quickly from origin to factory and to point of use.

People prefer cars over all other transportation methods simply because nothing else provides equal flexibility, comfort, and privacy. There are more than 97 million licensed drivers in the United States today, and we are adding nearly two cars for every three people. DOT (Department of Transportation) estimates that highway travel will grow to over 1.5 trillion miles per year by 1985, a 71 per cent increase over 1965. Until lately, pollution of our cities by cars has been largely ignored, though, for instance, smog in Los Angeles, mostly caused by car exhaust, has been a major problem for many years. The one-sided reliance on automobiles for transportation is influencing city form quite aside from pollution; it is determining how cities grow and it is changing the quality of urban life.

Transportation by car and truck is a vital economic factor for cities. Countless businesses have left downtown and are moving outside of city centers because of clogged transportation and because highways and truck transportation enable them to locate independently of railroads almost anywhere they choose.

Public mass transportation has been almost entirely neglected for the past thirty years in all U.S. cities. Commuter services, rapid transit and subways, where they exist, are poorly kept up, dirty, over-crowded at peak hours, and often erratic. Public transportation is mostly privately owned and therefore has to make a profit. But too often it does not pay. This is a growing dilemma, as cities simply cannot accommodate all the commuters' cars, and air pollution threatens everyone.

Public transportation, especially subways, work well in many cities in Europe and also in Tokyo, because they are financed by the government, maintained and run as a public service. Some of the largest cities in the world, London, Paris, and Tokyo, could not exist without an efficient subway service that is available at minimal cost.

Lately, there has been a good deal of interest shown by several U.S. cities in going beyond the improvement of their existing subway and public transportation systems. For instance, San Francisco is building a new public transport system, the Bay Area Rapid Transit, or BART, system. Washington is also beginning to build a subway.

Boston right now is engaged in a review of the entire metropolitan transportation situation. This came about as the result of citizens' protests against the "Inner Belt" highway project, which has been in the planning stage since the late 1940's. The Inner Belt was never built because it aroused such controversy and citizens' resistance. Of course, Boston citizens are not alone in protesting the building of highways through their urban areas: inhabitants of

San Francisco, Baltimore, Manhattan, and other cities have voiced similar protests with the same results.

The present dilemmas of highway construction in many of the cities go back to 1956 and the creation of the Interstate Highway Program, which proposed to build a total of 41,000 miles of highways to link 90 per cent of cities with populations over 50,000. Of the 41,000 total, 5,500 miles of these highways were to be built through urban areas, including city centers. The system consists mostly of four-lane divided highways which were to be widened to six or eight lanes in urban areas. Interchanges, overpasses, and underpasses do away with grade crossings and traffic lights. Since the federal government pays 90 per cent of all highway-related costs, the program becomes almost irresistible politically.

While in rural areas most of the planned system has been built, in city after city the highway builders encountered innumerable difficulties in the areas affected. Some programs, for instance in San Francisco, had to be abandoned. The opposition against the Embarcadero Freeway of San Francisco has served as a trigger mechanism in the "Freeway Revolt." San Francisco turned down two major freeways and a quarter-billion dollars of federal money.

In other cities, notably Baltimore, New York (the Lower Manhattan Expressway), and Boston (the Inner Belt), highway building has been stalled. Arguments went on for years (nearly twenty years in Baltimore and in Boston since 1948), but nothing was built. In turn, this indecision hangs like a destructive threat over the areas involved and slowly strangles their communities.

Since transportation is essential to the economy, some accommodations had to be found. The "Design Concept Team" approach was first devised as a compromise by Mr. Archibald C. Rogers, a civic-minded Baltimore architect and partner of a well-known architectural and planning firm. "The Concept Team brings together interdisciplinary professionals to plan an urban highway, not in isolation, but in full relation to the needs of the surrounding areas and the city as a whole." This is the description given by the Baltimore Urban Design Concept Team Project, the first of its kind. It is the responsibility of the professional members of the team to see that the highway does not overwhelm the city, that the human and individual scale is preserved, and to assure that the community interests are considered.

DISCUSSION

F.P.H.   Other cities have followed the Baltimore example, notably Boston and Chicago. In Boston, the Inner Belt stalemate has finally been broken through a series of decisions that have culminated in the BTPR, the Boston

Transport Planning Review, which started its work in summer 1970 and is to complete its recommendations by the end of 1972.

Secretary Altshuler, since you are closer than anyone to this new program, perhaps you could outline how and why this regional transportation review was organized and what it hopes to accomplish.

A.A.   The Inner Belt controversy has been going on since the late 1950's. It exploded after Governor John Volpe went to Washington to become federal Secretary of Transportation. Governor Sargent announced in the spring of 1969 that he intended to appoint a task force to advise him on whether the current highway plans for the region within Route 128—the circumferential highway which runs ten to fifteen miles from the core of Boston—took adequate account of:

The job needs of residents affected;

The housing crisis of the metropolitan area;

The effect on community life;

The balance of transportation needs; and

The effect upon environment

During the summer of 1969, Governor Sargent asked me if I would be the chairman of that task force. That was my introduction to the political system of Massachusetts

We put together a task force entirely composed of professionals in the field of transportation and related areas such as ecology, economics, and operations research. During the next four months, this team of professionals interviewed numerous private-group representatives and the senior officials of all the public agencies that had been involved in planning the proposed regional expressway network. In January of 1970, the task force reported to the Governor that the existing highway plans had been developed without adequate concern for the questions he had raised. The consequences of the highway projects as planned might be so harmful, we thought, that the burden of proof had to be on their proponents. We urged the Governor to halt all design work until a comprehensive re-examination of the transportation needs within Route 128 could be conducted. That is, the total needs of the region should be examined in terms of the kind of transportation that would be most appropriate for the area.

F.P.H.   Two points are important here, I believe: the regional needs and the comprehensive approach. Public and/or rail transportation is included in the review of the total transportation needs of the area to create a balanced transportation system.

A.A.   In February of 1970, the Governor adopted the recommendations of the task force. For the first time in Massachusetts history, the Governor went on prime-time television to say that he was planning to make a very major change in transportation policy. He announced that he was going to conduct a transportation planning review that looked at highway and transit alternatives simultaneously, that provided for citizen participation in the process, and that was free to consider the no-highway option.

F.P.H.   The BTPR, or Boston Transport Planning Review, which was the first result of Governor Sargent's new transportation policy, goes well beyond the Design Concept Team approach of other cities.

A.A.   The Planning Review is not unique in its inclusion of both highway and transit agencies. There have been quite a few other transportation studies around the country that have involved highway and transit agencies. It is unique in the extent to which local government and citizen-group participation has been solicited and given a major role in the whole process. Technical assistance has been available to enable citizens' groups to make more useful inputs.

The BTPR is also unique because it does not simply assume that the Commonwealth of Massachusetts must take advantage of every federal dollar that it may be able to get. One of the characteristics of almost all the transportation studies in the past has been their assumption that the interstate highways the federal government was willing to finance had to be built. The only questions that could be asked were where the highways ought to go and how they ought to be designed.

The Boston Planning Review is unique as well in that the Governor has given it a great deal of personal attention and support, and rather unusual in the degree to which it takes a broad urban-planning approach rather than a narrow highway-and-transit-planning approach. The study, furthermore, is noteworthy in that it has to come up with some very critical decisions for the future of the Boston region within quite a short period of time. At this point, only six months from the contract signing which enabled the Planning Review to begin, a number of key decisions have been made, including dropping all plans for the Inner Belt.

F.P.H.   I understand that Phase I of the review was completed at the end of December 1971. Phase I was primarily concerned with analyzing the existing plans made by the Department of Public Works and to consider and develop many new alternative transportation methods, besides highway construction, as well as modifications to existing plans. The help of interested groups was sought, for instance, from communities through which the highways were planned.

A.A.   Besides giving up the very controversial Inner Belt, all plans for eight-lane expressways in the Boston region have been thrown out. The maximum-scale expressways within Route 128 will be four lanes, with additional lanes for buses and emergency vehicles. We also have eliminated or changed a number of alignments to be more compatible with the urban fabric.

Another result of the end of the first part of the review was that the Governor recommended an improvement of the public transportation system to encourage more people to use it, as it simply is too expensive to build as many highways or parking lots as some think we need.

F.P.H.   Boston has one of the oldest and largest subway systems. Recently some improvements have been made in terms of new rolling stock and renovation of stations. Extensions to some suburbs have been opened using existing rail lines, and more are planned. Yet the Boston subway system, like practically all others in cities around the country, is in financial difficulties.

A.A.   We are looking at a number of transit proposals for additional development, including a circumferential light-transit system for the inner portion of the Boston area. We are also considering the substitution of exclusive busways for rail rapid-transit systems. A busway is a particularly attractive kind of transit to build when you have highway money available. Outside of peak hours, the roadway capacity can be used for some other purposes than simply carrying transit.

In the Boston region, we don't have the volume of demand in any particular corridor that makes it necessary to use the rail alternative. A rail system can carry forty to sixty thousand people per hour.

F.P.H.   You point to the primary dilemma about public rail transportation: in order to be economically feasible, it must have enough passengers. To pay for an extension of rail lines into the suburbs, specific density of living patterns is needed to make rail transportation useful and an investment that can be justified. But people generally have opted for dispersed living patterns that preclude the building of new systems or of extending existing ones—or at least we must wait until enough people live in a given area to make transit economical.

Buses are one answer, but even there you need enough passengers to run a frequent schedule. If people have to wait a long time for public transportation, they will use other means. The same is true of rail systems. The poorer and the less frequent the service, the fewer the people who use it, and the more it costs to run the service. As a result, service gets even worse, more people use other transportation, and so on. All our public systems, it seems to me, are in that situation.

A.A.   The problem is that even in those areas where public transit can do the job very effectively, we have not had the money to provide adequate service. It is also quite important for certain groups in the population that don't have automobiles or can't drive: the very poor, the crippled, the very old, the young.

In the Boston region transit is not a private function. The fact is that in the Boston region, the "fare box" covers less than half the actual cost of providing transit service, and the subsidy therefore is very high. The efficiency of transit depends on having economy of scale if you measure efficiency in cost/benefit terms.

In the inner portions of the Boston region, that is, from Boston to five or six miles out of the core of the city, a large market exists. When you go out beyond that area, transit service tends to be extraordinarily expensive per passenger served. One further point: the efficiency of a transit system has to be evaluated not only in terms of what it costs per trip, but also in terms of the comfort, convenience, and speed it provides the passenger.

F.P.H.   You mention that large public subsidies for transit are needed. But it is a fact that transportation by private car or truck could never function unless highways and roads were built, and they are constructed largely at public expense with federal moneys. The same, of course, is true of air transport—it requires expensive airports. Therefore, many people feel that transit also should be supported with public funds.

One of the latest proposals is to divert the highway funds, which are collected from gasoline revenues mainly to build more and better public transit, because otherwise cars will continue to multiply. Parkinson's Law as applied to highways says that space fills up in proportion to what is provided: the more highways you build, the more cars you get. Therefore, you can never solve transportation problems by building more roads. Besides, as you point out, a one-sided transportation system that relies on cars leaves out a large segment of the population. Costs per mile of private car transportation are increasing much faster than earned or disposable income.

A.A.   The federal provision of 90 per cent financing to build interstate highways, as you say, makes them politically almost irresistible, unless there are very powerful reasons not to build them. Those reasons, typically, in an area like the inner portions of Boston, Baltimore, Washington, and San Francisco, have to do with the number of homes and businesses that would have to be dislocated.

The federal program is pressing us to spend enormous amounts of money— at times up to $80 or $100 million for one mile of highway—though the cost/benefit ratio, even in narrow highway terms, often is very low. If we look at the major expressways within the Boston region, the traffic that uses these expressways during the peak hours—which is really what you are building them for—is commuter traffic, people going to work. That is, they provide little or no service for interstate traffic. But, in fact, the federal highway legislation which guides the interstate program says that equal concern shall be given to interstate and local needs.

The people who have argued for the construction of these roads have emphasized the economic benefits that the roads might provide within the region as a result of improved access and jobs that would be created by the construction of the roads themselves. Our position with respect to funding has been that we ought to have a flexible transportation funding system, one in which the federal government does not try to tell the states what projects to build and what balance to draw between highway and transit investment, but rather allows these decisions to be determined within the states, within the metropolitan areas. The intercity portions of the interstate system are by now essentially complete.

On the whole, we think that in respect to ground transportation, particularly highways and mass transit, if the federal government would leave the states more flexibility, we would get far better transportation policies.

F.P.H.   As I mentioned in the introduction, a number of cities are now making a major effort to build transit systems. The most notable is "BART," the Bay Area Rapid Transit system of San Francisco. This new system, which certainly will qualify in terms of providing comfortable, convenient, high-speed transportation, does not aim to replace cars, of course. It has been estimated that at best it can relieve the peak loads by some 10 per cent. Even that, however, is a very useful accomplishment, especially given the geography of the Bay Area. In New York, at least 80 per cent of the people who travel to Manhattan go by public transportation, and the city could not function without it, as we saw during the transit strikes. Yet the fares have been increased time and again with growing public debate.

Montreal has built an excellent, attractive, and quiet new public subway system and has managed to finance it. Tokyo, which has one of the best subway systems in the world, is constantly building more, and Paris is beginning to extend its extensive subway system into the metropolitan areas and beyond, to the new towns that are under construction in the Paris region.

That is, whatever the financing mechanisms—and the systems abroad are all publicly financed and run—the need for more and better public transportation seems clear, and responses are finally forthcoming. This no doubt is related to the growth of all metropolitan areas and their increasing densities. People no longer move into the inner city as in the past, but they move into the metropolitan areas where the jobs are. Therefore, the creation of viable, balanced transportation in metropolitan areas is especially important, and that is what the BTPR study is all about.

A.A.   Let me say a few words about the decline of the downtowns. First, there is nothing particularly surprising about old areas declining relative to new areas. It has always been cheaper to develop on vacant land than to develop on land where you had to buy and then tear down old structures. Cities like San Francisco, Boston, and New York, which have great density, have not been declining economically in recent years. If you look at the 1970 census data, for example, the economy of the Boston region has shown an increase in jobs during this period of time and a great increase in the dollar value of payrolls. Industry has been moving out. Economic users that have great space needs and great trucking needs have been moving out.

On the other hand, the general drift of the American economy is toward increasing the proportion of white-collar office employment, and the downtown areas have been getting a good share of that. In fact, the downtown areas that have transit and that also have the worst traffic congestion, have been the most thriving downtowns in that sense because they also have density which attracts more density. It is worth pointing out again that building transit does not eliminate traffic congestion. Transit makes high density possible. High density attracts more traffic, and the result is that in the cities with the best transit systems you also have the worst traffic congestion. Those downtown areas that have been the most dependent on automobiles have on the whole not done as well even though they have had less traffic congestion.

F.P.H.   The liveliness of a city, what makes the inner city attractive and also economically viable, means lots of people in a small area. Many inner cities recently have found it both attractive to people and economically profitable to create pedestrian malls, specifically streets, whole areas in some cases, where cars are eliminated. The merchants and shopkeepers at first resisted this idea, but in practice most have found that their business volume increased by keeping cars away from their front doors, because in a limited area it made more room for people. You can't shop from a car.

Cities all over the world have created such pedestrian areas, and more are experimenting with this idea. The most far-reaching proposal in this respect has recently been made abroad in Vienna, which has a very old city center. Vienna is also building a subway, though it has been losing population. The proposal made in conjunction with the new subway system is to eliminate cars from the entire historic city center and replace them with small pollution-free buses, much like airfield buses. These vehicles will operate at frequent intervals, probably free of charge. Victor Gruen's international planning firm is the consultant to the city of Vienna, and the proposal is going ahead. Victor Gruen has made far-reaching proposals of a similar nature in many cities in the United States, including Boston's CBD (Central Business District). Unfortunately, few cities have followed his advice, but many have regretted it later.

There has been a good deal of change recently in how we view the transportation problems of cities. Some of the programs and ideas we discussed certainly show a new and more balanced approach to the problems—balance in terms of using a variety of existing modes of transportation. Are we likely to get anything drastically new in the near future in terms of transportation technology?

A.A.   There is no revolution in the offing. In the field of the vehicles, we first have had a major and salutary regulatory movement in the area of safety which still has a long way to go. We are now in the midst of change with respect to the polluting effects of the vehicle. Industry, under pressure, is responding and will produce within the next decade either a minimal or zero pollution automobile. I think the next phase of development with respect to vehicles ought to be regarding the noise impact.

When we talk in terms of transit, most of the changes are incremental. There is no point in our getting into changes in rail systems. Monorail is not significantly different from a two-rail system. The issue of rubber tires versus steel wheel, two tracks, one track, whatever—these are not revolutionary matters. The fact is, if a vehicle runs at a given speed on a fixed right-of-way, from the passenger standpoint, it is pretty much the same.

Innovations in the field of transit that I consider more significant over the long run have to do with flexible use of vehicles which use the roads. We have tended in the past to think of transit as a rail system. People have talked as though the only alternatives were rail transit versus the private automobile. I think that actually the middle way is the path of the future, that is, transit vehicles that use the roads. The roads are there, and the marginal cost transit usage is negligible. But most important, you get the flexibility of the road system because rail rights-of-way can only go a very few places, whereas the road system goes everywhere.

If you have a vehicle which can carry large numbers, which can exploit the flexibility of the road system, which can travel at high speeds in the dense areas, using for instance an exclusive busway, you can probably carry the volumes of traffic that almost all corridors can generate. We have to focus on making the vehicles convenient, low-polluting, air-conditioned, and comfortable.

Then there is the concept of Dial-a-Bus which is a very attractive concept for lower density areas, for trips which are not radial in nature or headed toward the downtown.

F.P.H.   A few years ago MIT had a research contract to work out such a system, which they called CARS, or Computer-Aided Routing System. It really is a taxi system, directed by a computer which keeps track of all the cars in the system. As a consumer, all you do is phone for service. You are picked up at the given point and delivered where you want to go in a given time at a fixed cost. In fact, this system provides a door-to-door service at little more than public-fare costs. It has the advantage of being able to cope with our dispersed living patterns and can take care of non-drivers. It also works very well in conjunction with transit or rail services for suburban communities by taking care of the trip to the station.

A.A.   The idea actually emerged simultaneously in a variety of places and was developed in a variety of ways. It is possible for a good human dispatcher to keep track of up to eight or ten vehicles. When you get above that point, the complexity becomes too great for the individual. I think Dial-a-Bus is very promising.

F.P.H.   To sum up, you believe we should not rely on fantasies that new transportation technology will revolutionize life and change cities. Rather, we should expect that real innovations and improvements will come gradually, by incremental changes.

A.A.   The important thing is to have the money to invest, to develop new ideas the right way, to have the management skills to use them right, and to put them into the right circumstances so we don't discredit good ideas by misusing them in the early applications.

We are not about to have a revolution in transportation technology. The key questions are really questions of financing, of management, and of governmental choice rather than questions of technology.

F.P.H.   Thank you, Secretary Altshuler.

BIBLIOGRAPHY

BOOKS

Appleyard, Donald; Lynch, Kevin; and Meyer, John R. *The View from the Road.* Cambridge, Mass.: The MIT Press, 1964.
A most interesting study of noting the visual and environmental qualities of highway travel.

Fleisher, Aaron. "The Influence of Technology on Urban Forms." In *The Future Metropolis.* Lloyd Rodwin, ed. New York: George Braziller, 1961.
Influence of transportation on urban form, and vice versa.

"The Freeway in the City: Principles of Planning and Design." A report to the Secretary of the Department of Transportation by the Urban Advisors to the Federal Highway Administration. Washington, D.C.: U.S. Government Printing Office, 1968.

Halprin, Lawrence. *Freeways.* New York: Reinhold Corp., 1966.

Hosken, Fran P. *The Language of Cities,* 2nd ed. Chapter on Form and Movement. Cambridge, Mass.: Schenkman Publishing Co., 1972.

Meyer, John R.; Kain, J. F.; and Wohl, M. *The Urban Transportation Problem.* Cambridge, Mass.: Harvard University Press, 1965.
One of the most authoritative studies of present-day urban transportation problems, with an emphasis on cars.

Owen, Wilfred, *The Metropolitan Transportation Problem.* Washington, D.C.: The Brookings Institution, 1966.
A basic, informative book, discussing balanced transportation.

–––. "A Fable: How Cities Solved Their Transportation Problems." Washington, D.C.: The Brookings Institution, 1968.
A most whimsical story about the fictional urbanists and their transportation follies.

Pell, Senator Claiborne. *Megalopolis Unbound.* New York: Frederick A. Praeger, 1966.

"Phase I of the Boston Transportation Planning Review." The Commonwealth of Massachusetts, Executive Department, News Release No. 1/DC/72 (December 29, 1971).

"Report to Governor Sargent on Immediate Action Opportunities." Governor's Task Force on Transportation (January 1970).

"Study Design for a Balanced Transportation Development Program for the Boston Metropolitan Region." Prepared for Governor Sargent under the direction of the Steering Group on the Boston Transportation Planning Review (November 1970).

ARTICLES

Hosken, Fran P. "Highways to Create Life, Not Blight." *St. Louis Post-Dispatch*, October 20, 1968.

–––. "Vienna: A new future for an old city," *Boston Herald Traveler*, August 15, 1971, Section 7:9.

6

GOVERNMENT

A discussion with BARNEY FRANK*
Assistant to Mayor Kevin White of Boston

INTRODUCTION

City government today is one of the most complex and demanding jobs. Indeed, it has been said that it is impossible to run a city the size of New York; there are just too many problems and issues, too many demands and needs, too many conflicts and confusions, and too little money to get the whole interrelated bureaucratic machinery moving to where it will respond to growing crises on all sides.

What is more, the relationships are so complicated and so diversified that one no longer can predict the results of any one decision or policy. Often some decisions, for instance, those pertaining to housing, may have totally unexpected results in such areas as transportation or employment. Highways that cities decided to build with federal help to improve transportation, especially from home to job, resulted in destroying large areas in the cities and thoroughly upset and uprooted many urban neighborhoods. The decision by the federal government to insure mortgage payments to encourage home ownership and stability had as its unintended result the desertion of the cities by the middle class. The cities lost their most effective constituency and their best taxpayers, who went to the suburbs. Business followed the exodus of the middle class to outlying areas where taxes were low.

Most city governments find themselves with a shrinking tax base, an influx of low-income people, mostly blacks from the South or minorities from Puerto Rico or Mexico, and with rising welfare costs and rising costs for services and administration.

There are other public decisions within cities that have created many more problems in the wake of solving one. It is the interrelationship of the decision-making process of all government that is so difficult to deal with. Especially since, for the sake of management, the city's government and adminis-

*Mr. Barney Frank is now administrative assistant to Congressman Michael J. Harrington of Massachusetts, in Washington.

tration have been divided up in many different agencies and systems that often fail to communicate.

Perhaps with a topic as comprehensive and complex as city government, we shall have to do the same and divide it up into its most important components or problems because cities in the United States today seem to be a bundle of problems of every kind.

DISCUSSION

F.P.H.   Mr. Frank, you are in the best possible position as Executive Assistant to Mayor White of Boston to describe what some of the problems of city government are. It seems to me that one hears constantly about the need for more funds and the lack of money to carry out even the most necessary programs or to supply a satisfactory level of service.

B.F.   There is no question that money is the greatest problem, to the point where it dwarfs every other. This is a fact in Boston and I think it is substantially true in almost every other big city. We simply do not have the revenue to perform the basic services that we ought to be performing.

Leave aside for the moment the special problems of needy people in the areas of housing, employment, and related programs, or job training. Today, we don't even have enough money in the city of Boston to keep our streets clean, to keep our parks in good shape, to keep our municipal buildings in repair, to tear down vacant buildings, to give enough police and fire protection.

Boston, like most cities, has to rely on the property tax. We rely on it even more than most other cities, though most cities rely on it heavily. The property tax is regressive; it is unelastic; it simply is not adequate to the demands of the people today who want service. Especially in an inflationary period, the cost of city government is going way up, and the revenue that we have available to us is simply not increasing proportionately.

F.P.H.   The property tax makes difficulties everywhere. One reason the suburbs close themselves off from the city through zoning regulations is because if people with low incomes move to the suburbs, the property tax of every home owner automatically goes up. The school system, for instance, is paid for through property taxes, and education is the biggest part of any government's budget. Consequently, if low-income people with children move to a suburban town the tax rate automatically goes up to pay for the additional places in school.

B.F.   The property tax in every sense is an outdated and archaic fiscal tool.

It is not proportional to the ability to pay. The property tax is a major factor in rents. The cost of shelter through rents or home ownership for people on the lower end of the economic scale is a very high percentage of their income. Therefore, the property tax is terribly regressive. No big city has the resources to really deal with its own problems as a result.

We would be a little better off if we were allowed to experiment with our own income tax and perhaps sales tax, but even there cities simply do not have the financial resources.

The central cities today, as you have pointed out, have a disproportionate number of the poor. Middle-class people have moved out. We also serve as service areas to the whole region. And, a city like Boston contains vast amounts of tax-exempt land.

F.P.H.   Boston is a city of institutions, especially many educational institutions and hospitals, and all institutions are tax exempt. I understand up to 49 per cent of all the land of Boston is tax exempt.

B.F.   Probably over half now, for a variety of reasons. We have governmental bodies, the state and federal government, the Port Authority. We have universities, hospitals, museums, churches. The fact is that many of these institutions serve the metropolitan area. Yet, they are located physically within Boston and as a result tax revenue is being lost within Boston. But they serve Newton, Brookline, Lexington, Quincy, and more. In many cases they serve many suburbs and towns as much as they serve Boston.

Logan Airport has a vast amount of tax-exempt land within the city of Boston, very valuable land that would bring in a great deal of revenue. The city gets not one penny from that airport which, of course, is not a city facility. It serves the whole of eastern Massachusetts and sometimes the whole state.

F.P.H.   With much business now moving out of the city following the middle class, there is also a loss of jobs within the city. This also contributes to the problems because the people who live in the city have to travel outside the city to work, while the people who live outside the city travel every day into the city. But, in fact, the city gets nothing from either group in terms of taxes. The people who live in the city mostly do not own any property and the people who come to work in the city pay taxes in the suburbs.

It has been proposed to raise a payroll tax so that everybody who works in the city, who makes his living in the city, pays a proportionate share to the city for the services that he receives while there.

B.F.   There are two relevant points here. One is that in Massachusetts the

State Constitution forbids us to raise any such tax. That is peculiar to Boston because it is in the Massachusetts Constitution. But it also highlights another problem many cities have.

Cities are very restricted in their operations. States are much freer and have a larger range of public policies from which they can choose. Typically, cities are restricted by state constitutions and state legislatures. So even though we would like to help ourselves, we are restricted. And I know this is not just true of Boston. I recently saw the budgets of the mayors of Detroit and New York. In each case, to balance their budgets and to provide the level of service necessary, they had to go to their state legislatures for permission to propose new taxes. All cities have this in common: they are kept in chains by their states.

The second point you have made is that business has been leaving the city and people have been leaving also. One problem of the payroll tax, if applied only to Boston, would be that it would impose an extra cost on doing business in Boston. It would be a further incentive for people to move out, or for business not to come to Boston.

We would much prefer a more equitable distribution statewide; so that the taxes are the same, whether you are in Boston or in Quincy or in Everett. In turn, the city of Boston would be given, through a distribution formula, some share of the revenue earned by people in the city, because we have to provide services for them. We have to clean up after them, we have to provide police, we have to provide fire protection, we have to pave the streets and more.

The city provides a lot of services for the commuters and gets very little in return. We would like to get something from commuters, but not in the first instance. Our first preference would be for statewide revenue rather than a city tax, because of the economic disadvantage that would result.

F.P.H.   The political boundaries of Boston are particularly unfavorable for the city because Boston is a very old city and has not adopted or accepted suburbs for quite a long time. The suburbs all have their own administration, government, and tax structure. There are over one hundred cities and towns now in the metropolitan area of Boston, but there are less than 600,000 people in the city which serves a metropolitan area of over two-and-one-half-million people. This seems to be quite out of balance. The Mayor, time and again, has suggested that there should be much more metropolitan cooperation and working together on the problems that everybody shares.

B.F.   The figures you give are very relevant because the city of Boston is, I think, the second smallest big city, taking the city in proportion to the standard metropolitan statistical area. We are very tiny. It is not that we have not accepted the suburbs but that they declined to be accepted. I think the last annexation was early in this century. The town of Brookline, for instance, if we are looking at a map, is surrounded on three-and-one-half sides by the city of Boston. It really ought to be part of the city by any rational socio-economic distribution.

The problem of the city center servicing the whole metropolitan area is exaggerated by the imbalance in size. We have a lot of people coming in and working here, using our institutions, and then leaving at night. They don't provide either the economic support or the political leadership that they ought to be giving the city.

The Mayor, to combat that, has proposed a regional alliance of the metropolitan area governments. In the first instance, that would be a confederation of the existing governments, because we have to be careful in the central city not to frighten the suburbs into thinking that we are trying to swallow them up. We want to protect their autonomy. The Mayor has come forth with a plan that does that, but which would also allow us to cooperate at least in transportation and water resources, in air pollution, and in recreation.

F.P.H.　　Those concerns know no political boundaries, after all.

B.F.　　Absolutely. The fact is, we have metropolitan agencies. We have a Metropolitan Transit Agency, we have a Metropolitan Port Authority, we have a Metropolitan District Commission that handles water and sewers. While we have come up with a technological answer to deal with these problems on a metropolitan basis, we have no corresponding form of political control.

If you are talking about a state agency, it is controlled by the Governor and the legislature. If you are talking about a city agency, it is controlled by the Mayor and the city council. But if you are talking about the metropolitan special-purpose agencies, you are talking about agencies that are literally not subject to any direct vote or control. Now that in itself is an evil because I think you get arbitrariness and insensitivity to public problems because there is no mechanism for insuring the responsiveness of those agencies. The Mayor's plan for metropolitan cooperation is an attempt to make the cities and towns within the region work together and at the same time to democratize the special-purpose agencies that have been operating quite outside the democratic framework.

F.P.H.　　Since 1969 there have been several meetings of representatives of all the regional towns and the City of Boston. The framework for regional cooperation was provided by the Metropolitan Area Planning Council. This is a body created by the Commonwealth of Massachusetts that has existed for several years, mainly doing research and planning. They are an advisory body without any power. Unfortunately, all agencies concerned with planning on the metropolitan level are at the present time restricted to an advisory function and cannot take part in the decision-making process. They simply advise and write reports that get shelved.

B.F.   That is why the Mayor's plan would incorporate the metropolitan planning function but would also give this metropolitan agency operating control over transportation, over the airport, the seaport, the mass transit facilities, over water and sewer and natural resource planning, and air pollution. It would not be just an academic, abstract planning agency, to which nobody listened, but an integrated agency which planned and implemented their plans in the metropolitan area.

F.P.H.   Metropolitan government has been tried in other areas. Toronto has a metropolitan government and Dade County in Florida is operating on a regional basis.

B.F.   Indianapolis just adopted a metropolitan government plan.

F.P.H.   The greater London Council was recently created from the London County Council by adopting a large area surrounding the center of London. Greater London, which is now the second largest urban area in the world after Tokyo, just recently went through a major reorganization which involved a completely new look at London's city government, which became the government for the entire metropolitan area. Many previously centralized functions, for instance, housing, fire control, and other services, were completely decentralized. Others, for instance, transportation or water supply, which can be more efficiently managed by a centralized system, in turn were reorganized under one authority. The change from a city government to a metropolitan government was used to reorganize the whole system in terms of greater efficiency of services, as well as increased citizen participation and local control.

In Boston, as far as city government is concerned, we must draw a line with the year 1959. That was the year that Boston created an urban renewal agency, the BRA (Boston Redevelopment Authority). The BRA is based on the 1949 federal housing legislation. Though it took Boston some ten years to make up its mind to create the BRA, it has been going strong ever since. At this point it is almost impossible to divide the city government and the Boston Redevelopment Authority. In many areas they overlap, wouldn't you say so?

B.F.   Yes, they do. They have to if things are to function well, because you need integration of your Redevelopment Authority with all your other agencies of the city or you find yourself at war.

Unfortunately, HUD is in the process of cutting back funds for urban renewal, as well as other funds. This is one of the problems we face, which goes back again to the funding area. The Redevelopment Authority has a number of projects that are fairly well along. Some of them were originally quite controversial. But at this point they are in the construction phase rather than the demolition phase. Now we find that the Nixon administration has not put urban renewal and other urban programs very high on their priority list. So the Redevelopment Authority faces a very severe threat to its existence.

This is a good example of how tenuous the city's life-line really is. Budgetary decisions in Washington can create chaos here in Boston. We have thousands of units of housing that may remain unbuilt and building lots that remain vacant; buildings were torn down with nothing replacing them. The present administration simply has no interest in what we are trying to do in the cities.

F.P.H.   Boston, I think, has a most extensive and certainly one of the most successful urban renewal programs of any city of its size. Boston is a city where urban renewal really has something to show at this point. We are here in the new City Hall, which is one of the most interesting contemporary buildings built anywhere in the country. This would never have been built without the redevelopment program. Around us is the Government Center, which also was built due to redevelopment. The whole center of Boston is by now partly rebuilt. But this is only the first phase and a redevelopment effort has to be continuous.

Housing has always been a critical issue in any city and Boston is one city that has made a very serious effort to build housing concomitantly with redevelopment.

B.F.   Money is, again, the basic problem. Poor people cannot afford to live in decent housing unless it is subsidized. The construction industry's costs are such that they cannot build housing that low-income people can afford to live in unless there is substantial assistance. The assistance can come in the form of subsidies in the course of building so that the rental can be kept low; it can come in the form of rent subsidies to the individual; or it can come in the form of directly-built housing where rents are charged as a percentage of the tenants' income.

The number one priority in the city is housing for low-income people. I think it is unfortunate that some of the early phases of our urban renewal program were not as conscious of that as they should have been. Mayor White determined, when he came into office, that low-income housing and middle-income housing had to be given a much higher priority. We are trying as hard as we can to do something about this, but we are in a very tight money situation.

F.P.H.   At this point the federal funds are being cut just when you are really trying to build housing.

B.F.   We are in a position where we have acreage in the South End that is cleared. We have everything ready to go and now we are told the funds are being cut. We put together the "Infill Housing Program"—a scattered site, low-income program—which had several false starts, but it is now going ahead. We hope to get over seven hundred low-income housing units built within the next year or so, taking advantage of the leased-housing program. We are trying to take advantage of every federal and state subsidy program we can. It is a very difficult fight. At the present level of support by the federal government, it is simply not going to be possible to do very much about a very desperate housing crisis.

F.P.H.   The housing crisis has been made much worse through an increase in the interest rates, which have gone up enormously during the last few years until quite lately. The cost of the money to build a housing unit, plus the cost of the mortgage, is the largest part of all housing costs. For instance, every half per cent of increased interest payments raises rents of the finished building some 15 per cent. By now the rents are entirely out of proportion to what people can pay. As a result, you have to increase the subsidies if you want any housing at all for low-income people. It becomes a vicious circle. Besides the high cost of money, inflation has contributed much to the housing crisis: the construction costs have gone up quite out of proportion to other industries.

B.F.   We have had some projects that were just about ready to go when the rise in interest rates threw the financing into chaos. They had to be refinanced and, of course, that causes the rents to go even higher.

F.P.H.   One very interesting program I think we should talk about is the Mayor's decentralization effort, in terms of creating Little City Halls in different parts of the city. The purpose is to enable people to participate more directly in the political process, or at least make themselves heard. It shows people what city government is all about. They can take care of their problems in their own neighborhoods without going downtown. This program has been very effective. It would be interesting to hear more about this from you.

B.F.   There has been a change in public thinking in the last few years. Twenty years ago the concept of democracy was that people went to the polls every stated number of years and elected their representatives, instructed them, and then sat back until the next election. They might occasionally contact their representatives, but that was really the limit.

Now, especially in urban government, since governmental action very directly affects many peoples' lives on a day-to-day basis, they want more involvement. It is necessary to preserve the government structure, but also to provide mechanisms for more continuous participation, and we have been experimenting with a whole range of ideas.

The Little City Hall network, which you mentioned, covers the whole city. There are about thirteen Little City Halls which serve a number of functions as decentralized service centers. They also hear complaints. One of the most frequent problems people complain about is that streets are not clean or that a street light is out. To remedy some situations you may find that four or five departments are involved, maybe the water department, perhaps the sewer department, or the parks department, or others. The people get completely frustrated trying to understand that merry-go-round. But at the Little City Halls they need to speak only to one person.

F.P.H.   Sweden has tried to remedy this same situation by creating the function of an ombudsman who helps people unravel the red tape and who has direct access to all departments.

B.F.   Well, that is what our Little City Halls do. You don't have to find out which department is responsible, but you tell the official in the Little City Hall what is wrong. It is his job to track it down, and to crack department heads over a jurisdictional dispute. It usually means some part of a public service is not being performed.

You can also go to the Little City Halls to get services, tax forms, etc. Equally important, the Little City Halls have begun to serve as a nucleus for community organization. We have found that our Little City Hall managers within the councils of the administration have become very zealous advocates of the neighborhood viewpoint. Little City Hall managers from East Boston and Jamaica Plain were instrumental in persuading the Mayor to come out against a proposed highway network which threatened those areas. The manager in the Brighton area alerted us to the need for rent controls. There have been a number of issues in which the Little City Halls' managers have functioned as the representatives of their areas, and we have decided to institutionalize that by getting some advisory committees elected. We are still experimenting.

Boston also has a large Model Cities Program. The Model Cities Neighborhood Board in Boston is an elected board that has a great deal of power over the program.

F.P.H.   The Model Cities Program of Boston is one of the most comprehensive and effective ones anywhere in the country. The Model Cities area here is very large, about 10 per cent of the city. The program in Boston really is quite a remarkable experiment in democracy, in self-determination, on the part of a large area in the city. The people in the Model Cities areas want to decide their own fate and future and they participate in planning for the services they need.

B.F.   It is working very well. One other point is that the Model Cities Neighborhood Board is racially integrated. When racial tensions are increasing, when separatists and segregationists of various hues are gaining strength, it is useful to note that the Model Cities program is integrated. The whole area is integrated. The previous board, which is just going out of business, had eleven black members and seven white ones, I think. The racial breakdown will be approximately the same on the new board, and they work very well together. That is important because it shows that people with the same economic problems, and the same social problems, black people and white people, though very different in some respects, are able to work together in a very democratic framework within the city government.

The good relationship that the Mayor has with the Model Cities Neighborhood Board has demonstrated conclusively to us that citizen participation and a degree of community control can be a genuine asset for everybody. One should not look at the Mayor and at the community groups as adversaries. In fact they can work together very well.

F.P.H.   This experience has really proven to be excellent for Boston. Politically and socially, Boston is interesting from many points of view. As you point out, race relations have been on the whole quite peaceful and well-handled, certainly from City Hall. I believe Boston does not have some of the acute racial problems that some other cities have. Boston also can serve as a model for the rest of the country, since the black-white ratio is just about the national average, or a little more than 12 per cent of the total population. There are many more children among the black community; therefore there are many more black children in school, but, on the whole, I believe the population is approximately balanced in the same proportion as nationally.

B.F.   It is now growing toward 15 per cent or more, because we have a certain number of whites moving out. This is certainly much closer to the national average than Cleveland or Detroit or Washington, D.C., or Philadelphia or any of the other cities. Martin Luther King said Boston probably had as good a chance to make it in the racial sense as any city. There are a number of factors that make it an easier situation. There has been much less inmigration. Boston is sort of out of the way and it is cold. In other cities the population has grown very rapidly. People have moved in who were not used to city living and the city was not able to provide the services they need.

F.P.H.   Boston recently has had many new Spanish-speaking immigrants from Puerto Rico and always had a large Jamaican population group.

B.F.   There are greater problems with the Spanish-speaking immigrants because of the language barrier. We have to set up more Spanish-language schools and classes. We don't think that the black people of Boston or the Puerto Rican people of Boston are very well treated. There are grave defects in the ways in which society responds to their problems and the ways we overcome them. We need a lot more money to do it better.

But I think it is true that the situation in Boston, because of the small size of the black population, is easier, and also because many of the people have been here a long time and are familiar with city living and with Boston. As a result we have made very real progress. Take as an example the Model City Neighborhood area. We know the Model Cities program in many cities is in all-black areas, while here it is integrated. In many cities there is a great deal of tension between the mayor and the Model Cities board.

F.P.H.   Here it has worked out remarkably well and I think this is much to the credit of Mayor White, who seems to get on with all the minorities extremely well.

B.F.   We find that in a lot of cities the mayors are pressing hard to cut back on community participation. In Boston we want to give our model neighborhoods more power than HUD wants us to; Mayor White as administrator understands that this is the best way to run Boston.

F.P.H.   Perhaps we should take a look into the future. At this stage, unfortunately, it seems to me the future is very much in doubt. The financial problems seem to be overwhelming, which brings us back to the beginning of our conversation. The debt service is increasing each year, while the city services are cut down. The taxes must be increased, which drives more business out of the city. More people are leaving because schools are inadeqoate and do not offer the kind of education people want for their children. There are more and more strikes by teachers and city service employees, more and more budget difficulties in every area. The whole situation seems to defeat itself.

Yet we need the city. I do not see how we can get along without cities. But nobody seems to realize that our present national system, or really non-system, destroys the very basis of cities and especially their ability to raise taxes. As a result they can no longer provide the services people demand. On top of that, they are physically aging and in need of many repairs. What do you think of the future of Boston in particular?

B.F.   My prognosis has to be both pessimistic and optimistic. Pessimistic if you project the trends into the future as they now seem to be going. That is, most cities as we both said, do not have the money to do a good job.

In Boston, I would say, if there are not some drastic changes in the near future, if there are not some really great infusions of money from outside, you can expect a rising tax rate that will further oppress the poor. A rising property tax rate will help drive more of the middle class out of Boston. Yet you can expect no improvements, because even with the rising tax rate the income has so dwindled or failed to keep pace that it will not be able to provide the services that are needed. I think that will increase the unpleasantness of city life and increase tension and alienation. On the whole, the near future will be very bleak.

My optimism comes from the fact that this does not have to be. I do not think anyone questions that this country has the resources to solve most of the problems of the American city. Racial tensions and other social ills certainly are going to be around for awhile, and money alone will not solve that. But we have enough money to build decent housing for every American; there is no question about that. We must have enough housing for people to have a decent life. We have enough money to have a decent mass-transportation system and clean streets. The fact is that the political majority in this country at this point has not been willing to commit the resources to the city; it takes the cities for granted. It is also taking for granted that the cities should produce most of the federal taxes without getting anything in return.

F.P.H.   The city still is the center of government and administration, of service jobs, of the professionals, of business management, of cultural affairs and communication, of education, of universities, and of hospitals.

B.F.   I think here is the answer. The national administration unfortunately does not appreciate the magnitude of the city crisis. Hopefully, we can do some educating there. Things look bad, but they don't have to be bad. I think our problem is not that we lack the resources but that the political decisions have not been made on the right levels to employ the resources toward the problems of the city.

F.P.H.   We are also increasingly aware of pollution problems. We should realize that it is not only a matter of ecology but that we are facing some very fundamental problems as far as the quality of urban life is concerned. The man-made environment, the way it is built, is one of the greatest contributors to environmental pollution.

B.F.   My greatest fear is that suburbanites are going to forget the city, and that the ecology is going to become the new cause, while the city will be last year's issue.

F.P.H.   But everybody lives in a man-made environment. I can never understand why people who spend their days in an urban environment so completely neglect and abuse this environment. Their own lives, as a result, are made miserable, unpleasant, unhealthy, and polluted. All these problems are man-made, and therefore they can be dealt with and eliminated.

B.F.   Why do people want to ignore the city to the point where they feel that they have to live an hour-and-a-half's drive from the city? Yet they want to work in the city and they spend three hours going back and forth each day. They could save themselves a good deal of time and wear and tear if they would help to make the city into the kind of place that they would want to live in. As you say, the problems are man-made, and they can be man unmade, and that is why there is some hope.

F.P.H.   Thank you, Mr. Frank.

BIBLIOGRAPHY

BOOKS

Abrams, Charles. *The City is the Frontier.* New York: Harper and Row, 1965. The U. S. city as the location of change, analyzed by one of the outstanding pragmatic urbanists of all times.

Adrian, Charles R. and Press, Charles. *Governing Urban America.* 3rd ed. New York: McGraw-Hill Book Co., 1968.

Baker, John H. *Urban Politics in America.* New York: Charles Scribner's Sons, 1971.
A well-organized, comprehensive view of city politics.

Bundy, McGeorge. *Strength of Government.* The Godkin Lectures at Harvard University, 1968. Cambridge, Mass.: Harvard University Press, 1968.

Carmichael, Stokeley, and Hamilton, Charles V. *Black Power: The Politics of Liberation in America.* New York: Random House, Inc., Vintage Books, 1967.

Dahl, Robert A. *Who Governs? Democracy and Power in an American City.* New Haven: Yale University Press, 1962. Paperback.

Downs, Anthony. *Urban Problems and Prospects.* Chicago: Markham Publishing Co., 1970.

A pragmatic discussion, including suggestions for solutions of urban problems pragmatically, seen by one of the most experienced experts.

Eldredge, H. Wentworth, ed. *Taming Megalopolis.* 2 vol. New York: Frederick A. Praeger, 1967.

The largest collection of urban topics, with a large choice of contributions.

Gans, Herbert J. *The Urban Villagers: Group and Class in the Life of Italian Americans.* New York: The Free Press, 1962. Paperback.

Glazer, Nathan, and Moynihan, Daniel P. *Beyond the Melting Pot: The Negroes, Puerto Ricans, Jews, Italians and Irish of New York City.* Cambridge, Mass.: The MIT Press, 1963. Paperback.

Greer, Scott, *The Emerging City.* New York: The Free Press, 1962. Paperback.

———. *Governing the Metropolis.* New York: John Wiley and Sons, Inc., 1962.

Handlin, Oscar. *The Newcomers: Negroes and Puerto Ricans in a Changing Metropolis.* Garden City, New York: Doubleday and Co., Inc., Anchor Books, 1962.

Lindsay, John V. *The City.* New York: W. W. Norton & Company, Inc., 1970.

Weaver, Robert C. *Dilemmas of Urban America.* New York: Atheneum, 1965. Paperback.

Wood, Robert C. *1400 Governments.* Garden City, New York: Doubleday & Co., Anchor Books, 1964.

A city government consists of hundreds of overlapping and conflicting jurisdictions, 1400 in New York.

ARTICLE

"The Conscience of the City," *Daedalus.* Journal of the American Academy of Arts and Sciences. Fall 1968 issue.

7

EDUCATION AND SCHOOLS

A discussion with Dr. DAVENPORT PLUMER
Manager of Educational Services for Training, Development
and Research Associates, Inc., Cambridge, Massachusetts

INTRODUCTION

Urban education and schools have been the subjects of hot debate, accusations, and controversies of all kinds in every city in the United States. Schools and education are a foremost political issue despite the fact that the structure of the American school system was designed especially to keep schools out of politics. The political issues of administering, financing, building, and running schools, the issues of community control and decentralization are often inseparable from the education that schools provide. Schools exist for the purpose of educating children, but in most cities they have recently become prime political battlegrounds.

The cost of education and schools is the highest budget item in most communities. The cost of schools directly affects the level of property taxes, which in turn influences the cost of housing and, therefore, the cost of living.

The local control of school systems is a hallowed prerogative in the United States. The result is that schools differ greatly from one community to another. Frequently, inner-city and suburban schools, sometimes only a few miles apart, are worlds apart.

The inequality of the financial base of schools, which depends on how much property tax each community can raise, has recently come under attack and been declared "illegal" by some court decisions. That may well revolutionize the whole basis of school financing in the near future, as well as change the property tax system, which has been termed regressive by most experts.

Since schools and education are such a broad and controversial topic, priority will be given here to issues that directly affect the education of urban children, especially inner city schools. Each issue is discussed with this question in mind: How does it affect the urban child's education and life, especially the child of the inner city, whose education has become the center of so much controversy?

DISCUSSION

F.P.H.   What is education doing for the urban child, Dr. Plumer? What in your opinion is really happening now in education, and specifically in city schools?

D.P.   To answer this question, I think it is worthwhile to look at what people have thought education was doing in the past. Perhaps this will give us a clue to the way people are reacting to educational offerings that they find in cities today. One of the main illusions about the education of the past is that it performed the function of a great melting pot. People of all nationalities, different ethnic backgrounds, and diverse academic abilities came to school, mixed with one another, learned each other's ways and, according to the illusion, accepted one another.

This notion is also associated with the notion of upward mobility as a product of education. When we think of upward mobility, we think of the able child from a deprived minority. The able child goes to school, does well academically, goes on to some form of higher education, then moves up in the social ladder, and, finally, advances to a position beyond that of his parents.

What is causing people dissatisfaction and concern about education today is that these two benefits do not seem apparent in the experience of many people who go to school in the cities today. They do not find that the school offers the opportunity for either upward mobility or social integration. Particularly in the case of black students, they find that even doing quite well in a city school has depressingly little to do with success in the world later on.

F.P.H.   Have the city schools fallen behind the schools in other parts of the country, say for instance suburban schools?

D.P.   Yes, and there are several reasons for this, it seems to me. Let us take an uncontroversial reason to start with. A student in a city school frequently will have what appears to him, and perhaps to his parents as well, a very good academic record. He will have A's and B's. But when he goes to take standardized tests that might have to do with his entrance to college, he finds out that he does very poorly and does not qualify for entrance or scholarship aid. The problem is that the standards that apply in city schools are often much lower than those in competitive suburban schools.

Another reason, and this is a somewhat more controversial one, is the often sharp differentiation between the expectations and attitudes of the teachers and administrators and the expectations, experience, and needs of the students and their parents.

F.P.H.   The city school problems with educational standards are well-known. Perhaps, for a start, we could outline the problems and then discuss solutions.

It seems to me that the problem is the lack of money to do what is necessary for the recent immigrant to the city who hopes that the school system will provide what a family cannot provide: to get the child used to the city and a different way of life, to stimulate upward mobility, and to perform the melting pot function, which you said turns out to be an illusion though it is widely believed, especially by parents. At this critical moment so many people depend on the school system to provide what the family cannot do.

D.P.   This failure is particularly acute because the majority of white and black immigrants to the city depend upon the institution of the school (rather than, for example, the church or some other institution) for success in later life. They come from rural areas where the norms for social roles and interactions and the demands of making a living are radically different from the demands made upon them by the city. This is different from the early 1900's, when some immigrants to the city at least had the advantage of coming from other urban settings.

Now, most city school administrators and policy makers have accepted (grudgingly and doubtingly in some cases) the role of principal socializing institution for disadvantaged immigrants to the city. They have also said, "We need more money to do this exceedingly difficult job." Some of that money has flowed from the Elementary and Secondary Education Act of 1965. But this depends upon the vagaries of national policies and thus the bulk of the money for inner-city schools must still come from the overburdened urban property owner.

In this connection, it is worth noting a second problem plaguing city school systems. As urban property becomes increasingly expensive and important to the city's tax base (especially in a city like Boston where about all of the city's acreage is tax exempt), it becomes harder and harder to find and to justify taking land for public schools from the city tax rolls. New York and other cities have taken some imaginative steps in reducing this problem by laying the legal groundwork for multiple occupancy. That is, a private developer might build a school into an office complex and take a tax reduction in payment for leasing the school to the city. A variation of this idea has been proposed for Boston whereby the city would require that the usual school construction be halted and that no new privately-owned, income-producing building be put up unless it contained a school. Such a move would not only alleviate space and financial problems; it would accomplish a very decisive kind of decentralization.

F.P.H.   The financial situation has many more implications than lack of money to build city schools. Suburbs pay for their own school systems. But immigration of people from the city, especially low-income people, directly affects the tax rate, since the costs of educating their children are not offset by the local taxes they pay. The suburbs are protecting themselves with zoning regulations in order to keep low-income people out. Large-lot zoning makes it too expensive for poor people to move to the suburbs. Low-income families with many children immediately affect the tax rate of every home-owner in the suburbs, and most suburbs therefore refuse to build any housing for low- and middle-income people.

D.P.   One of the results of this segregation in housing is that there is tremendous inequality in per pupil expenditure for education. To cite just one example, the difference between the annual expenditures in the inner city of Houston, Texas, and its surrounding suburbs comes in some cases to as much as $350 per pupil. This financial inequity is bound to cause all manner of social and educational inequities, some of which we have not even been able to measure yet. It is also difficult to measure the extent to which federal programs like Head Start, Follow Through, or Job Corps have been successful in compensating for the inequality in educational spending that stems from the unequal real estate tax base of suburban, urban, and rural areas. The recent California Supreme Court decision declaring the local property tax an unacceptable basis for educational spending may go far to close the gap in educational spending.

F.P.H.   The property tax is a most regressive tax in every way. The Federal Education Act of 1965 has tried to compensate for some of these inequalities by providing more financing where it is needed, mostly in the city schools.

D.P.   Yes, this was the intent of the Act; particularly Titles I and III were intended to do just that. For the most part they have not had conspicuous successes. This may, however, not be because the concept of compensatory education is inappropriate to the situation but that it has not been given an adequate trial. For example, some of the expenditures for city schools have gone into a reduction in class size.

F.P.H.   Fewer pupils per class, however, is one of the demands of all teachers.

D.P.   Yes, and it is a perfectly legitimate demand. It is a demand which teachers' unions, especially, have pressed for. But the difficulty is that, even with a tremendous increase in the expenditure per pupil, the end result is miniscule in terms of effect on a given pupil. For instance, you can have what appears to be a large expenditure that, when it is broken down into the effect on a given pupil, may result in only the reduction of a class size from thirty-two to thirty. Or, it may result in the addition of fifteen to twenty minutes' time on the part of a teacher, to deal with a given child over a period of a week. Now, these two kinds of changes are hardly adequate to deal with the multi-problem child who normally inhabits urban classrooms.

F.P.H.   One recent experiment pertaining to classroom size is to add teachers' aides. It seems to be quite successful, for instance, in the Boston school system and it is also stimulating community participation. I imagine school systems elsewhere have tried the same thing.

D.P.   Teachers' aides are one way of dealing with the high pupil-teacher ratio that you find frequently in city schools. It seems to make good sense, certainly from the political standpoint. There are two main advantages. One is the fact that a teacher's aide, at least in theory, comes from the same background as the pupils and is able to bridge the gap in understanding and experience between the teacher and the pupil. This frequently has a very beneficial effect, at least in terms of the general atmosphere and tone of the class. It has yet to be proven that it has an effect on the children's academic performance.

The second advantage, of course, is the advantage to the aide. Teacher aides are frequently people from the local community who may not have a very full educational experience themselves, but who often have an intuitive ability to deal with children. If the experiments showing the importance of teacher expectation have any validity at all, it seems to me that teachers' aides can have a profound effect on what goes on in the city schools. For instance, if you find a situation in which a teacher's expectations for his pupils is not as high as it might be, it is at least possible that a teachers' aide can influence both the teacher and the student. The teachers' aide can convey a sense of higher expectation to the child and the teacher and thus influence the child's sense of confidence and, over time, his performance.

F.P.H.   The first experiment in teacher expectation you refer to was made inadvertently, I believe. The records of some pupils got mixed up—between children of high I.Q.'s and low I.Q.'s. It was found at the end of the year that the children whom the teacher expected to perform well due to the wrong I.Q. scores did indeed perform well, while other children of whom the teacher didn't expect performance fell behind quite markedly. The expectation of the teacher is very important because it also shapes the child's own expectation of himself in regard to performance.

D.P.   The same thing happened in the army where several men's computerized records were inadvertently changed. Eventually, after the computer was corrected, it was found that the person at the low end of the scale was performing very well in the complex role he had been put into by mistake. This it seems is a principal argument for the movement toward more community control of schools and getting parents into a position where they can influence the teachers' expectations for their children.

F.P.H.   By taking an active part in this way the community can have an effect on education. There is a continuous debate about decentralization and community control. The two, however, are not the same. Considering that the American school system was based originally on the prerogative of individual communities to control and to finance their own school systems, it seems obvious that the city schools should be controlled by their own communities. The city no longer is one community, as in the past, but has grown enormously. Cities are made up of many different communities and neighborhoods and most often city school systems are just too large and don't reflect the needs and wishes of the many communities within their system.

City school systems, though very large, are centrally controlled. Suburban school districts are much smaller and more flexible, enabling them to respond better to the needs of different students. As a result, students there often see schools as less restraining and unresponsive and more able to change and innovate.

D.P.   Yes, but I think that this is not exclusively because suburban schools are more directly controlled by the parents, though this is a very important feature. It is very clear that the centralization of a large city school system, like New York for example, dramatically limits what can be done in terms of individualizing schools or classrooms. You do not have to do any more than read David Rogers's book *110 Livingston Street*[1] about the organization of New York City schools to realize that it is virtually impossible to effect any changes in individual schools, much less the system as a whole.

One attempt to effect an organizational change, namely to give the Ocean Hill-Brownsville district and the other demonstration districts in New York City a measure of self control, ran into innumerable difficulties. Many of these were due to centralization and bureaucratization of schools in New York City. There are simply too many people who place a higher value on bureaucratic convenience than on educational flexibility and experimentation.

[1] David Rogers, *110 Livingston Street* (New York: Random House, 1968).

Another stumbling block in the efforts to establish demonstration districts has been the uncertainty in people's minds about the relationship between community control and decentralization. Under decentralization, the professional administrative personnel retains primary control over the fundamental decisions about schools, mainly hiring and firing, expenditure, and curriculum. Under community control, these issues become the responsibility of parents or parent representatives. This was the reorganization that the local governing body in Ocean Hill-Brownsville was trying to bring about. Because of the publicity and because the dispute eventually led to a ten-week teachers' strike, the whole notion of community schools has received a bad name and is considered unworkable by some people. However, it should be pointed out that there is another example of a community-controlled school that works within the framework of the public school system, namely, the Morgan School in Washington. There, the concept of a community school has taken hold and is working out much better. The school has received much less publicity, though it has done very well and should be considered a model for the concept of community-controlled education.

F.P.H.   The Philadelphia school system during the last few years has been planning to decentralize. This effort, I understand, goes on with the help and cooperation of the central school administration and affects the entire public school system.

The concept of community schools also implies the use of school buildings as community centers for all sorts of community activities afternoons, evenings, weekends, and during vacations. It seems a pity to have a good school building empty and unused much of the time in a community that frequently lacks facilities. Schools are shut at least three months out of the year and every weekend, while children have no place to go or play. Most schools keep parents out altogether. If nothing else, this is a great waste of expensive facilities.

Many new city schools are built with community facilities so that the schools can lead a double life: one for the pupils and their teachers in the morning, and one as a center for the rest of the community. Sports and recreation facilities such as swimming pools, auditoriums, and meeting rooms —also classrooms, cafeterias, and workshops—can in many cases be used by all people in a community and programs can be organized by community groups.

In Boston there are a number of new schools just completed that have facilities which are available for all kinds of community-oriented programs and for afternoon recreation programs for children. These community schools are also used evenings, weekends, and the year round. One problem is financing these activities. Most school systems are hard put just to finance basic education or to keep the buildings open six or seven hours a day, five days a week. If they have to be open twelve or fourteen or more hours a day, seven days a week the year round, this puts an enormous financial burden on the city; and schools are paid for by the property tax.

D.P.   Yes, it clearly adds to the problem. I think, though, that the underlying problem here is only partially financial. The closing of schools at 3:15 and the closing of schools on weekends and in the summer is representative of an attitude on the part of the teachers, professionals, and school administrators, which stresses the sharp differentiation between them and the parents. This differentiation, or even unwillingness to work with or associate with parents, and particularly poor parents, is symbolized by the closing of the city schools, which are really "closed" to the surrounding community. By and large, this tendency on the part of professional teachers and administrators to exclude parents from the activities of the school tends to be accentuated when the parents happen to be poor and black and recent immigrants to the city.

The most obvious manifestation on the part of professional teachers is an attitude of low or minimal expectation towards poor black children. The assumption is that a child who is poor and black is not going to succeed. This child will either be allowed to slip through the school with a minimum amount of work or will be treated as a person who simply cannot do the work to start with. Various solutions have been proposed for this problem; one of these is community control of schools. As you observed, many schools are now being built that have community facilities. In the long run this is going to have a beneficial effect in breaking an artificial and negative barrier between the professional teacher and the administrator on the one hand and the parents and other residents of the urban school district on the other.

F.P.H.   From the point of view of many community spokesmen, the school should be the natural center of the community and a place where everybody should be free to come and go. This ought to be reflected in the physical plan of a community. In fact, this is the case in many new towns abroad that are planned around their schools. Most of the new towns in Great Britain, for example, are organized into neighborhoods around their schools. Land for school building is designated from the start, with housing and community facilities arranged accordingly. Also, children don't have to cross any streets and can walk to school from where they live.

Certainly the school should be a place to spend your leisure hours constructively and pleasantly. A true community school could enhance the entire social life of the community. It should fill leisure hours with new pursuits and ideas, and be a place for the whole family to go. This concept could restructure many city communities.

D.P.   Before we move on to other considerations, there is a third kind of community school that we have not talked about. It is a small enterprise as far as schools are concerned, but I think it represents many people's sense of dissatisfaction and frustration with public schools as they now exist in the cities. The kind of community school I mean is a private school set up by parents to meet the specific needs of those parents and their children. Most of these schools are small. Probably Boston has more of them than many other cities, but I think the concept is important. The school that is probably best known is the First Street School in New York. George Dennison, in his book, *The Lives of Children*,[2] wrote about this school which is supported by private sources. The emphasis in this kind of school is on the needs of very poor children, many of whom are not able to succeed in public schools.

There are three community schools of this type in Boston, each of which operates outside the public school system. They are all having financial troubles, but they are successfully developing the concept of a community school as an entity outside the public school system which is able to meet the special needs of a small population of children who are usually left out.

F.P.H.   There are many new ideas in education now, probably due to the dissatisfaction with public schools and the monopoly they exercise over education. One idea concerned with opening up schools to the surrounding city, the "school without walls" as it has been called, has gained popularity. This kind of school involves students in the activities and life of the city. Schools too often shut children off from the life of the community around them. A prime requirement for positive change is to establish a connection between schools and community life. Children learn in different ways, and there are different things that children ought to be involved in. However, schools have often turned their backs on changes taking place in the surrounding community and city.

In addition to those we just mentioned, there are other interesting new educational concepts, such as team teaching, schools without formal classrooms, and non-graded schools where children progress individually and work at what they are interested in pretty much on their own.

D.P.   There are many new ideas that should be tried. Team teaching is a way of structuring teaching and learning that holds some promise for a city school—if only because it means that the city child is less likely to be faced with a different substitute teacher several days in a given week. In some schools children have as many as twenty different substitute teachers in a given year. This problem can be alleviated by team teaching.

[2] George Dennis, *The Lives of Children* (New York: Random House, 1969).

However, the difficulty with any new scheme is that it requires a willingness to change on the part of the teachers who actually are doing the teaching in city schools, and this has been very hard to achieve.

F.P.H.   There are other new ideas and new methods being discussed about how to effect change in education. The tuition voucher is an idea that has been much discussed lately. It would ensure that every family receives enough money for the education of each child, which they could spend on any school of their choice. As a result, it is believed that there would be competition and many different schools would be set up. Schools might be organized by business corporations that would offer a great variety of educational programs. Such a scheme would certainly change the whole idea of education and the existing school system.

D.P.   The tuition-voucher idea is one of the most fundamental blueprints for educational change to come along in a long time. As I understand it, it does not rule out public schools; each child's voucher, which is the equivalent of a certain amount of money, could be used at any school he wanted to attend within a given price range. At least theoretically, this would exert a great deal of pressure on public schools to become responsive to their communities or else run the risk of having no children to teach.

F.P.H.   Another innovation is the Philadelphia Parkway Project, which has been quite successful. It is especially interesting in this context, because we are concerned with city problems and city schools. In the Parkway Project, the city is being used as a resource for the school. The Parkway Project, which is for high school students, has no school buildings or classrooms. The students use the institutions of the city, such as museums, libraries, or any other institutions' educational and training programs where they participate. The students meet three times a week to discuss their progress with a tutor; other than that, they write their own schedule. I should mention that a student, first of all, must develop his own program, which has to be approved by the Parkway Project. Other students must be willing to join this program, which is offered as a "course," if enough students want to participate. I understand it has turned out to be quite a success. A school without school buildings also saves the community quite a lot of money.

D.P.   The Philadelphia Parkway Project is particularly interesting because it achieves the effect of individualizing instruction, and this is one of the difficulties that a great many schools face now. Because of their size and because of the tendency to become committed to a set of textbooks or a program, large city schools have very little opportunity for individualizing instruction.

It seems to me that one of the most promising aspects of the Parkway Project is that it does allow the student to determine his course of instruction.

F.P.H.   At present the Parkway Project is entirely for high school students. I understand a similar experiment will be started with elementary schools.

Perhaps we should now look at the city's education and school problems in a racial context. Integration versus segregation has been one of the prime issues in the schools, especially in the city schools. It certainly is one of the prime national political issues at this point, despite the fact that integration in schools has been the law of the land since 1954. How to achieve integration and quality education has been the cause of much controversy. Education stands for excellence in our culture and in our life; but it also furnishes the basis for economic success. Without education you cannot get a good job, to put it into basic terms. This has been realized by the black communities— hence the pressure for better urban education.

D.P.   There are a couple of things that anybody who is going to seek to improve urban education is going to have to deal with. The most obvious one, as you mentioned, is the problem of segregated education versus education in an integrated setting. Now, it is clear that the laws of many states and the law of the land is that education should be carried on in an integrated setting.

F.P.H.   Unfortunately, the housing patterns really deny this. The housing patterns, particularly in the northern cities, have resulted in segregated schools. Hence the controversy about busing.

D.P.   The patterns of segregation are often very subtle. Given an integrated neighborhood, what we frequently find is that the white children from a somewhat higher socio-economic bracket are in the higher achievement tracks, and the black children are at the bottom, even though they come from the same neighborhood. This pattern can be found whether the housing patterns are integrated or segregated. I think the issue is more than a legal one, however, because there is a clear moral issue here.

The issue is: What does the country stand for? What are its commitments in terms of human values? There is also the complicating factor of the whole direction, quality, and tone of the school and its effect on the student's performance. In other words, there is some evidence from *The Coleman Report*[3] that a student's performance and his attitude toward school and himself depends a good deal on the socio-economic status and background of

[3] James S. Coleman, *The Coleman Report* (Washington, D.C.: U.S. Government Printing Office, 1966).

his fellow classmates. If you are going to group students, either inadvertently or by some sort of testing arrangement, and you find them ending up in groups that are organized by either social class or race, then this apparently puts a ceiling on what these children can achieve.

Therefore, there are compelling reasons for pursuing integration. However, there are some difficulties here. One is the geographic one; integration is very difficult to achieve in a city the size of Washington, St. Louis, Los Angeles, New York, Philadelphia, or any large city where the population of black students is very large and concentrated. It is very difficult to foresee a time when you are going to be able to integrate the schools either through busing or other means.

There is the additional difficulty that many black people feel that they are not getting their fair shake in the public schools. They feel that the only way they are going to get quality education suited to their own needs is by having some sort of control over the schools that their children go to.

Now, this raises what I think is the other primary issue that education in the future is going to have to face, the issue of local control versus decentralization. If you decentralize, and if you consider a smaller unit as basis for educational decisions, you achieve two valuable ends. One is that from the racial standpoint you put the schools much closer to the parents who have a clearer understanding of the problems, the advantages, and the potentials of their own children than perhaps a more distant school administrator or school teacher might have. In addition, you have the advantage of a greater likelihood of individualizing a given child's program.

On the other hand, if you look at a larger organizational unit you have the opportunity of providing much more complete technological advantages, such as closed-circuit television, more sophisticated and complicated scientific equipment, computer terminals, and a variety of expensive learning aids. Furthermore, in schemes for educational parks and larger school complexes you have the opportunity to integrate schools by drawing children from a larger geographical area.

Any attempt to solve, or at least alleviate, the problems of urban education and city school systems is going to have to establish a very delicate balance between these issues, the issue of segregated versus integrated education, and the issue of localized versus metropolitanized education. A look to the future, I think, is going to find legislators, administrators, and teachers working out a new balance between these factors that are at the root of much of the profound discouragement that now pervades urban education.

F.P.H.   To summarize, there are two opposing arguments that will have to be resolved that are both dictated from valid points of view. Perhaps they can be correlated to preserve the advantages of both. One is the argument for community control and decentralization, which we discussed at length. The other is the argument for creating educational parks and larger units to achieve integration, to offer much more variety to the students in terms of programs, and to take advantage of some of the new educational technology which is available but can be used only in a large system.

Perhaps, these two directions do not conflict as much as it seems on the surface. Educational technology can be made available on a metropolitan or even regional basis to local school systems by subscription, as those tools are usually not location bound. But determining what tools to use or what kind of education to have, including the choice of teachers or whether to use team teaching or traditional classrooms, should be a decision that is made on the local level by parents in conjunction with those who know the local educational needs.

But, whatever the future holds for the education of the urban child, we cannot get away from the racial context which, in the foreseeable future, will become decisive in the city schools as white people continue to leave the cities every day. Racial issues increasingly influence all metropolitan schools; therefore, any solutions to education problems clearly will have to be found in that area.

Thank you, Dr. Plumer.

BIBLIOGRAPHY

BOOKS

Bendiner, Robert. *The Politics of Schools—A Crisis of Self-Government.* New York: Harper and Row, 1969.

Coleman, James S. *The Coleman Report.* Washington, D.C.: U.S. Government Printing Office, 1966.
The most comprehensive social study every undertaken to determine the correlation between education, race, and financing of schools.

Dennison, George. *The Lives of Children.* New York: Random House, 1969.
A most imaginative book about new educational ideas, as well as a critique of existing schools.

Dentler, Robert A., et al, eds. *The Urban R's.* New York: Center for Urban Education, 1967.

Gittell, Marilyn. *Participants and Participation: A Case Study of School Policy in New York City.* New York: Center for Urban Education, 1967.

Gross, Ronald and Beatrice, eds. *Radical School Reform.* New York: Simon and Schuster, 1969.
An anthology of short chapters, each written by a different expert, explaining briefly their philosophies and ideas.

Holt, John. *How Children Learn.* New York: Pitman Publishing Company, 1967.
Holt has written several books about children and education: a "must" for anyone really interested in education.

Illich, Ivan. *Deschooling Society.* New York: Harper and Row, 1970.
The basic thesis of this book is to disestablish formalized schooling altogether.

Koerner, James D. *Who Controls American Education?* Boston: Beacon Press, 1968.

Kozol, Jonathan. *Death at an Early Age.* Boston: Houghton Mifflin Co., 1967.
This book deals with the devastating experiences of Kozol as a new teacher in the Boston school system.

Levine, Naomi. *Schools in Crisis: A Case History of Ocean Hill-Brownsville.* New York: Popular Library, 1969.

Mayer, Martin. *The Teachers Strike New York, 1968.* New York: Harper and Row, 1969.

Miller, S.M., and Riessman, Frank. *Social Class and Social Policy.* New York: Basic Books, 1968.

The Politics of Federal Aid to Education in 1965: A Study of Political Innovation. Syracuse, New York: Syracuse University Press, 1967.

Rogers, David. *110 Livingston Street.* New York: Random House, 1968.

Schrag, Peter. *Village School Downtown.* Boston: Beacon Press, 1967.
How a typical city school system functions, explained by using Boston as an example.

Silberman, Charles. *Crisis in the Classroom.* New York: Random House, 1970.
A devastating critique and some new ideas about teaching and schools, done on the basis of a national survey.

ARTICLES

Cohen, David K. "The Price of Community Control." *Commentary* (July 1969), 22-32.

Hamilton, Charles. "Race and Education: A Search for Legitimacy." *HER.* Fall, 1968: 669-684.

8

RACE RELATIONS AND COMMUNITY

A discussion with WHITNEY M. YOUNG, Jr.*
Executive Director of the National Urban League

INTRODUCTION

When we talk about urban problems in the United States cities, usually the first problem that comes to mind is race relations. The difficulties that minorities face today in the cities are overwhelming. Segregation—economic, social, and physical separation—dominates our urban living patterns everywhere.

Yet one purpose of the city is and always has been to create communities for people. People, as Aristotle stated, come to the city to lead "the good life," to find safety, to prosper and grow and realize their full potential. Face-to-face contact and personal interchange is the essence of the city. Diversity and variety are the spice of the city's life.

But, in American cities today, that purpose is denied. The way cities are built and used, the housing and living patterns, employment, transportation, recreation and schools, deny that original purpose of community and personal contact and deny variety and diversity. Our cities separate person from person, group from group, neighborhood from neighborhood—economically, ethnically, socially, and, finally, physically.

Discrimination and segregation, racism and apathy, have left their mark on all United States cities and their life. The ugliness of large areas of our cities reflects appalling social and physical neglect. Poverty problems aggravate race relations, especially in cities, where in the overcrowded ghettoes people often live very restricted lives.

Poverty and race problems are not only related, but they reinforce each other. Many old deteriorating areas in the cities, abandoned by the middle class who are moving into the suburbs, have become the homes of blacks and minorities. Poor housing with all the attendant problems of unhealthy living conditions and inadequate city services are a major problem of the urban poor and racial minorities.

*Mr. Whitney M. Young, Jr., died in March 1971.

Job opportunities increasingly are moving to the suburbs, especially manufacturing jobs which in the past provided unskilled urban immigrants with employment. Cities are left with increasing numbers of welfare recipients whose ranks have grown further due to the recent increase in unemployment which is worst in the cities. Blacks and minorities living in the cities have the highest unemployment rate while transportation to the suburban jobs is more and more expensive due to the lack of public transportation facilities.

School problems of every kind are on the increase in every city school system, from serious financing problems to drug abuse, from educational deficiencies to a deteriorating school plant, and lack of community involvement or community control.

The economic problems of cities greatly aggravate the problems of minorities who are dependent on public services. In turn, racial discrimination not only aggravates poverty, but affects the tax income of cities, which are unable to spend enough money on schools and services which could help the urban poor and minorities gain some economic independence.

DISCUSSION

F.P.H.   Mr. Young, in your recent book, *Beyond Racism,*[1] you outline many typical race problems that are also typical urban problems because more and more cities are increasingly inhabited by blacks, minorities, and poor people. You propose some solutions. Perhaps we could first talk about some of the problem areas that have weakened the sense of community in our cities and then discuss some remedies.

The main problem areas, I think, are the traditional ones of housing, education, and jobs. To this we should probably add insufficient social and city services, lack of health care, expensive and poor transportation, and more.

W.M.Y.   The problems of housing are paramount. Out of housing patterns develops the question of educational opportunities. In view of the fact that many of the jobs are moving into the suburbs, there is also an economic aspect. I would say that housing is the major problem.

There is no question at this time that we have the know-how, the technology, and the resources to build housing. The issue is the will, and that goes beyond the use of the technology to such things as zoning laws. Availability of land is another question. Code enforcement is a part of the answer; another part is the appreciation by the American public of the great benefit of diversity in their neighborhoods. I speak of diversity in terms of differences in economic level, cultural backgrounds, race, and life style.

[1] Whitney Young, *Beyond Racism* (New York: McGraw-Hill Book Co., 1969).

F.P.H.   One result of the FHA legislation is that middle-class people are able to leave the city for the suburbs. As a consequence, segregated housing patterns have been considerably reinforced for the past twenty or more years. People from the rural South, primarily blacks, lost their jobs due to the agricultural mechanization. They started to move into the northern cities in search of work and a better life. While the FHA legislation enables white, middle-class people to buy a house in the suburbs, blacks and minorities move into the inner-city housing where they can rent. This results in completely segregated housing patterns.

W.M.Y.   Yes, this situation is a paradox. The so-called "white noose" around the mostly black central cities is a result of official action on the part of the federal government, and not just through the FHA making it possible for white, middle-class people to move out of the central city. but also through the establishment of public housing only in the central cities. This makes it almost inevitable that this housing for the most part is filled by low economic groups, mostly blacks from the South and a few poor whites.

The FHA cooperated with the historic restrictive covenants to create "racially homogeneous" housing. Even after restrictive covenants were outlawed by the Supreme Court, the so-called gentlemen's agreement between banks, real estate operators, and builders continued, which assured that neighborhoods would be racially homogeneous.

All this works together to make the city become poorer and blacker. I do believe that more people are beginning to see the dangers inherent in this situation, which will affect all the inhabitants of metropolitan areas if central cities are permitted to deteriorate further and people are completely separated by race.

F.P.H.   In some metropolitan areas an effort is being made to open up some of the suburbs to build subsidized housing. However, this is going to take a long time, and I don't think we have that much time.

It is interesting to see that housing patterns in other industrial democracies have gone just the opposite way. Both in Great Britain and Sweden, and most European countries, the postwar housing built with government subsidies is in the suburbs and not in the inner cities, particularly for poor people from the overcrowded slums. In the United States the government policy has worked the opposite way.

W.M.Y.   At the present time, I am not sure that poor people or black people would necessarily benefit from moving out into the suburbs. I am thinking particularly of New York where the problem of transportation and traffic is paramount. Many white people who moved into the suburbs now have to spend a great deal of time going to work. I understand they would be quite willing to take over some of the slum areas in the central cities, clean them up, move back into town, and let the blacks move out into the suburbs.

Some of the most expensive property in terms of land value, and also buildings, can be found in some of the slum communities in the ghettoes. I think of Harlem, for example. The housing is terribly overcrowded and in bad condition. But the basic buildings often are solidly built. In terms of distance to work and to the cultural centers, this is very desirable housing. I would not want to see a program that in effect replaces slums with high-rent rehabilitated housing or highrise, luxury apartments. Then all of the suburbanites would move back into town, only to send the blacks all out to the suburbs.

F.P.H.   What you mention has happened to some extent in Washington, D.C., in Georgetown, which from a slum has become one of the most expensive upper-class residential areas. A similar movement is under way in Boston's South End. The original brick housing was well built and suitable for rehabilitation. It is attractive and close to downtown. The blacks in many such areas are pushed out, usually to worse areas in the city.

However, the answer, it seems to me, is to create integrated housing from the point of view of white people, as well as black people, so everyone can live near where they work, because this unnatural separation simply does not work economically, socially, or in any other way. For instance, the transportation patterns you mentioned—at this stage, large numbers of white middle-class people and professionals commute from the suburbs into the city every day to work, while black workers who live in the cities go out to the industrial plants in the suburbs. This double commute means an enormous amount of waste of energy, time, effort, and productive capacity.

W.M.Y.   There are two things to consider. We are talking about more than just the improved quality of housing. In the ghettoes we are talking about density. If all the population of the New York Metropolitan area lived as closely together as people live in central Harlem, you could put more than 200 million people into the five boroughs of New York. We are talking about density also in terms of the impossibility of providing amenities, recreation, and services for that many people in that small a space.

Secondly, we are talking about the concept of diversity. I think all too often people see integrated housing as something that would be of benefit only to black Americans and brown Americans. They do not see the great benefit that would come to white Americans. One is also culturally deprived by growing up in some of these bland, sterile, antiseptic, all-white ghettoes where there is nothing but sameness in terms of cultural and economic background. I think that this sameness turns off so many of our young. It is one reason why youngsters in Greenwich, Connecticut, want to come to Greenwich Village.

F.P.H.   To go back to public housing—which is the only housing program for low-income people—this program originally was not started to house the poor but as a means to produce jobs during the depression in the 1930's. The lesson that we have learned from this experience is that buildings alone cannot do the job. The housing projects have lacked in social services, which are the prime need of low-income people, particularly where recent immigrants from rural areas are involved. We certainly need more community facilities of every kind, besides good housing. And finally, we need much more subsidized housing that is economically and socially mixed.

Plurality and diversity are the essence of the city. Unless we provide socially and economically mixed housing, one of the purposes of the city is denied. People must have a chance to get to know different people, in order to respect each other, starting from the time they are children. This can only be achieved if housing patterns are mixed and integrated socially and economically.

W.M.Y.   The National Urban League recently started a National Housing Program to assist local Urban Leagues to build housing. The National Urban League, as a nonprofit organization, has traditionally dealt with the problems of urban immigrants; these immigrants now are mostly blacks and other minorities, frequently from the South and not equipped to deal with the complexities of our cities. They need help in many areas to become economically independent, from job training and education to social services of all kinds. Recently, due to the deterioration of the housing stock in the cities, the supply of physical housing has become an overwhelming problem for the minority immigrant and is affecting all other areas of concern. Therefore, we have taken on the building of housing as a priority program of the National Urban League.

The Housing Division of the National Urban League assists, with technical advice, local Urban Leagues, which are established in some 101 cities all over the country, and with resources to establish local housing corporations to actually build housing.

One of the major concerns today in developing housing is the involvement and the participation of the people who live in the community where the housing is to be built and of those who will live there. As a community-based organization, the Urban League is qualified to do that.

There also has not been sufficient employment of black people in building. I refer not just to construction workers and to skilled trades, but architects, lawyers, and black contractors and builders. We hope through the National

Urban League housing effort not only to get more housing built, but to get it built with more black participation. We want to involve black citizens both in the planning and design, as well as in the actual work opportunities.

F.P.H.   The community aspects of housing have always been linked with schools. One reason many middle-class people have moved out of the cities is the poor school situation, particularly their failure to educate children.

W.M.Y.   This gets back again to community control. Historically, in many of the northern cities the schools have been for the most part administered by people who do not live in the community. White people living in the suburbs have been the principals. Most of the teachers have been white and from outside of the community. There has been little opportunity for parent participation or for the community to exercise any kind of control.

It is also quite apparent now that these inner-city schools have not done a good job. The schools have not helped the young people to reach national achievement levels and reading levels. Very few, less than five per cent in the Ocean Hill-Brownsville section in New York, were able to go on to college, as contrasted with 65 to 70 per cent in other sections of the city.

F.P.H.   In the Ocean Hill-Brownsville area in 1969 and 1970, the first attempt was made to implement some decentralization as far as the New York School System is concerned. One of the first decentralization plans in the whole country was made there. This had considerable political repercussions in the whole school system of New York and in other city school systems. I understand that you believe firmly that decentralization is the only way to success and that, in the long run, it is going to prove itself.

W.M.Y.   I am convinced that you cannot exercise discipline in a community from the outside. I am convinced that we have to provide the people that live in a community with resources and authority so that the people who serve them, whether they are teachers or social workers or policemen, know that they are accountable and must be responsible to that community. As long as the people who provide the services feel that they don't have to be responsive to the people in the community, we are always going to get inferior services.

It was unfortunate that in the Ocean Hill-Brownsville struggle the basic concept of local control got lost in the union's issue of teacher job security. Then the ugly problem of anti-Semitism raised its head. But I feel that this was not a major issue at all. The major issue was to what extent were the parents and the people in the community going to have direct, specific control over the educational destiny of their children.

In the long run, I believe local and community control will succeed in many city school systems. The black communities also want to see educational institutions not as little isolated islands, but they want to see educational institutions relate to the community and engage in activities to help the entire community and to prepare people to go to work in that community, not just prepare people to go to work on Wall Street.

F.P.H.   I believe young people today—and this is evident in high schools and colleges especially—reject the extreme competition and individualism that prevails in many schools. They reject one-sided achievement; they prefer cooperation and want to learn to work together. To learn to get along with different people is especially important in our plural society and this is one value our schools can teach the youngsters in the urban schools. Therefore, it is especially important that the schools should not be segregated.

W.M.Y.   Education as we have known it is vulnerable as to its relevance to life today. It is not enough any more for education simply to perceive of itself as the perpetuator of culture and to reflect the *status quo*. As black communities point out, education has historically ignored the black contribution. There is very little in education that gives to the black child a sense of roots, of dignity, and of history. Education conveniently forgot the great contribution of blacks. So in addition to young people now wanting to know more about the social, the human, and the philosophical values, there is also a great desire on the part of the young blacks to see themselves and their ancestors in the history books.

I would like to make one point very clear. Quality education as far as I am concerned cannot be achieved in a segregated school, either for whites or for blacks. The sooner we recognize that the old criteria for determining potential or intelligence are no longer valid, the better. Most of the tests that are now used are based upon white middle class norms and are not real indices to measure the intelligence of ghetto youngsters. I think the fact that a kid survives to the age of five in the ghetto shows he is educable. The problem has been that most of our teachers have expected nothing from the poor children, whether they are whites from Appalachia or blacks from the rural South. Given the low expectation, the children did not feel challenged; they did not feel that they had to prove themselves and perform.

We have had some red herrings raised, such as the issue of busing, when, in fact, busing has been an activity that this country has engaged in since it started education.

F.P.H.   Children could never go to school in a suburb if they did not have a school bus. Every suburban school system also maintains a complete transportation system, because otherwise children simply could not get to school.

W.M.Y.   That is right. In many cases, however, we have bused white kids past black schools in order to achieve segregation. Nobody got upset or excited about those long distances that children had to ride. They only get excited when we want to bus to achieve integration. Then people start talking about the neighborhood school being so wonderful.

F.P.H.   In higher education, particularly at the universities, a great effort has been made in recent years to attract more blacks and minority students. Probably the students deserve more credit for that effort than the university administrations. A college degree today is an economic necessity to get a good job.

W.M.Y.   There has been progress, not just through increasing the number of students, but also the number of black faculty members. The contributions that black people have made throughout history are being taught in Afro-American studies. You are right when you point out that the students ought to get most of the credit for this. What annoys me most is that all these recommendations were made to university administrators 15 to 20 years ago by people like myself—nothing happened. The students, through aggressive methods, were able to get something done. So I don't get nearly as upset with the students who engage in some of these disruptive activities as I do with the administrators, who seem only to respond to confrontation.

F.P.H. Perhaps the final issue we ought to discuss is the employment situation. You certainly are one of the experts in that area. You have done more than anyone else, for a longer period of time, to open up employment opportunities for black people and for other minorities. The National Urban League also has been responsible for job-training programs of all kinds.

W.M.Y.   Economics, I think, is pretty basic, particularly in a materialistic society like America. For many years the Urban League has made jobs, that is, employment, its primary preoccupation. On the other hand, I do want to point out that today the work of the Urban League is very much involved in housing and education, because we live in a highly technological industrialized society. Unlike the past when the white immigrants came to this country, all you needed then was a strong back and a willing man. Today one needs education, and one obviously gets a better education in the less crowded neighborhoods of the metropolitan area.

We have made strides as far as the employment opportunities are concerned. There are much better opportunities than ever before for the black who is educated and who has some skills. Things are worse though for the unskilled. The majority of black people, due to historic discrimination, find themselves lacking in the skills and the education that are needed for today's world. For them the situation is worse than ever before. Most of the modern work-world requires skills.

We are facing a situation where the administration has used unemployment to control inflation. There has been a cutback on jobs, many industries have laid off people, and the blacks and minorities have been hit hardest of all. Unemployment in the inner cities among minorities is higher now than ever; many who have been unemployed for a long time are no longer even counted. But the cost of living is still going up. The tight money market hurts the unskilled black worker; no money is available for training or education; and there are cutbacks by the federal government, including loans to go to school. So the man at the bottom of the totem pole is the last hired and the first fired.

F.P.H.   I understand some of the training programs of the Urban League have been far more successful than the government-run programs.

W.M.Y.   The on-the-job training programs, for example, we do for about one-third the amount of money the government needs for the same training. We have a much better job retention rate, that is, the number of people who are still working a year after they have been placed. The same is true in our labor educational advancement program, which is a program designed to increase the number of black apprentices and journeymen in the construction trades.

F.P.H.   The building industry traditionally has offered low-skilled or unskilled people entry into the industrial job market. Many cities all over the world have been virtually built by the labor of the urban immigrants. Therefore, the position of many of the building trade unions—of limiting employment opportunities—has seriously affected entry into the job market, especially by low-skilled black urban immigrants.

In the construction industry, therefore, the opening of the craft unions to minority employment has become an area of constant controversy. The recent "Philadelphia Plan" was devised to hire more black people in the construction trades in the city of Philadelphia. I understand this agreement has been used as a model for other cities.

W.M.Y.   The posture of the construction unions has been quite irritating to us, because the public position and historic rhetoric of unions has always been in support of integration and concern for the little man. Yet we find in the construction unions particularly, as contrasted with the industrial unions, that many have become guilds and protectivist associations. They are concerned about keeping the number of skilled people at a low level so that they are in a better bargaining position. Many of them are almost totally white, for instance, unions like the plumbers or electricians or sheet-metal workers.

Union leadership for the most part claims that it is helpless. They are elected and they are not like corporations. The leaders saw among their rank-and-file union members a great deal of backlash and prejudice and resistance to increased opportunities for black people. They see blacks as threats to their own security.

F.P.H.   The high cost of money in 1969 and 1970 has caused a setback in the building industry and has affected employment in that industry. Would you say that any progress has been made lately in this area as far as hiring minorities is concerned?

W.M.Y.   Not much. The administration has been inconsistent and contradictory. They pushed for the Philadelphia Plan, which was designed to open up more jobs in the construction trades. Then a cutback of public building was ordered. The tight money market was due to government policy. All this has affected building jobs.

The recent lowering of interest rates has improved the job situation and we do have more black people as apprentices now, and also more journeymen. But we are still talking about 2, 3, 4 per cent instead of talking about 12 to 15 per cent, or what black people represent in the population.

F.P.H.   In the end, I think we should also talk about health care and social services which are in many ways related. I understand you have been very active in this area. Today, for anyone to get sick and to be hospitalized is an economic disaster as well as a physical one because of the enormous costs of hospitalization, which are increasing all the time. It seems strange that at the same time the hospital workers, many of them blacks and minorities, get the lowest pay. There have been numerous strikes, particularly in the South, to upgrade the position of the hospital workers.

W.M.Y.   Taking health care first, one of the strange paradoxes about this country is that we spend more money on health care than any other nation—around $60 billion—yet we rank about thirteenth or fourteenth in terms of infant mortality, a most telling statistic.

The problem is first the organization of health care and then the delivery system. There is great waste; there is much overlapping. The very rich get more than they need and the poor get very little. Middle-class Americans suffer a great deal, too. We reached the point, due to the high costs of care, where most people don't get medical care until it is too late in many cases, or until they have become terribly sick.

F.P.H.   You are saying that we ought to have preventive care and clinics where people can go before they get really sick, which would in the end be a much more economical way of dealing with the problem.

Also it can be proven statistically that the health care the inner-city inhabitants receive, often blacks and minorities, is worst of all. Though in many cases they live close to some of the largest hospitals, they have no access to their health services nor can they afford to get any medical care.

W.M.Y.   That is why I belong to the Committee of 100[2] which Walter Reuther of the United Auto Workers initiated. The committee is composed of very prominent citizens who are pushing for national health insurance. I think this type of insurance is essential. But a lot of people are opposing it today, primarily the American Medical Association. But they have often opposed all innovation; they even opposed Blue Cross at one time, and now they support it.

Now about welfare. We have retained in this country a punitive welfare system with all of the old English Poor Law concepts of the means test and eligibility. Everything is designed to make the receipt of welfare as humiliating and as dehumanizing an experience as possible. The notion is that if it is made as humiliating as possible, and people are given as little as possible, then they will not apply. The assumption is that people basically are lazy and that they are chiselers, that there is work but they just don't want to work. Well, this just is not true.

F.P.H.   Of course, most of the people on welfare are either children or too old to work or people who are unable to work. In fact, HEW just recently published and widely distributed information showing who the welfare recipients really are. Most of them are unable to work.

W.M.Y.   In fact, 95 per cent are too old or too young or too sick to work. In addition, you have an awful lot of people who are working full time who have an income below the poverty line. The working poor in this country represent a real problem. You mentioned some of them—the hospital workers, the laundry workers, some of the agricultural workers. These people work hard, full time, and still don't make enough money to take them above the poverty level.

*Committee of 100 or Committee for National Health Insurance, sponsors of Bill S-3 (HR 22).

F.P.H.   Will a guaranteed minimum income—the bill that is still in Congress awaiting action—remedy the situation?

W.M.Y.   It is called the Family Assistance Plan or Income Maintenance Program; it has various names. I support the concept of an economic floor for all Americans. The government has the responsibility to see that income maintenance is available to all citizens wherever they live. At present, many states have residency requirements in order not to pay welfare or keep poor newcomers out. But we are such a mobile society that the people who are ill-educated, ill-housed, and ill-fed in Mississippi this year live in Chicago and New York next year. At present, welfare payments greatly differ from city to city and one state to another.

There are parts, though, of the legislation for family assistance that I am very unhappy about. The floor that has been established is much too low. The least we can do is have a floor that takes us up to what has been established as a poverty level in this country. I am also very much concerned about the mandatory work provision in this legislation.

F.P.H.   At the present time, unemployment is so great that the work requirement will be impossible to fulfill.

W.M.Y.   That is true, but you also have a situation where somebody has a potential for being a great architect or physician who is forced to do menial work. At the same time, if we say that there are no jobs, we forget all the needed services that are not provided now, for instance, in cities because local government cannot pay for them. There are plenty of jobs that need to be done.

F.P.H.   What do you think the future will bring? Will we learn to deal constructively with the community and racial problems in the cities, where most of our difficulties arise?

W.M.Y.   I think in the long range these problems will be met forthrightly. But in the short range we are likely to have the same rhetoric, the slick propaganda, the press releases, and very little change.

We must see changes in our priorities of spending for the domestic area as we have been spending in the past for the military and defense budgets. I feel that things probably will get worse for a while before they get better and that seems to be characteristic of America. We seem to respond to crises and to tragedy. We don't act on the basis of logical review of facts and of history.

I anticipate that due to the inaction of officials, due to the lack of courageous leadership and due to the fact that many of our leaders are more concerned about getting re-elected than about addressing themselves to the serious domestic problems, we will see escalating problems especially on the economic front. The young whites who are the sons and daughters of affluent America have a different value system and are cynical and contemptuous of what is happening. The answer is to move courageously to eliminate the great areas of deprivation and denial and poverty in our society.

F.P.H.   The worst problems of our society—poverty, racial discrimination, neglect, and deterioration—are concentrated in our cities where most of the blacks and minorities live. But it is a fact that the cities still produce most of the tax income for the federal government. Yet the present administration is ignoring the cities and minorities and utterly neglecting their very real needs while living conditions in cities get worse from year to year. This cannot help but lead to serious trouble.

Mr. Young, you have given some of the best leadership in this country to the cause of social justice and equal opportunity, which truly is the cause of the cities. Thank you.

BIBLIOGRAPHY

Young, Whitney. *Beyond Racism.* New York: McGraw-Hill Book Company, 1969.
A pragmatic outline of the problems and a proposal of remedies in the form of a "domestic Marshall Plan."
———. *To be Equal.* New York: McGraw-Hill Book Company, 1964. Also in Paperback.
A now historic statement of the U.S. race problem.

BOOKS

Clark, Kenneth. *Dark Ghetto.* New York: Harper and Row, 1965.
All of Kenneth Clark's work as the foremost psychologist analyzing race problems is a "must" for any serious student of race problems.
Committee for National Health Insurance. 806 15th St., N.W., Washington, D.C. 20005. Bill S-E Senate (Kennedy), Bill HR-22 House (Corman and Griffiths).
Fried, Joseph P. *Housing Crisis USA.* New York: Praeger Publishers, Inc., 1971.
The housing crisis seen firsthand by a newspaperman who tells it as it is.
Harrington, Michael. *The Other America: Poverty in the United States.* Baltimore: Penguin Books, Inc., 1964.
This little book laid the foundation for OEO and many other programs.

Kaiser, Edgar F., Chairman. "Report of the President's Committee on Urban Housing: A Decent Home." Washington, D.C.: U.S. Government Printing Office, 1968.

The best available background information on housing problems.

Kerner Report. *Report of the National Advisory Commission on Civil Disorders.* New York: Bantam Books, 1968. Paperback.

The best available study of the U.S. race problem.

Piven, Frances Fox, and Cloward, Richard. *Regulating the Poor.* New York: Pantheon Books, 1971.

An excellent critical analysis of poverty and society's way of dealing with the poor, by the two foremost scholars in this field.

Rose, Arnold. *The Negro in America.* New York: Harper and Row, 1964. Paperback (Harper Torchbooks).

A revised and updated summary of the classic study of the U.S. race problem of Gunnar Myrdal by his collaborator.

Silberman, Charles E. *Crisis in Black and White.* New York: Random House, 1964. Paperback.

———. *Crisis in the Classroom.* New York: Random House, 1970.

These two books by Silberman are the best written and researched studies of each field by a most perceptive observer.

9

PLANNING AND URBAN RENEWAL

A discussion with EDWARD LOGUE
President, New York State Urban Development Corporation;
formerly Administrator of the Boston Redevelopment Authority

INTRODUCTION

Planning and urban renewal are closely related. In fact, in Boston, where Mr. Edward Logue was Administrator of the Boston Redevelopment Authority from 1961 to 1967, the Planning Commission and the Redevelopment Authority are combined. In Philadelphia, which besides Boston has one of the most effective and comprehensive redevelopment efforts under way, the planning agency and the renewal authority work in close cooperation.

Urban renewal is an activity that has been going on for centuries in every major city everywhere. It simply means replacing and renovating old, obsolete, and worn-out structures and rebuilding whole areas in a city with new buildings that fit the demands of the present. But urban renewal is also the name of a federal program, of the Department of Housing and Urban Development (HUD), which was started in 1949. That is, in that year's housing bill, federal subsidies were made available to cities for the purpose of replanning and preparing for the rebuilding of certain deteriorating areas in each city or town, after designating them as "blighted areas." The initiative, that is, the creation of a renewal authority and the designation of a specific project has to come from the individual city, which also has to put up a certain percentage of the necessary funds.

Before 1949, the federal government had made money available for public housing; but under the urban renewal legislation, federal money was made available for area-wide renewal in cities that created a renewal agency and made their own plans. These renewal funds include planning grants and funds for the execution of whole projects, including changing and rebuilding streets and renewing the infra-structure. Federal funds are made available for the buying and assembling of land, with powers of eminent domain to create new property lines.

These new replanned land parcels are then resold, usually at a reduced price, to developers who won a competitive bid from the urban renewal agency for redevelopment of the land. Each individual proposal has to be economically feasible, it must have community participation and support, and it has to meet certain design standards set by the agency.

Design and quality control are the best assurances that redevelopment will not make the same mistakes that often caused the original buildings to wear out prematurely and be torn down. One of the reasons, of course, why many downtown areas are obsolete is that they were never planned for a future that is now here. Most of the cities grew piecemeal, according to how the developer could make the highest profit regardless of the broader needs of the city and its citizens.

DISCUSSION

F.P.H.   Mr. Logue, you have the reputation of being the most effective urban renewal administrator in the country, and now, as president of the New York State Urban Development Corporation, you have extended your activities from the city to a whole state.

How are planning and urban renewal related? It seems to me we could say that urban renewal is the inner-city part of a broader metropolitan, and, in your case, statewide planning effort. In the case of the New York State Urban Development Corporation, you deal with both urban renewal efforts in the cities and a statewide planning effort concerned with all kinds of development, including the building of new cities and towns.

E.L.   The New York State Urban Development Corporation is the first agency to have a statewide responsibility for urban development. It has become essential to consider the state as a whole and to develop policies accordingly.

What we have chosen to do is to work in cities, that is, inside traditional city boundaries, through the urban renewal program. We are assisting some twenty-six municipalities (75 per cent of the state's population) by planning and carrying on urban renewal activities in most of these communities. Over and beyond that we have to look at larger geographical areas like counties and regions. For example, the mid—Hudson region is the next developmental corridor in the New York City metropolitan area in New York State.

We combine looking at the very small urban renewal project with a hundred units of housing to areas of several hundred square miles. We try to do both and keep them in balance. Finally, we are just at the very beginning of this effort to see that the balance provides a better pattern of growth than the rather haphazard one that is traditional in our country.

F.P.H.   Actually, the New York State Urban Development Corporation was fairly recently created: nothing of this kind existed before, and you are its first administrator. What are the goals and objectives, and why was it created?

E.L.   It was created in 1968 by the Legislature of New York State, at the urgent request of Governor Rockefeller. And his reasons, as he stated them then, were entirely valid. He said that New York State and several cities in the state were not making the progress that they should be making in the struggle against slum housing and blighted areas. It was Governor Rockefeller's notion that these frustrations at the local level were the responsibility of and could be overcome by the creation of a new state agency with a new state public policy behind it.

F.P.H.   Many people all over the country consider the New York State Urban Development Corporation a model for other states. It is quite unique, and no other state has created such an agency as yet. In other ways it is also considered a model for national development, particularly in its planning and building of several new towns in upper New York State.

E.L.   Yes, we happen to know that our legislation is being examined with a great deal of interest in Massachusetts, Connecticut, New Jersey, Pennsylvania, West Virginia, Ohio, and several other states because of its unusual combination of powers and its use as an instrument for developing new towns. In the New York State Urban Development Corporation, we put a good deal of stress on new towns, their planning and development.

F.P.H.   In 1969 I reviewed the book *The New City*[1] which was sponsored by Urban America, Inc., a private organization sponsoring urban research, action, and education programs. This book publishes the work and recommendations of the National Committee on Urban Growth, formulating a national urban-growth policy. In the expectation of a hundred million more people in this country in the next thirty years, it was suggested that there was an urgent need to plan the environment nationally in order to absorb this increase in population. This is an alternative to the current non-policies of haphazard growth and land development by individual corporations and builders who are only concerned about their own profit.

We have seen the problems of haphazard growth in every city, first in the overcrowding in the inner city and then in the enormous expansion of the

[1] *The New City*. Published for Urban America, Inc. (New York: Frederick A. Praeger, 1969).

metropolitan areas. This is creating ugly, uncoordinated commercial and industrial developments that pollute large industrial areas as well as large numbers of speculative housing subdivisions of small, box-like, repetitive houses that cover more and more land. The National Committee on Urban Growth suggests that, nationwide, we ought to plan about a hundred new towns for a hundred thousand people, and ten new towns for one million people, all with their own industries and jobs, that is, coordinated economic, physical, and social planning. How far do you believe these ideas are removed from reality?

E.L.   Personally, I would be satisfied with an adoption by Congress and an acceptance by the President of that Commission's report. The book, *The New City,* is a first-class piece of work. It explains the background, the need, and recommends the policies. I do not think we need to look any further.

We are also finally making some progress. The Senate of the United States has passed legislation which calls for a national council to create an urban growth policy. The same legislation has cleared the House Banking and Currency Committee. I suppose that some time in the next year or two we are very likely, at long last, to have such a policy.

It is a shame that we did not have the wit to do this the way the British did in World War II. With all the troubles they had, they still managed to create the Town and Country Planning legislation. They do have a national urban-growth policy, and have had one for over twenty years.

F.P.H.   *The New City* builds very strongly on the British experience. After seeing some of the new towns around London and also in Scotland, I think it is rather remarkable to consider that all this was built in the short space of twenty years. Nevertheless, the metropolitan area of London still keeps on growing.

However, in the absence of any organized growth policy in this country things are much worse, especially since the population growth here is much greater. What in your estimation should we learn from the British experience, and from the British policies?

E.L.   We must learn that an urban-growth policy must be a national policy, that it needs to have a strong support from the national government, that it needs to move very quickly from plans and theories to reality, something people can see and enjoy, something useful and attractive. There is quite a lot to be learned from the new towns in the United Kingdom and also quite a lot from the civilized way in which the Swedes have organized the Stockholm metropolitan area. And there is a lot to learn from what the Finns have done in Tapiola near Helsinki, to create one of the world's most delightful suburban communities. There is much to be learned in Western Europe and maybe even in Eastern Europe, although that is not so clear.

F.P.H.   In Paris, the national land management agency, l'Amenagement du Territoire, has been working for the last ten years toward decentralizing the growth of Paris in an organized fashion. After a decade, the effects of its work are only just beginning to show. This points to our need of moving rapidly to do something before it is too late.

In France, two things have been done. The whole country is divided into eight regions which receive differing amounts of tax support as incentives to persuade business to locate there rather than in or near Paris, as most of them would. In turn, the Paris region itself is decentralizing the city of Paris by creating incentives for business to move out of the city to certain areas in the larger metropolitan region which are planned to become new growth centers. Specifically, five new towns have been identified in the Paris region and are now going ahead with planning and building coordinated urban settlements. The French government says, if you have a business in the city of Paris, you are not permitted to expand beyond a certain percentage of floor area. As a result all expanding businesses are moving out of the city and are creating new jobs in towns designated for growth. Is this the type of growth policy that you think should be initiated in this country?

E.L.   I think these are the basic elements. It is a call for a shift from the private decision-making process to the public decision-making process. And I do not think we should be bashful in saying that. We should say that it is time that we organized our great metropolitan areas and our regions in a way that will maximize our opportunity to enjoy them over many generations.

F.P.H.   As the Administrator of the Boston Redevelopment Authority, you never were very bashful, and with very excellent results. The new City Hall is completed and in use, while more and more buildings are going up downtown. The new Government Center was just finished. It initiated this renewal of the city. Despite the present economic recession, the buildings are there, and a positive direction has been established.

You taught Bostonians two valuable things: the importance of preserving historic buildings of the city as part of renewal, and methods for effectively establishing design control over new buildings and entire areas.

E.L.   Well, I enjoyed the work I did in Boston, and I enjoy, in a very different way, going back and looking at it. It is a painful reminder of how long it takes to get something planned, built, and done.

The striking new City Hall building in the center of what used to be Scollay Square fits in very naturally with Beacon Hill and the North End. The relationship between these areas and buildings is comfortable; the views are better than they have been in the past.

This shows that it is worthwhile to think about design and to back it up with controls. No man should have the right to say that, because he is using his money, he has the right to do with the skyline of a city whatever he pleases, particularly since buildings are getting taller all the time. This has happened too often in New York, and I am glad we have been able to keep it under control in Boston.

F.P.H.   You touch on something very important here, which is the public interest. What is the public interest? Who speaks up for it? City planning, which depends on exercising effective controls, has very little political support in this country and even less political clout. People and business are always afraid of being regimented by bureaucracies or dictated to by officialdom. On the other hand, the private developer and entrepreneur, to make a profit for himself, is allowed to do almost anything to a city. As you point out, he can build a highrise building which may be visible from miles away and ruin the view for thousands of people, spoil a whole section of town, and create traffic problems. It seems to me that planning is the only way, that is, planning in the public interest, to deal with this effectively and to control development.

E.L.   You cannot trust a private company to consider the public interest first; they consider their own selfish financial interest, and put that first. That is why we are going to have a monstrosity in Copley Square in Boston, the new John Hancock Mutual Life Insurance Company Building, which is under construction now. I can say flatly that it would not have happened if I had been in Boston. It is sixty stories high and one great big glass mirror. The biggest mirror in the whole world. It will make the Prudential Tower, which is only two or three blocks away, look like a superior work of design.

F.P.H.   The building of the Prudential development in Boston with its fifty-two story tower was opposed by many people who cared for Boston. It is quite out of scale with its environment, particularly as it lacks any relationship to the area of Commonwealth Avenue, one of the few attractive unified avenues still left in the country. However, I suspect the new Hancock building will be infinitely worse. How can this sort of thing be prevented?

E.L.   The city administration has to care enough to prevent it. It was perfectly obvious the Hancock Company was going to build a taller building than the Prudential, since their home office is in Boston. They did at first propose a very handsome sixty-story building which I personally thought would have been a marvelous addition to the cityscape. But in 1967-68 they changed their minds and had this dreadful thing designed instead.

We learn from these mistakes. There is a great resurgence of interest in design here in New York City. Too bad it did not come earlier. Certainly one of the finest things Mayor Lindsay of New York has done is to say, "I am the mayor of this town, I care what the city looks like, and my people are instructed to care what it looks like." That has made a difference and has persuaded real-estate speculators to improve the quality of their product. I regret to say, however, that none of the new buildings come up to the quality of Rockefeller Center.

F.P.H.   Rockefeller Center certainly is one of the historic examples of how sound planning and design have created the type of environment that even now, so many years later, is enjoyed by millions of people. Every time you go there, regardless of the time of the year, it is full of people; they are enjoying themselves and their environment, they are getting together in an area re-served for people outside the traffic. There are too few places in New York where this sort of thing happens.

You spoke about design control in Boston, where an excellent system was initiated at the Boston Redevelopment Authority. You mentioned the City of New York is practicing the same. Can you describe how this was done and organized?

E.L.   I should point out the City of New York has not gone anywhere near as far as we did in Boston. The midtown area is controlled by the City Planning Commission's right to approve or disapprove development; they may grant an exception from the zoning code, or allow exceptions as a reward for open space plazas at the street level. But this is a clumsy tool compared to what we developed in Boston. Yet, it is a major step forward for the public interest, and it will lead to further progress.

F.P.H.   I understand the New York Urban Development Corporation is trying both to preserve the quality of the city and to decentralize. But Mayor Lindsay is upset if any businesses move out because of the tax loss. On the other hand, all efforts in many cities around the world have been directed towards decentralization, simply because life in the cities is becoming over-burdened with traffic and pollution, too many people, and all the waste they produce.

E.L.   In this country, because we have the property tax as basic revenue for the financing of public city services, commercial and industrial property is a very important asset for any city. Commercial and industrial property produce the most revenue with the least expense.

But what is most difficult for all mayors is the fact that the cities are being left with the poorest families, the ones with the least education and the ones least equipped to take care of themselves. The more prosperous members of society, the strong new industries, office parks, upper-income families, have moved out; yet they still use the basic services of the city, the cultural resources in particular, the transportation networks, the recreation and amusement resources. But they contribute very little. This and the wrongly-ordered national priorities are the reasons why central cities are in such desperate financial condition.

F.P.H.   Planning, hopefully, might create a counter-balance to this. But on the other hand, planning cannot control the property taxes, which are really the reason why businesses and people move out of the city. The problem is that we need a new attitude towards inner cities and particularly towards planning and environmental controls. In this sense, taxes are one of the most formidable instruments to achieve planning goals.

E.L.   In the United States we have an artificial distinction in our statutes in federal program financing, and also in the way we organize our local government, which separates the planning function and the urban-renewal function from fiscal controls or incentives. I think that this is perhaps an important reason why we have made relatively little progress in the rebuilding of our cities in the twenty-one years that the national urban renewal legislation has been on the federal statute books.

In Western Europe, in the United Kingdom in particular, but also elsewhere, the implementation of plans is tied very closely to their preparation. I am hopeful that without losing too much more time, we shall come to understand the necessity of putting planning, renewal, and development together to create one system for carrying out the plans that are made, including a sounder revenue structure than the local property tax.

F.P.H.   Many of the best-made plans change with implementation, which is a difficulty. At a recent conference of the American Society of Planning Officials, as keynote speaker, you urged the professionals to reconsider the whole role of the planning profession and the planning function in our society.

E.L.   Planning, as an academic discipline, is with few exceptions not an important part of any university curriculum in the United States. I shall never forget going to a Harvard commencement and watching various recipients of degrees stand up. The undergraduates were largest in number; the Law School and the Business School members were substantial; when it came time for the recipients of a degree in city planning, you could hardly see them in the crowd. The same is true at other universities. Planning is not taken seriously enough by our universities even though the presidents of the universities, their faculties, and the students are increasingly concerned about urban problems.

Going beyond that, planners in the United States, unfortunately, are not concerned with implementation of their plans or the political arrangements that are needed to assure implementation. Frequently, their plans cannot be used in practice. That is in sharp contrast to Western Europe and many other areas in the world where planners are responsible for the execution of their plans on a continuing basis. As a result, planning in the United States is strikingly ineffective, and plans are seldom followed. It seems to me that the time has gone by when we can afford to behave that way as a society.

F.P.H.   You urged that planners should become politicians and should take care of their plans in the political environment. They should see that plans are implemented. Planners should not just act as advisors to politicians, but become active politicians themselves.

In your present position as head of the New York State Urban Development Corporation, you have moved planning into quite a new role; you are trying to show that planning is, in fact, extremely important to our society. Nobody stands up effectively for the public good but the planner. To be effective, planning must receive not only much more money but more power as well and thus be able to act for the public interest, not just talk about it.

E.L.   The public interest must become paramount in the use of land, in order to prevent its abuse. I do not want to put too much blame on the planning profession as such. I think the people in public life, elected officers and others, and certainly the business community, are equally to blame. We have never had a President of the United States who was committed to the solution of the urban crisis. We have never had an administration in Washington, nor a Congress, which put the resolution of this problem at the top of the priority list, as has been done in other countries.

Until we put cities and urban living on the top of the national agenda, I think we are also going to continue to see pollution of the environment. Solving the problems of the central cities will go a long way toward solving pollution problems.

F.P.H.   Most of us live in an urban environment and we all live in a man-made environment. It seems to me the pollution of the man-made environment is something that we could, with adequate controls, take care of very speedily and very quickly; it has been done in other countries. In the future, we shall live closer together, as ever more people are moving into the metropolitan areas. As a result, we will have to enact some controls, simply to be able to live together peacefully. The newly built urban environment, located on the outskirts of cities, unless it is properly planned and controlled creates a never-never land of sprawl and of high taxes, of commercial ugliness and huge parking lots, of congested traffic or, alternately, a lack of transportation. The degradation of the quality of life, which we all deplore, is a function of development without any plans, without any regard for controls that would protect the public interest.

E.L.   The debate about pollution of the environment is proceeding in a way that emphasizes the cosmetic nature of the problem. The idea is that we somehow or other improve the sewage treatment facilities, that we invent new ways for solid-waste disposal, and new internal combustion engines with less air pollution. But none of these inventions and improvements will keep pace with the increasing pollution that comes year by year through greater use of automobiles, and with the absurd transportation patterns we have for getting in and out of our metropolitan areas, which are the result of lack of planning and rational coordinated development.

In short, I think it is safe to say that the pollution problem will get worse until the urban development problem is put at the top of the national agenda, and we begin to change some of our national public policies on transportation, on housing, and on the location of industry.

F.P.H.   While we talk about pollution of nature, we seldom consider that *what* we build, and even more important *how* we build it, is the greatest active pollutant. *How* we develop land and *how* we build the man-made environment in the first place, determines the quality of life and determines if an area becomes polluted. People make these decisions, and in the final analysis it is the people and their behavior that pollute the environment.

E.L.   It is too much, it seems to me, to expect individuals who, it is perfectly true, are the source of pollution, to change their habits. That is a responsibility of society; that is what government is for.

The same thing is true with private real estate. It is too much to expect the rogue who is putting up an office building and the architectural firm that has put its name on it to behave in a responsible way. That is a societal function —a responsibility of the city or the state or the federal government.

It is, of course, absurd that we and other nations of the world, through the absence of positive urban-development policies, seem to encourage the gathering together of people and industry and commerce in ever-larger conglomerations. We even had to invent a new word, "megalopolis," to describe this phenomenon. The rather ugly term, "Bos-Wash," (Boston-Washington) is the great megalopolitan city of the future; it seems to me an undesirable and unnecessary kind of growth.

F.P.H.   Basically, the development of our economy from an agricultural to an industrial and finally now a service economy is responsible for the ever-growing metropolitan areas. In a free market situation, growth attracts more growth—this is precisely why we need controls.

E.L.   I think we have to look first at why it happens, and we have to recognize increasingly, not only here in the United States, but elsewhere in the world, that we need fewer and fewer agricultural workers to produce the food that we must have to live.

The extractive industries are also being mechanized, and we need a smaller and smaller work force. For example, only about one-fifth of the United Mine Workers are presently engaged in active work digging coal, as compared to the 1930's under John L. Lewis. The manufacturing processes year by year become more automated, and the percentage of the population relatively engaged in manufacturing goes down. What does go up in order that we may all have something to do Is moving paper around.

F.P.H.   In fact, service jobs are increasing constantly, and service jobs are located in cities and urban areas.

E.L.   Service jobs are increasing, and the vast flow of paper moves efficiently over short distances and gets more specialized. This is a natural and indeed worldwide phenomenon, and it is centered in cities—almost all new jobs are in urban and urbanizing areas. We need to do something about this; we need to have a national policy of urban growth. We need this for many reasons, particularly for the long-term political and social stability of the nation.

We are finding in the great heartland of the United States, away from the Great Lakes, that by and large the cities are declining in population, and we are not utilizing the existing infrastructure. Many facilities in upper New York State, in the Midwest, in eastern Connecticut, in many parts of the United States are used at far less than capacity, while people pour into these great metropolitan centers, like the one from Washington up to Boston.

F.P.H.   This is another example of an absence of planning in the regional and national context. National planning or any national urban-growth policy must be supported politically and economically, that is, by fiscal policies. It would effectively improve the quality of life of everyone.

To return to the context of the individual city, housing, or the absence of decent housing all people can afford, is the greatest problem cities and metropolitan areas face today. They especially lack housing for low- and moderate-income groups.

E.L.   Well, I have suggested a solution that I will offer here. In the suburbs, I think we need to adopt what I call the concept of "fair sharing." Every suburb ought to be willing to provide within its borders housing for low-income families, to the same extent that those low-income families are present in the rest of the metropolitan area.

If you take the case of Boston, for example, 5 per cent of the people in the Boston metropolitan area are minority families, largely low income. Twenty per cent of the City of Boston are minority families; then you look at the suburbs exclusive of the city, and only 1 per cent of the population of the suburbs are from minorities. When minorities have difficulties getting housing outside the central city, you are bound to have very serious problems. If all the suburbs of Boston took 5 per cent of low-income people, by building housing, the problem and the segregation that goes with it would disappear very quickly. Then, it seems to me there is an opportunity for a fresh start by building new housing.

F.P.H.   New towns, I believe, could start with a balanced population, balanced not only economically but integrated without the restraints we have in cities, in terms of segregation. When you start out fresh you can set policies. What sort of policies do you think could be effective here?

E.L.   At the New York State Urban Development Corporation we have a housing policy stating that 70 per cent of all housing in a given area is for middle- or moderate-income families, 20 per cent for low income, and 10 per cent for the elderly. We think this is a mixture that will work and make a major contribution.

F.P.H.   Massachusetts passed a so-called anti-snob zoning law recently. In the suburbs a great deal of activity started instantly, aimed at considering ways to build housing that would anticipate the effect of this law. It directs that a certain percentage of the area of each suburb, in relation to population, will be rezoned for multi-family housing, some of which will be subsidized using state or federal programs.

E.L.   I am familiar with that statute. Its principal effect is, just as you described, to encourage local communities to take the initiative rather than have the statute used against them. I also think, speaking as a lawyer, that it is entirely possible for zoning which excludes low-income families to be found unconstitutional by the United States Supreme Court. It has already been found unconstitutional by the Supreme Court of Pennsylvania, and I am confident that that view will be held in other states as well, before too much time goes by.

F.P.H.   Perhaps we should finish our discussion with a word about the future. You were not very optimistic about achieving some of the goals we discussed. What do you think the future holds in terms of regional development and controlled urban development which will remedy some of the problems we have seen in the past?

E.L.   We have many opportunities, but I look around and I see the size of the problems here in New York State or around the country. When I see how much is required, I have to say to myself that, until this war in Indochina is over and until there is some kind of reduction in the expenditures for armaments, this country is not about to change its national priorities. We need to adopt new kinds of tax legislation that would have for its objectives a decent home and a decent environment at the top of the list. I wish that more Americans who care about this could see the new towns that you have seen, and look at what the Swedes have been able to accomplish in what is not a basically very rich country.

I am not optimistic at the present time, because I do not see the war ending quickly or the cost of maintaining the Department of Defense going down. But I am totally confident that, given the funds and the commitment, we can do it. The techniques are there, the knowledge is there or available; we have the productive capacity and the architectural skills to build a whole new environment.

F.P.H.   My favorite idea is to shift all the capabilities that have been developed for the military and the space programs into building a new environment and new cities. Many of the technologies that have been developed for those areas are perfectly applicable, particularly in terms of computer techniques or control techniques or social development, to some of the more complicated problems of how to run cities and their transportation and disposal systems. This also would create millions of jobs and a new economic base. It would be a great challenge to reorganize the defense establishment's know-how towards building a variety of different new cities and towns using all kinds of new technology and ideas.

E.L.   That suggestion has a great deal of value.

F.P.H.   Thank you, Mr. Logue.

BIBLIOGRAPHY

BOOKS

"Annual Reports." The New York State Urban Development Corporation. Central Office: 1345 Avenue of the Americas, New York, N.Y. 10019.

Cities. A Scientific American Book. New York: Alfred A. Knopf, 1965. Paperback.
Written by some of the most knowledgeable people in the field, this book, though old, is well worth reading.

Elias, Gillies, Reimer. *Metropolis: Values in Conflict.* Belmont, California: Wadsworth Publishing Co., 1969.

Gottman, Jean. *Megalopolis.* New York: Twentieth Century Fund, Inc., 1961.
The author created the term "Megalopolis." A most interesting research study.

Gruen, Victor. *The Heart of Our Cities.* New York: Simon and Schuster, 1969.
A pragmatic approach of how to deal with cities by an actively involved international planner.

Jacobs, Jane. *The Death and Life of Great American Cities.* New York: Random House, Vintage Books, 1963. Paperback.
This is a classic and a must—dealing with the diversity of the city and very critical of planners.

The New City. Donald Canty, ed. Published for Urban America, Inc. New York: Frederick A. Praeger, 1969.
A "must" for everyone seriously interested in the topic of this discussion and especially urban growth.

Scott, Mal. *American City Planning.* Berkeley, California: University of California Press, 1969.

Vernon, Raymond. *The Myth and Reality of our Urban Problems.* Cambridge, Massachusetts: The MIT Press, 1966.

Weaver, Robert C. *Dilemmas of Urban America.* Cambridge, Massachusetts: Harvard University Press, 1965.
The Godkin Lectures of 1966. A critical, pragmatic approach to urban problems by the first Secretary of HUD.

Wilson, James Q., ed. *Urban Renewal: The Record and the Controversy.* Cambridge, Massachusetts: The MIT Press, 1966.

ARTICLES

"The Conscience of the City." *Daedelus.* 97:4 (Fall 1968).

Hosken, Fran P. "Are new towns a cure for urban ills?" *Christian Science Monitor* (September 17, 1971), p. 11.

———, "France: New Towns point the way." *Christian Science Moniter* (September 27, 1971), p. 13.

———. "A New Town Within London." *St. Louis Sunday Post-Dispatch* (March 1, 1970), p. 5B.

10

HEALTH CARE AND THE CITY

A discussion with John H. Knowles, M.D.*
General Director of the Massachusetts General Hospital

INTRODUCTION

The health care situation in the nation's cities has been deteriorating steadily for years. At a conference on "Medicine in the Ghetto," in the summer of 1969, Dean Ebert of the Harvard Medical School challenged President Nixon to address his administration to the urgent need of devising an equitable health policy directed toward the nation's poor, most of whom are urban dwellers. He urged the President to rectify the piecemeal approach and correct the injustices of a failing health-care service.

In 1971 the administration introduced a health-care plan that is neither comprehensive nor able to serve the poor. It is designed to perpetuate the present system built mainly on private health insurance by making employers and employees responsible for insurance costs. But it does not correct the inefficient, costly, and unequal health delivery system in any way and does not include those who are unemployed. The administration's bill was introduced in competition with the Health Security Act of Senator Edward Kennedy, which in the opening sentence makes this commitment: "Every individual in the United States will be eligible to receive benefits."

The costs of health care and hospitalization have increased so drastically that not only the poor but also middle-income people are facing financial ruin if they require hospitalization. The absence of any coordinated, rational health-care policy is greatly contributing to the health-care costs. It has been pointed out time and again that there is no rational system of any kind underlying the health-care industries of this country, and even now there is no coordinated planning of health-care facilities or hospitals for any given metropolitan area.

But health care has also been neglected by previous administrations, despite frequent warnings that the nation must plan for and coordinate its health

*Now: President-elect, Rockefeller Foundation.

needs. The health-care situation has been neglected for a long time, especially in the inner cities. As it stands, it cannot be improved except with massive federal help.

Medical costs, and especially hospitalization costs, have risen out of proportion to other services. There is an increasing shortage of physicians and trained medical personnel. The cost of hospital beds has recently doubled; in many areas it has reached more than $100 per day and is still rapidly increasing. These facts are aggravated by the general overcrowding of medical facilities.

Thus, in this richest country of the world, the life expectancy of the people has fallen behind many other industrialized nations of the world. From 1959 to 1966, for instance, the life expectancy of males in the United States dropped from thirteenth to twenty-second place among all countries. According to recent U.N. statistics, while life expectancy is increasing in all countries, the rate of increase in the United States is falling behind many other nations. Infant mortality statistics, the other index of the health care situation of any one country, show that while infant mortality rates are declining all over the world, in half the world's countries infant mortality rates are declining faster than in the United States.

What are the reasons for this situation, and how is it possible that the most affluent society in the world, that prides itself on its organizational efficiency, is seemingly unable to provide decent health care for all its citizens? It is evident that there are some very serious defects in our present medical and health-care systems, defects that require more than superficial remedies. The statistics of life expectancy and infant mortality furthermore reveal that the people most affected are the black and other inner-city inhabitants. Despite the fact that most large hospitals are located in cities, the poor inhabitants of the city receive the worst care.

One reason is that the population is increasing beyond the financial ability of health-care facilities to expand. There are more people, especially more elderly and more children, who need regular health care and who deserve quality care; but there are not enough professionals, nor have sufficient facilities been added over the years.

In many ways, the present methods by which medicine is dispensed are their own worst enemies. Medical facilities are not coordinated, whether locally or regionally. Hospitals build specialized facilities, though the same facility, for instance, a heart-lung machine, may be available and unused in another hospital a few miles away. In the meantime, the urgent need to improve and enlarge outpatient departments almost everywhere goes unmet. The absence of any coordinated planning in the health-care facility field is one major reason for its inability to meet the demand. Existing facilities must be more rationally used and enlarged, or new ones built, to cope with the increasing numbers of people who need care and are presently left out.

Another major difficulty that greatly contributes to the overcrowding and the skyrocketing costs of health care is that, generally, health care is still interpreted as care of the already sick. It would be far less expensive and would greatly improve the health of the population if regular preventive care would be stressed and available. Most health conditions can be remedied before they are acute, or before there is need for hospitalization, if they are discovered in time by regular checkups.

Furthermore, all medical insurance systems at present work in such a way that a patient gets reimbursed for the cost of hospitalization. Yet some conditions could be better taken care of in the patient's home if nursing care or some home care were available or reimbursable to the patient. But the way all insurance plans presently read, a patient, to benefit, must occupy a hospital bed.

Special hospital facilities, such as operating rooms, are generally scheduled for use only at certain times of the day. Except for emergencies, they are unused on weekends and at night. Patients are generally asked to come to the hospital and occupy a bed twenty-four hours before a scheduled operation. The result is that fewer people obtain the necessary care at much higher cost because of a scarcity of facilities, which is largely created by inefficient or under-use of these facilities. Much of this could be changed by more efficient scheduling and use of existing facilities.

Add to this the fact that too few physicians have been trained in the United States for at least the past thirty years as a result of the restrictive practices of the AMA (American Medical Association). Like any trade union, the AMA argued that scarcity would increase the income of doctors and they succeeded admirably. Physicians are the highest paid professionals in the United States today. Furthermore, many routine services that could be handled by para-medical personnel, and often are (for instance, in the Army), must be reserved for physicians, according to the AMA rules. The result is that physicians often are not available when needed and that the overall public health situation is steadily deteriorating as the statistics show. The poor in the cities receive the worst care or frequently no care at all—as has been found by examining youngsters in the schools and children participating in the Head Start programs.

DISCUSSION

F.P.H.   Dr. Knowles, you have been actively involved in the health-care situation of the nation for a long time. Is the situation as bad as I see it? In particular, what is the public health situation in our cities?

J.H.K.   The city concentrates the largest number of people with very large health needs. Neighborhoods with impoverished people in inner cities today have staggering health needs. Since a large percentage of the city population, for a variety of reasons, is disadvantaged, they also often have the highest health needs; many are unemployable for reasons of poor health, which is a vicious circle.

For example, we did an OEO (Office of Economic Opportunity) study here in Boston and its environs, and of a thousand youths between the ages of fifteen and twenty-one over one-third had undiagnosed diseases or conditions that required follow-up. We commonly found cases of hypertension and streptococcus infections in the throat. We found venereal disease, which was rampant. We know that the health statistics in this country are as dismal as they are, specifically because of inner city conditions.

F.P.H.   Have Medicare and Medicaid made any difference? Both programs were finally enacted in 1965, despite vehement opposition by the AMA. I understand Medicare and Medicaid have put more pressure on the existing health facilities in terms of numbers of people, so that facilities are even more overloaded now. On the other hand, we obviously need such programs desperately.

J.H.K.   Well, the programs have helped in a variety of ways. First of all, they have reduced economic barriers for people who need health services, but who are afraid to try to obtain them for fear of having to move from the hospital or the doctor's office into the poorhouse. Medicaid for example, by paying physicians for what they traditionally did for free, has at least kept some physicians in inner-city areas where they are accessible to the poor people who need their services.

Medicare has reduced economic barriers for people over sixty-five. But Medicare today only covers a total of about 45 per cent of the health costs of these older people. Another 15 to 20 per cent is covered by Medicaid. Of course, once Medicare runs out, you can go on Medicaid. The rest of it is essentially coming out of pocket.

Now, you must bear in mind that with twenty million people over the age of sixty-five in this country, there are roughly eight million people under the present level of Social Security benefits who qualify or live on the border of poverty. There are also two-and-one-half million to three million widows whose income is somewhere around $1800 to $2000, and who are therefore definitely living in poverty. When only 45 per cent of their health needs are paid for out of Medicare, they have a problem.

One of the things that Medicare does not cover, for example, is medication. Now, chronic disease is seen most often in aged people. The cost of drugs for an aged person with heart disease or arthritis or mental illness may be as much as four, five, or six hundred dollars a year, or one-third of their total income, a cost that Medicare does not cover. Yes, Medicare-Medicaid has solved some problems, but, first of all, they have not revised the system of medical care; secondly, they have not reached expanded numbers of people.

F.P.H.　Again, many of the elderly live in the cities. I understand that many of the state governments through which Medicare-Medicaid is funneled have found it necessary to increase the premiums quite aside from the fact that the individual only gets a certain percentage of his costs reimbursed. From your point of view, what could we do to improve the Medicare-Medicaid services as far as the whole country is concerned? And, further what can we do to improve the health-care delivery to those people who are poor or old or very young, who need health care most?

J.H.K.　First of all, we must build standards and quality controls into Medicare and Medicaid. Medicare has a requirement of a so-called utilization review committee, which requires that participating hospitals have a definite, visible committee that keeps records and minutes and reviews the need for hospitalization of people who are admitted to the hospital. It does not require quality review. At the Massachusetts General Hospital, we have added quality controls into this requirement.

Medicaid requires neither quality review, utilization review, nor standards of any kind. Therefore, the total amount of money spent on Medicare and Medicaid have essentially perpetuated the present system. They have frozen it in a certain direction and have not taken the opportunity for change that capital financing, or operational financing of hospitals, could have provided.

Now, what kind of revisions are we talking about in this system? Medicine in this country in the past fifty years has evolved as essentially an acute, curative, after-the-fact operation. We have not stressed programs that would go into communities to make health services accessible, to give health education to the people, so they can understand how best to use physicians. And medicine has not taken the opportunity to keep people out of high-cost hospital facilities.

F.P.H.　In fact, you are saying that we would be much better off if we could treat people before they are so ill that they must go to the hospital. We should institute some organized preventive care, because by the time you go to the hospital, your situation is acute; quite aside from what that does to you, it also overloads the system. Because there is no preventive care, there are many more people who finally need hospital care, which is much more expensive for the individual and for the government that pays for much of it.

Therefore, the rational thing to do would be to institute not sick care, but health care, in the real sense of the word—care that keeps people healthy and prevents them from going to the hospital.

J.H.K.   There are two forces that mitigate against this. First of all healthy people are not interested in preventive medicine. A healthy person has a view of himself as being essentially immortal: "It cannot happen to me. I feel well today, so why should I go see a doctor or do something to prevent disease." Besides this basically "consumer" attitude, you have a profession that has geared itself to only acute-curative medicine and not to rehabilitation, preventive medicine, or those services with a very high benefit-to-cost ratio. You have got to do two things: you have to change the behavior of the producers of health services—doctors, hospitals, nurses, and so on, and you have to simultaneously change the behavior of the people.

What we have done here at the Massachusetts General Hospital is to decentralize our services. In one instance, we extended our services into the community of Charlestown, an area of Boston with seventeen thousand people, where we set up an easily accessible health center. From there we deal with the health education of the people—how to prevent disease, how to maintain health, when to see a doctor, and for what purposes. By being accessible to people, we have been able to reduce the Massachusetts General Hospital admissions from Charlestown, which is one of the communities of the city that we serve.

F.P.H.   What you point out, I think, is also reflected in the education of doctors. In the past, increasing numbers of medical students wanted only to specialize, instead of taking care of a community or going into general practice. I understand that now, particularly, the Harvard Medical School and also other top schools have instituted a new specialty, which is called "community medicine." If you decentralize service into the community, a reform very badly needed, the first thing you need is doctors who are general practitioners and the personnel to staff these clinics.

J.H.K.   That is right, and that has been another problem. We are so short of manpower right now that it is very hard to find doctors and other health workers to staff such services. However, as you point out, we have to change medical education, and we have to generate these types of people by enlargement of training. We have to do both. We must produce specialists who are needed desperately right now in this country, as well as generalists and community health people who will be practicing as much public health medicine as acute-curative medicine.

F.P.H.   I understand that one major problem in the city hospitals is the shortage of interns and young doctors. Due to the fact that our medical schools simply have not graduated enough doctors to fill these staff positions, we are largely dependent on foreign-trained personnel, that is, doctors who come from abroad and spend several years in American hospitals. I have been told that a number of the large city hospitals would have to close their doors tomorrow if these foreign-trained doctors could not continue in this service.

There has been a great deal of concern about this, I understand. It was felt on the one hand that M.D.'s from abroad could not provide the right type of service for the patients, as the AMA claims their training is not as good as in the United States. On the other hand, we are depleting badly-needed specialized manpower by attracting professionals from all over the world from countries that cannot afford to lose them, while we don't seem to be willing or able to train enough of our own doctors for our own use.

Medical education is very expensive; but it seems to me that the federal government should support medical and paramedical training on a much larger scale, which is really the only way to deal with this problem. I understand that the AMA has prevented the education of more doctors and paramedical personnel by not accrediting enough medical schools and by preventing paramedical personnel from doing routine tasks.

J.H.K.   The AMA has steadfastly denied that there was any shortage of physicians in this country until two years ago. For the last fifty years, they have prevented the expansion of medical schools, and have lobbied against any form of state or federal subsidy to allow such expansion. Only two years ago, I repeat, did they finally make a public statement allowing that there was, in fact, a shortage of physicians.

Now, all the other organizations, public health, nursing, and everyone else knew there was a shortage twenty years ago, but were unable to override the power of the AMA to prevent expansion of medical schools. Today, as a result, about one-third of all newly-licensed physicians in this country are graduates of a foreign medical school. We cannot tolerate this forever, nor can the countries that need their own doctors in their own countries go on tolerating this.

What is going to happen? Unfortunately, right now the present administration in its fight against inflation has reduced the support of medical schools and teaching hospitals, while at the same time asking us to increase the output. We cannot increase output unless we are given additional funds. So right now we are walking a tightrope. We are being told to do one thing, while the money is steadily taken away from us. There is much to be done by both the public and the private sector.

In the last analysis, it is the amount of money and the programs that are developed in this country that produce results. The present administration says there is a shortage, and the schools have got to expand and increase their output. I agree with that. At the same time, the Bureau of the Budget, at the direction of the White House, has reduced support for training and research to the medical schools of this country. This could have serious, adverse results.

F.P.H.   It is the same situation with many federal programs designed to help cities: funding that is already past due is delayed, while prices rise, or the programs are deferred. This does not really save anything; but, on the contrary, costs more, as we have seen particularly in the area of health care and medical training. Because costs go up continuously, you are simply deferring to the future what you ought to take care of now. It will not only be more expensive later, but in the meantime many people suffer. Often the damage is irreparable, especially since these are matters of human physical health.

Looking at the problem purely in financial terms, you see that the number of people who are unable to earn a living due to poor health is increasing. This increases welfare costs, as well as health costs. You are not saving any money at all by saving on health care expenditures.

Can we learn anything from Europe? Many countries in Europe have had well-functioning health-care and health-delivery systems for many years. Austria, a small and relatively poor country, has had publicly financed health care since the 1920's. We have heard a great deal about the health-care plan of Great Britain that was started after the war. It has had many growing pains and many difficulties. It seems to me we could learn a great deal from the practical experience of these countries.

J.H.K.   Their situation is not quite comparable to the political and cultural problems in this country. For example, England has fifty million people in quite a small area. Culturally and ethnically, the people are not nearly as diverse as the people in the United States. The same is true in Scandinavian countries. So some issues are quite different.

Nevertheless, they have fully regionalized systems of medical care in England, and in Scandinavia and other European countries. We have much to learn from them for we have not regionalized medical care in this country, and we should. It would help to improve quality and reduce costs. For example, a hospital like the Massachusetts General Hospital should be a highly technical, acute, curative, highly specialized hospital; but it should be serving a ring or a satellite of smaller community hospitals which are low-cost, curative hospitals that do much simpler procedures and take care of the usual ailments. We don't have that in this country today. The Scandinavian system, interestingly enough, and the British one, too, have found that their costs have risen tremendously, because they are relatively short of manpower in certain areas. But, nonetheless, they have rationalized the political arrangements, and that we have yet to do in this country.

F.P.H.   You point out one very important factor, the regional coordination of health care and of health-care planning. We seem to duplicate services frequently at hospitals. On top of that, there is the dichotomy between the university hospital and the community hospital, which frequently are not even on speaking terms, I understand. The majority of hospitals are quite small, and many of the community hospitals cannot provide needed services and are short of help; it would seem reasonable to make them larger and more efficient.

There seems to be a failure in communications and in planning in most areas. The state of New York, for instance, has gone about organizing a statewide planning effort for health care, which certainly is an important step in the right direction. However, it takes a very long time to translate the best plan into political reality, and New York State is unique with this plan.

J.H.K.   This is one of the problems we face. I certainly agree that we have not had the regional planning that we should have in this country. The traditional liberal view is that you create state or federal agencies to provide for regional planning, and all will be well. In fact, in New York State I have no evidence whatsoever that the cost of hospitalization or the rational use of health services, even with their state law, has necessarily been improved or is any better than it is in Massachusetts without such a law.

Furthermore, when you set up regional planning, it is a double-edged sword. You are trying to save money and avoid duplication. But what you do is to show the inadequacy of the existing health services—the need for more manpower, the need for more capital expenditures in certain areas.

It is going to be necessary through state and federal legislation to pass laws that demand that local plans are regionally coordinated. That is, hospitals will have to submit their plans to both professional and lay groups before they are allowed to expand their facilities. There are hospitals in this country today that add a wing and another hundred beds, when right down the street there are unused beds, and that is wrong. The costs are too high to allow that to continue.

F.P.H.   I understand that at the present time people are thinking along insurance lines with respect to the expansion of health care. For instance, labor unions certainly have pioneered in this area. There is Blue Cross/Blue Shield, one of the best-known insurance systems, and there are many more private insurance plans. It seems to me that most of these insurance plans work in the same direction, perpetuating rigidity of the system. For one thing, they pay for service. You get paid for being in a hospital bed. You don't get paid for preventive care, and you don't get paid for nursing service at home. Therefore, these plans overload the hospitals further.

The other point I would like to make is that obviously all the insurance plans leave out people who have no jobs or work for businesses that have not joined any insurance plans. Even if it becomes mandatory to join an insurance plan, which in essence is what the new health care bill by the administration suggests, there are temporary workers and certain categories that are still left out, quite aside from the people who are unemployed. And unemployment is very high in all areas, often through no fault of the unemployed, but because of the economic recession. The point is that insurance plans do not cover anywhere near the number of people who need health care, and least of all those who need it most, the poor. Obviously, the urban poor cannot pay the premiums for health insurance.

J.H.K.   All I can do is agree with every point that you have made. I am also always amused by our union leaders of the AFL-CIO. They will stand out at the front door here at the Massachusetts General Hospital and tell us to reduce our costs when they know that three-fourths of our costs are accountable as wages and fringe benefits of our employees. Then they go to the back door to unionize us and increase our costs further. Right now we face a union movement in this country that is taking the minimum wage in hospitals from about $2.00 an hour to $3.00 an hour. When you do that, your hospital-bed costs go up from $100.00 a day to $150.00 a day. Furthermore, I don't like the rhetoric of the AFL-CIO saying that the house of medicine is sick, that all doctors are chiselers, that all hospital directors are inadequate managers, and that the people are getting rooked.

Our job first of all is to save lives and not money. Secondly, the health-insurance plans should stimulate the use of low-cost facilities, preventive medicine, and health education. Thirdly, all citizens should strike at the roots of disease. Disease is the result of a combination of factors such as inadequate food, bad housing, inadequate education, lack of jobs, inequality, poor city services, abortion laws that should be repealed, and not enough birth-control information. We have 300,000 illegitimate births a year in this country. If you want to reduce the welfare rolls and the sick rolls in this country, reduce the 300,000 illegitimate births.

The point I am making is that the whole system in this country is going to have to get healthier, not just the health system, *per se.* Health insurance, through the lever of money, can change this system. But the federal government, in its wisdom with Medicare and Medicaid, was so scared of organized medicine, the pharmaceutical industry, and other powerful lobbies in Washington, that when they wrote the act they did not seize upon the opportunity to make the great change in the system that is needed. Now they are going to have to do that, and I think everybody recognizes this. I think the pharmaceutical industry and organized medicine themselves now recognize this must be done, and I would count on their help to do it.

F.P.H.   The Massachusetts General Hospital, I understand, is one of the hospitals that has initiated new techniques and automation in many areas. This should give the patients much better care, by freeing the nurses, for instance, to really nurse, instead of keeping books. I understand that you have done a pioneering job in that respect, from using TV monitoring in patient rooms to automated drug distribution, two-way call systems, monitoring of patient conditions, instant distribution of test results, more efficient scheduling of facilities, and so on. This should show other hospitals what can be done, as well as saving money or using manpower much more efficiently, which is the same. Could you describe that a little?

J.H.K.   Well, we are constantly looking at ways to reduce or contain costs here. A number of these innovations, the decentralization of the pharmacy to the floors, the development of floor managers, which frees the nurse for more critical nursing work, the automating of our chemistry labs, have materially reduced costs. We have automated the radiology department in various areas so that when you have an x-ray taken, it is automatically developed and given to the physician to read. We have automated view boxes so that our radiologists can read large numbers of film in a short period of time. We have a variety of labor-saving devices and employee-incentive programs.

At the same time, by virtue of decentralizing our services to the local community here, we are trying to keep people out of this hospital by being available to them, by detecting their diseases in their incipiency, treating them "on the hoof," so to speak, so they will not have to come into the hospital. All these things combined are important and make a great deal of difference.

F.P.H.   The Massachusetts General Hospital has the reputation of being a pioneer in that area. The answer seems to be that this kind of approach should be used in many more hospitals all over the country. However, to use automation, you need a certain size hospital. The small, community hospitals really cannot effectively deal with this in terms of capital investment.

J.H.K.   That is where regional planning comes in again. Regional laboratories can save money. A number of hospitals can group themselves together so that they can achieve economies of size and afford jointly the capital equipment that they need. Those are important issues.

A place like Massachusetts General Hospital is expected to be a pioneer and to be at the forefront. Every week we have people coming from all over this country who run hospitals and various types of medical care institutions to look at our automated laboratories or other systems that we have developed here to reduce costs, and they take those ideas back to their hospitals. Also, all of us here publish articles all the time.

F.P.H.   Perhaps there should be a stronger incentive system in terms of financing by the federal government. If we put money and a reward system behind the idea of planning on a regional basis, behind modernization, the automation of facilities, we may get it done much faster. From what you pointed out, there will have to be much more money spent if we really want to give health care the priority that it needs and deserves. Therefore, the right incentives must insure that the money is spent the right way, that is, on innovation instead of perpetuating past mistakes.

In summary, what do you think of the future?

J.H.K.   Well, I think the future is a healthy one. I think the future of the whole country, despite what the prophets of doom and gloom say, is relatively good. We have had crises like this both in medicine and the country at large in the past. In 1890 we had a massive loss of national nerve, inflation, and a deep recession. Forty years later, in 1930, we had the same thing again, and here we are again.

To sum up: We have a nationwide crisis in health care now, but as a result, in this coming decade many of the things we have been discussing will be changed. We have to expand the output of manpower. We have got to contain costs. We have got to stimulate the use of lower-cost facilities and initiate a system of preventive medicine. In fact, we have to resystematize the whole field. This means we must begin immediately; and I think that is what will be going on in the next decade in this country.

I have great confidence in the future because I believe we shall get this done.

F.P.H.   Your prescriptions are far-reaching and important and in a large measure depend on more people understanding and learning more about the complexities of health care problems.

Thank you, Dr. Knowles.

BIBLIOGRAPHY

BOOKS

Knowles, John H. *Hospitals, Doctors and the Public Interest.* Cambridge, Mass.: Harvard University Press, 1965.

—––, ed. *The Teaching Hospital.* Cambridge, Mass.: Harvard University Press, 1966.

—––. *Views of Medical Education and Medical Care.* Cambridge, Mass.: Harvard University Press, 1968.
A detailed pragmatic view of hospitals and medicine and medical education, lucidly written.

Editorial Research Reports on Health Topics. Washington, D.C.: Congressional Quarterly, Inc., 1967.

Education for the Health Professions. A Report to the Governors and the Board of Regents from the New York State Committee on Medical Education. June 1963. Copies available from the Board of Regents, New York State Education Department, Albany, New York.
A detailed study of the future of medical education.

Feingold, Eugene. *Medicare Policy and Politics.* San Francisco: Chandler Publishing Co., 1966. Paperback.

Health Security Act of 1971. 92nd Congress, January 1971. For information write: Committee for National Health Insurance, Suite 410, 806 15th Street, N.W., Washington, D.C. 20005.

"The Health Services." Pamphlet published by the British government, detailing the British health-care plan. For copies, write to British Information Services, 845 Third Avenue, New York, N.Y. 10022.

Love, Albert and Childress, James Saxon, eds. *Listen to Leaders in Medicine.* New York: Holt, Rinehart and Winston, 1963.

McKeown, Thomas. *Medicine in Modern Society.* New York: Hafner Publishing Company, 1966.

Pollack, Jerome. "Health Services and the Role of the Medical School." Prepared for Seminar on Health Policy, Institute for Policy Series. Washington, D.C., April 5, 1966.
Dr. Pollack is the foremost health service economist of the United States.

Report of the National Advisory Commission on Health Manpower. 2 volumes. Washington, D.C.: U.S. Government Printing Office, November 1967.
A detailed technical study of the health manpower field.

Rutstein, David D. *The Coming Revolution in Medicine.* Cambridge, Mass.: The MIT Press, 1967.
The best book on technical innovations available (but often not used) in the medical field, by the best expert in the area.

Wilbur, Muriel Bliss. *Community Health Services.* Philadelphia: W.B. Saunders Company, 1962.

ARTICLE

Penchansky, Roy, and Rosenthal, Gerald. "Productivity, Price and Income
Behavior in the Physicians' Services Market—A Tentative Hypothesis."
Medical Care 3:4 (October-December 1965).

11

CRIME, LAW, AND ORDER

A discussion with ALBERT M. BOTTOMS
Former Director of Operations Research Task Force, Chicago
Police Department; Research Associate, Joint Center for Urban
Studies of M.I.T. and Harvard

INTRODUCTION

Crime in the city streets has become a major concern for every urban citizen, for all city police departments, mayors' offices, and the federal government. Crime control, the enforcement of law and order, is a constant controversial news topic and the subject of political campaign promises. It also is the goal of stern new legislation, which is called repressive by many who have studied its effects.

Mayor John Lindsay of New York, in his book *The City*, asks:

> What happens if Supreme Court decisions are overturned, if police are ordered to shoot a looting thirteen-year-old? What happens, if after this victory for "law and order," we find—as we will—that the crime rate is still going up, that the streets are still not safe, that more and more lives have been lost, and that America is being divided into armed camps?[1]

But crime in the cities has increased at an alarming rate. According to a recent *U.S. News and World Report* survey, crimes of violence in the United States are rising ten times as fast as the population.

In the nine years from 1960 to 1969, murder has increased 66 per cent; rape has increased 115 per cent; robberies have increased 180 per cent; and aggravated assault has increased 103 per cent.

One reason given by most authorities is the drug addict, who needs money to supply himself with drugs. But there are other, more long-range social ills, which define the condition of our inner cities, where the highest crime incidence exists; in the congested, physically dilapidated, economically deprived,

---

[1] John V. Lindsey, *The City* (New York: W.W. Norton & Company, Inc., 1970).

and socially abandoned ghettoes. Lack of jobs and of any satisfying occupations combine with miserable housing, poor schools, overcrowding, no recreation, family disintegration, and, as a result, a sense of hopelessness.

All studies of crime show the highest delinquency rates nearest the center of the city, the lowest ones farthest out. This occurs regardless of which ethnic group occupies these central areas. Many neighborhoods that had the highest crime rates in 1930 also had them in 1900, and they have them still today. Too little has been done in all this time to correct the living conditions in the city slums.

The white middle class is leaving the cities, while poor Southern blacks and minority immigrants, unused to city life and unskilled in urban industrial and service jobs, are moving into the decaying inner-city areas. This is a recipe for trouble, and crime is the most visible result.

One fact should be mentioned here: The vast majority, or 90 per cent, of all violent crime victims are of the same race as the offenders. Furthermore, contrary to what most people believe, most violent crimes take place between family members or people who know each other.

Another fact also quoted in Mayor Lindsay's book is that the Supreme Court decision which requires suspects to be informed of their constitutional rights by police has had no discernible effect on the conviction rate, contrary to what has been claimed.

The Report of The National Commission on the Causes and Prevention of Violence, "The Eisenhower Report" as it is called, warns that:

> Violent crimes are chiefly a problem of the cities of the nation, and these violent crimes are committed mainly by the young, poor, male inhabitants of the ghetto slums.
>
> In the slums increasingly powerful social forces are generating rising levels of violent crime which, unless checked, threaten to turn our cities into defensive, fearful societies.
>
> An improved criminal justice system is required to contain the growth of violent crime, but only progress toward urban reconstruction can reduce the strength of the crime-causing forces in the inner city and thus reverse the direction of present crime trends.[2]

The reconstruction of our cities must be started now, but it will take time to be effective. However, there are some urgently needed, immediate, and tangible reforms that must and can be dealt with immediately. First, more police are needed on all city streets, and there must be more efficient use of existing police. Next, trial must quickly follow arrest. It now often takes more than two years between arrest and a jury trial. Most of this time elapses

[2] National Commission on the Causes and Prevention of Violence, Milton Eisenhower, Chairman. *Report on Civil Disorders.*

between indictment and trial and is often spent in jail by the alleged offender if he is poor and unable to raise bail.

And finally the whole prison system needs fundamental reorganization and a change of goals. Instead of reforming people, prisons turn out hardened criminals and recidivists.

More visible policemen in the city streets and the modernizing of police departments, using modern communication systems and computers, walkie-talkies, and other new techniques, including contemporary management methods, can do much to give the citizen better protection and better service for his tax money.

DISCUSSION

F.P.H.   Mr. Bottoms, as director of the Operations Research Task Force of the Chicago Police Department, you have direct experience with all these problems.

A.M.B.   Yes, that is right. We can use the advanced techniques of the management sciences to get the following specific benefits: improved control over the allocation of financial, equipment, and personnel resources; identification and evaluation of alternatives for action, employment, and for the purchase of new hardware; improved response to citizen calls for service; and improved effectiveness of the preventive-control function. These things should confer enhanced police-community relationships, because of the apparent increased professionalism of the department.

The management sciences are attempting to reduce the burden of the police administrator by helping him assess the potential costs and benefits of various alternative courses of action.

F.P.H.   It has been said that we no longer have adequate police protection. But what adequate police protection entails is hard to define, though it is usually linked to more manpower. The cost of what is termed adequate police protection, meaning many more visible police in the streets at all times, is quite astronomical. I think you have proposed as an alternative a more efficient use of existing police manpower. In fact, as you point out, more modern management techniques could do much to accomplish that.

A.M.B.   No city government in the United States can afford to match the increased public demands for police service with just increased manpower. More police, more hardware, higher-powered guns, and so forth are *not* the answer.

The answer is to use what we have in the most intelligent, effective way. It may be worthwhile to consider the police problem a little more broadly. You cannot separate the law enforcement function from the courts and correction. You cannot separate the criminal justice system from the community, the social fabric at large. Therefore, you have to see where the police fit in. The technique known as systems analysis helps to structure the best use of police resources.

We find, for example, that the main jobs are the protection of life and property, the maintenance of peace and order, and the providing of public service. There are some tasks that are less important but still resource-consuming: traffic control, special functions, control of man-made disasters.

It is significant to think that in a major city like Chicago we dispatch 9000 cars (units) on a typical summer weekend. Of those 9000 answers to public calls for service, 74 per cent do not specifically involve enforcement of felonies or law enforcement. The great majority are public service calls. They range from helping somebody get a cat out of a tree to the transport of a sick child. Clearly, some of these things must be done. Equally clearly, some of these things represent luxuries in the face of the rising demand for service. Every city in the United States has seen public demand for service rising at rates from 10 per cent to 20 per cent each year.

F.P.H.   This is true in all service areas in the cities. Certainly in the police protection function, one of the greatest increases in demand for service has occurred simply because of the increase in crime.

But, as you point out, a policeman's job is really a most diversified one. We tend to see it only from a very limited point of view. In fact, most people associate police service with trouble of some kind.

There should be different people available in each police department for the different types of jobs the police fulfill. They require a totally different type of person and orientation. Do you think that this approach holds some answers?

A.M.B.   Experimentation is going on in just that area. For example, in control, and similar jobs. It seems to work very well, and it frees the fully-trained manpower for other law enforcement tasks.

However, when you get into the inner city, the police officer is a sort of ombudsman. He must be prepared to handle almost anything. He is the only representative of the city government on duty sixteen of the twenty-four hours of the day. So he has to handle and know how to do a great many things.

In New York City, for example, the Family Crisis Unit has proven to be an outstanding success. Specially trained teams work with the family problems that can so often result in homicides.

F.P.H.   Of course, a policeman today has to be a psychologist, sometimes even a doctor or nurse; you always read about policemen delivering babies in taxis or police ambulances. He has to settle family problems; he has to convey children across the street and often help them with their troubles; he has to rescue animals and pets. All this quite aside from dealing with crimes and theft. It seems that a policeman is required to do more different jobs than any other public official. It must be very difficult, also from a recruiting point of view, to find persons who can fulfill all these different demands. The recruiting problem, therefore, is understandably difficult.

A.M.B.   Policemen don't do all these jobs on a professional level. But they are trained to handle them until help arrives. They fulfill really a first-aid function. There is a strong argument for having them continue in this function, because by being helpful to the people of a community, they establish rapport and develop community support.

The police cannot run a city like an occupying army, although it sometimes appears that this is exactly what is happening. They have to be there to help and to encourage the people in the inner city to help themselves. However, this great multiplicity of jobs we talked about results in some extremely serious problems for the police administrator. He has to figure out how to allocate his resources among all these different tasks.

We must recognize right from the start that he also has to allocate his resources in response to political pressure—the word commonly used is "clout," in reference to the power and the influence that some residents exercise. You are often likely to find a lot of police representation in the neighborhood where the mayor lives, or an influential alderman, or an influential businessman. This allocation may be quite incorrect when you look at the crime statistics. For example, in Chicago a resident of the ghetto is over 30 times more likely to be the victim of a serious personal assault, robbery, rape, or homicide than a resident of one of the white suburbs. And the police allocation does not reflect that. Police resources are essentially uniformly spread throughout Chicago.

F.P.H.   The distribution of protection has been one of the problems. Another basic issue implied here is the residency issue. The policeman should be a member of the community. What has been resented most of all is the police as a sort of occupying force. On the other hand, each community should be partner to the decision of who their police will be and where policemen are recruited.

Do you know of any communities that have some direct say in the kind of police protection they have and in the selection of recruits? After all, communities pay for police through their taxes.

A.M.B.   In many cities, and certainly in Chicago, the community has impact on the kind of policing that goes on through the interchange at the police-community workshops, through calling on the district commander, through the press, and of course through the elective process. It is recognized that sometimes this is not enough. The Deputy Chief of Police in Chicago, who heads the Community Relations Unit, points out that often we are not talking to the people to whom we should. The very fact that somebody is at a police-community workshop almost says that we don't really need to be talking to him, that he is with us. We are not talking to the hard core who feel that they are not represented.

Now, the police as a para-military organization find it very, very difficult to accept the concepts of civilian review boards, local control, and neighborhood control.

F.P.H.   In New York the civilian review board has been defeated.

A.M.B.   It was absolutely defeated. In Washington, the attempt to create a model precinct that was to have some of these features has resulted in terrible tensions.

F.P.H.   Would you please explain what a model precinct is, and what the model precinct in Washington is attempting to do?

A.M.B.   The model precinct in Washington wanted to place police into storefront police sub-stations. They would have been ombudsmen in every sense of the word to work with the citizens. In addition to law enforcement, they planned to work very closely with the citizens to raise the whole standard of life in that community—and they were going to be under the direction of a neighborhood council. This was where the concept came apart. The election of that council was very hotly contested by radicals on both sides, and the project, as far as I know, is at a dead stop.

F.P.H.   This is unfortunate because it certainly could have yielded some important new information and guidelines; at least it should have been tried out.

A.M.B.   Experimentation in law enforcement is an absolute must if we are going to make any progress. Whenever anyone wants to experiment, they should be encouraged and supported.

F.P.H.   To date, as far as I know, there has been no progress made in terms of decreasing crime in the streets, so that new ideas and experiments are especially important. It was also pointed out that to make police operations more efficient, it is necessary to apply modern administrative techniques. Automated communication, walkie-talkies, and other innovations should be used by police departments, and other city services as well.

A.M.B.   The police are not alone in their lack of sophistication in their approach to management. Most other city departments are as bad or even worse. However, we find that the police do not have a body of knowledge in written form. If you ask the police: Why do you do certain things that way?, they answer: We have always done it that way.

The systems analysis method, which I mentioned earlier, helps to identify the major programs and the major police and community goals. This sounds easy, but it took the Chicago Police Department eight months to get an agreement as to what those goals are. However, once you have an agreement on goals, you can identify the programs where the resources are to be spent.

I think it is important to remember that in any police department in the United States the personnel costs are the major item. Personnel costs in the Chicago Police Department amount to 96 per cent of their $180 million budget, that is, 96 per cent goes for employees. Obviously, expenditures for people have to be carefully managed. The other 4 per cent deals with automobiles, telephones, and other hardware. It is most important, therefore, to find out where the 96 per cent of that money is going.

In the Chicago Police Department, 70 per cent of the 96 per cent goes to the Bureau of Field Services, that is, to the street forces, the infantry of the police department. These are the men who do the street work.

F.P.H.   These are the policemen who walk around in the streets, who ride in the patrol cars, and whom you see every day.

A.M.B.   They are the task force, the visible part of the police department. The detectives are also in the Bureau of Field Service. The detective division is only about a thousand strong, out of twelve thousand in the Chicago Police Department. Overall administrative support of the department runs at about 20 percent of the budget, and that includes such things as the Crime Lab.

A.M.B.   It is not so much to make savings, but to insure the right utilization of the resources that counts. First, we have to find out where our efforts are going. Using the techniques of systems analysis to find out what is really happening, why and how, we developed what we call a "resource analysis budget." This tells the police administrator how much he is spending on crime prevention, on public service, on parade supervision, and elsewhere.

Having found out how much is spent on what, you try to develop alternative ways of fulfilling the same goals. For example, could you not use community service instead of police to assist in marshalling Boy Scout parades? And there are other alternatives for accomplishing many of the same tasks. In time, through the use of various techniques in analysis, we will be able to tell how much it is worth to put on officer on one task as opposed to another. We may even be able to tell the kind of officer that should be put on the different tasks, because we shall know something about how those jobs ought to be done. There are jobs that call for an aggressive police officer. There are other jobs, like the "Officer Friendly" program, that call for the father image, the patient, kindly officer who captures the imagination of the children before they become clients.

F.P.H.   The relative distribution of activities within the police department, as you point out, has a major effect on the overall efficiency of the service that is rendered to the citizen. In the past, I suppose nobody has really looked into this in terms of operations research, analyzing what distributions and procedures would be best under certain circumstances. This probably also differs from city to city. What kind of a force should each community posess in order to best carry out the necessary functions?

A.M.B.   This does differ somewhat from city to city, although there are marked similarities. The work that has been done, operations research work, by the Rand Institute in New York, by our group in Chicago, by students at M.I.T. working with the Boston Police Department, and on the West Coast, has shown up remarkable similarities in the nature of the problems and therefore in the nature of the solutions.
There are, of course, certain differences. One question that arises in parts of Chicago, and in fact in every city with highrise buildings, is how to patrol a vertical beat. That is, how to control in terms of security the elevators, corridors, and lobbies on the many floors which are virtually public spaces, yet not to interfere with the privacy of the tenants.

F.P.H.   Many of the large office complexes or groups of highrise buildings, mixed office-housing complexes, have their own private security forces, from the doorman to the elevator operators, as well as private detectives. But the crimes that have occurred time and again in the corridors or elevators seem to point out that these buildings are really lacking in security due to improper organization. We really don't know how to deal with the problem of verticality in our cities.

A.M.B.   It is partly organization, partly policy, and partly hardware. It depends on what the people in that particular community want. For example, in a luxury apartment-hotel in Chicago the relatively well-heeled residents would welcome a patrol strolling through the corridors. They don't mind being screened as they go into the entrances. In many buildings, they have to identify themselves and have to use a special passkey. This kind of thing does not appear to them to be unwarranted surveillance.

In another community in Chicago, the very appearance of a police officer or even the Chicago Housing Authority patrol officers causes near rebellion. In some buildings, the officers cannot go above the first floor with any safety.

F.P.H.   One question that has been asked time and again, especially due to frequent violence, riots, and trouble in the inner city is: Should our police carry firearms? In the United States the police have always carried firearms. But we are the only western democracy, I believe, where police carry firearms at all times. Certainly, the British police do not, nor do the police in most of the central European countries. They have never carried firearms except in special cases of emergency. Would you say that this is a practice that we should reexamine in the United States?

A.M.B.   It probably needs continual reexamination. But I wonder if we are not in the chicken-and-egg dilemma. Unfortunately, the other side appears to be armed to the teeth. For example, in the Second Police District in Chicago, using the stop-and-frisk law on police pull in as many as two to three hundred hand guns every week. The great majority of these guns are not registered, nor is the owner a registered gun owner. This is a clear violation of the law. This in an area that had 2500 robberies in a recent year.

The question now is: Is it practical to send a law enforcement officer into an area where the populace is already armed and has shown every willingness to use these weapons? If we can, through gun-control legislation and through public education (which is even more important), persuade people to turn in their guns, then I think the police will exercise restraint in direct proportion. They will not be thinking about automatic weapons and shotguns and will hopefully go back to the billy club or something of this sort.

F.P.H.   As you point out, the police cannot disarm in face of the fact that so many criminals seem to possess guns and other weapons. The public must be protected. Perhaps this problem should be tackled through public safety education and gun control rather than through police disarmament.

There are other factors that seem to contribute to crime, such as the very long time it takes to bring a suspected criminal into court. Though this is an area in which the police are only indirectly involved, by the time a case requiring police testimony comes into court, it is hard to reconstruct the details of each crime and the credibility of the police is damaged and much police time is wasted.

A.M.B.   The cost to the police of the endless continuations and delays in the courts is staggering. In that same second district in Chicago that I mentioned before, where more than two hundred offenders of the firearms act are apprehended each week, we found that an officer had to make an average of four to five appearances in court for each case brought to trial. This means a loss of almost five days' work just to sit around in the courtroom to hear the judge grant a continuance.

We have found that there is a great deal of necessary investigation of the crime itself and of the background of the offender, who may just be carrying a gun because he is afraid. For the police, this is another expense and a drain on manpower.

Finally, in a sample of something like eight hundred offenders, less than 1 per cent spent any time at all behind bars. Our efforts tend to seem like an absolute waste of time. Certainly police investigation and apprehension has not changed the robbery rate. This raises some questions about the effect of straight law enforcement as a method of control.

The police complain bitterly about the turnstyle courts. They bring in an offender whom they have caught in an act of robbery. Two hours later he is back out on the street. We had a case in Chicago where the same youth was arrested twice in the same night for armed robbery. The explanation on the second arrest was that he needed money to pay a lawyer.

F.P.H.   This, of course, involves the whole court and trial system. Law and order must be tackled from a comprehensive point of view. Efficient performance of the police is not enough if the law cannot deal with proven criminals once apprehended. However, in the majority of cases, crimes are never solved at all.

Preventive detention is part of the new anti-crime legislation in the District of Columbia. Washington is one area where street crime has greatly increased recently. The new legislation has the power to detain people even though their court cases may not come up for weeks. It means that people can be put in jail for an extended period without a trial. Wire tapping, electronic surveillance, and no-knock searches have been authorized recently as anti-crime measures. A number of people reacted to this legislation and claimed that this would only aggravate the situation.

Professor James Vorenberg, from the Harvard Law School, who was the head of the President's Commission on Law Enforcement, warns against simplistic solutions of curtailing civil liberties and unleashing police. He seems to feel that the police lately have overstepped their limitations, encouraged by new legislation that abridges the rights of the citizen before the law. These stern measures, he suggests, will make the overall situation pertaining to crime, law and, order worse rather than better, and former Attorney General Ramsey Clark [3] agrees with him.

A.M.B.   Take the criminal justice system as a whole—law enforcement, prosecution, courts, and correction: To develop improved information link-ages among all parts of the system may prove to be one part of the solution. Improved communication with the rest of the community is just as necessary, so that decisions about arrest, about prosecution, about detention and the method of rehabilitation will be made with all available information about an offender.

There are a number of decision nodes that occur as an offender is processed through the system. You should not want to treat a juvenile the same as a felon. You don't want to treat an addict like a felon. On the other hand, you don't want to treat a felon as merely somebody who is a nuisance.

We should develop ways of structuring the flow of information so that everybody has the information he needs: the judge, for example, needs to know the background of a case instead of having to process it in a supermar-ket-type of courtroom. At present, the judge often does not have the infor-mation or it is not available, or the social worker was not able to make it into court that day. There are many causes why the administering of justice seems to be at best extremely uneven or quite capricious. I think it is possible to rectify this situation. Management of information is one of the things that computers can do for you.

F.P.H.   In the matter of invasion of citizens' rights, for instance, you point out that it is not just the police who are at fault, but the interrelated systems of police, law enforcement, and prisons: they will have to be reformed con-comitantly. Better communication between all the above people or groups must be established, and some positive goals must be set.

Much of the crime situation is caused by the inhuman conditions imposed upon the inner-city inhabitants. People who live in great discrimination, den-sity, and poverty have always been crime-prone, quite aside from the rela-tively recent escalation. The social, economic, and physical neglect of many inner-city areas is frequently a cause of crime. We have done little that is positive for the inner cities; our society has neglected housing, education, jobs, recreation, and all that produces a decent life for inner-city inhabitants. As a result, the inner-city areas form the natural breeding ground for crime.

---

[3] Ramsey Clark, *Crime in America* (New York: Simon and Schuster, 1970).

Finally, I should like to quote a statement from Chief Justice Earl Warren that he made after his recent retirement:

We have people in our big cities who are living in ghettoes without employment of any kind. They are ignorant, they have had no schools, they have no skills with which to compete in the economic market, they are easy prey to all kinds of bad influences in the community.

I think one of the things that must be done in order to eliminate much of that is to improve the conditions of our cities. We must get rid of the ghettoes, we must see that every youngster who comes into being in our country is afforded a decent education and is given some skill through which he can compete in the market.

Then, I think, he must not only have that skill, but he must have the opportunity to get a job, he must be able to join a union. We must eliminate the discrimination that is so prevalent in many places if we are to have a society that will accomodate itself to the law.[4]

Thank you, Mr. Bottoms.

[4] Anthony Lewis, "A Talk with Warren on Crime, the Court, the Country," *New York Times,* October 19, 1969, pp. 34 ff.

BIBLIOGRAPHY

Bottoms, Albert M., and Nilsson, Ernst K. "Management Sciences and Law Enforcement: The Results of the Chicago Demonstration Project." Unpublished paper.

BOOKS

"Anti-Crime Proposals." Hearings before Subcommittees No. I and No. 3 of the Committee on the District of Columbia House of Representatives, September 22, October 1, 7, 14, and November 4, 10, 17, 1969. Washington, D.C.: U.S. Government Printing Office, 1969.

"Anti-Crime Proposals." Supplement to Hearings before Subcommittee No. 1 and No. 3 of the Committee on the District of Columbia House of Representatives, January 29 1970.

Clark, Ramsey. *Crime in America.* New York: Simon & Schuster, 1970.
A pragmatic approach to dealing with crime from the experience of one involved on every level, including as Attorney General.

Demaris, Ovid. *America the Violent.* New York: Cowles Book Company, Inc., 1970.

Lindsay, John V. *The City.* New York: W.W. Norton & Company, Inc., 1970.
A well-written, pragmatic book, written from the unique basis of the direct experience of running New York.

National Commission on the Causes and Prevention of Violence, Milton Eisenhower, Chairman. *Report of Civil Disorders.*
  A comprehensive document researched by the best people available in this field.
Report of the National Advisory Commission on Civil Disorders. *One Year Later.* Published by Urban America, Inc., 1969.
Wilson, James Q., ed. *The Metropolitan Enigma: Inquiries into the Nature and Dimension of America's Urban Crisis.* Cambridge, Mass.: Harvard University Press, 1968.

ARTICLES

Leahy, Frank J. "Planning Programming Budgeting." *The Police Chief,* July 1968, 16-27.
Lewis, Anthony. "A Talk with Warren on Crime, the Court, the Country." *The New York Times* (October 19, 1969), p. 34.
"Why Streets are Not Safe: Special Report on Crime." *U.S. News and World Report* LXVIII:11 (March 16, 1970), pp. 15-21.

12

VIOLENCE

A discussion with JOHN P. SPIEGEL, M.D.
Director of the Lemberg Center for the Study of Violence,
Brandeis University

INTRODUCTION

Violence has become a continuous preoccupation of our time. At present, violence is used as a means to settle problems in areas where, previously, peaceful means prevailed. It seems that our ability to deal with the constantly sharpening problems of our time has in part been replaced by a heightened inability to postpone gratification or wait for solutions. The result is polarization and the resort to violence, as people lose faith in settling grievances peacefully. In the international area, it has been learned by most countries that warfare is no longer a useful or acceptable method of solving problems. Nor does violence in civil disputes yield lasting, useful solutions, though many claim it is the best way to gain the necessary leverage for change.

Since the term "violence" has been very loosely used as a result of recent political events, perhaps we should first of all define here what we are talking about. The definition proposed by Dr. Spiegel and the Lemberg Center for the Study of Violence is as follows: "Violence is the maximum arousal of aggression for destructive purposes, including the killing of members of one's own species." This definition implies that there is a good deal of aggressive behavior, including repression, constraint, deprivation, resistance, and even disruption, that must be distinguished from violence, or the open use of force. Violence, the way it is defined for our purposes here represents the strongest manifestation of aggression.

DISCUSSION

F.P.H.   Dr. Spiegel, since it is so important to clearly define such a controversial subject, could you please add some qualifications to your above-quoted definition?

J.P.S.   Well, I think it is important to keep in mind that violence is often used by people to describe things they don't like. When people say, "We are a violent society," they frequently have in mind such facts as people suffering from deprivation or from other forms of oppression, which, so far as the studies carried on by our center are concerned, would not be included in such a definition.

Nevertheless, we would tend to include all forms of oppression and misery under the label of "aggression." But it is important for us to distinguish non-violent aggression from violent aggression. Violence is at one end of that whole spectrum of behavior and has been reserved in the course of evolution as the kind of behavior available to the human species only in extreme circumstances. We are now living in a time in which we see a greatly accelerated use of violence. This tends to mean to us that the social circumstances under which we are living are becoming more extreme, and that therefore violence tends to be aroused more frequently.

F.P.H.   There are many different conditions which you describe in your work that contribute to violent behavior, such as biological conditioning and the rapid feedback of information that is possible now through the communication media. What is socially acceptable now is very different from the traditional way of looking at things, and this also creates tension. Our value structure, as far as society as a whole is concerned, is changing, and this makes for uncertainty and difficulties.

We also have a long history of violence that we tend to forget, as history books are largely silent on that subject. Violence seems a new phenomenon to many today, but historically this is hardly the case.

J.P.S.   It is important for all of us to realize how confused Americans are on the moral question of when uses of violence are acceptable and when not. We have no clear set of ethical principles about it. So far as one can learn from a study of history, there are at least two positions that can be outlined. One we can call the absolutist position, which is to say that violence is never permissible under any circumstances, not even in international struggles. And, of course, this speaks for all the pacifists and all of the religious sects who take a very firm and clear position that violence is never justified.

But for most Americans the position is a relative one, and this is where the difficulties come in. There is, I think, a majority point of view that Americans support, which is that violence is justified under some situations. For example, in the conduct of a "just war" or in self-defense or in similar circumstances.

The problem here is that circumstances that are used to justify violence as a relative matter are like a rubber band. They can be extended and stretched out so that today we fight a supposedly "just war" in Vietnam, but we know to what degree that rubber band may be stretched to cover Laos and Cambodia and perhaps all of Indochina and perhaps other international engagements. The same thing is true where violence in the streets and protest are concerned, that is, it can be indefinitely stretched out in terms of justification. As a result, all of us tend to lose our bearings as to what we will be able to tolerate and what we feel we must condemn. For this reason, I think it is very important for us not to be hung up on the question of moral or ethical justification. We must try to be as analytical as possible about the conditions that give rise to violence and the possibility for non-violent solutions of those conflicts that do instigate violence.

F.P.H.   The Revolution was one very violent cycle in our history. Everyone refers to the Revolution as a completely justified application of violence. There have been other violent cycles in our history, for instance, the beginning of the labor movement, when the labor unions were first organized. The strikes that resulted aroused a great deal of violence. Now the labor unions are anything but violent.

Time seems to have a very de-escalating influence on violence. What happened in the past seems far less violent. The fact is, however, that our background, or history of violence, which is in our consciousness, supports the concept of violence.

In your writing, Dr. Spiegel, you point out that the present social conflict is brought about by the incompatibility of our democratic ideals with the authoritarian practices that are prevalent in our society.

J.P.S.   In approaching our history to find out where the current cycle of violence fits in, it is important to avoid two extremes. One is the sort of Utopian extreme, which would take the position that if we are just clever enough, if we do enough research, we may be able to get rid of all violence and solve all conflicts peaceably. The other extreme is the pessimistic one, that man is violent by nature, that the United States has always been a violent society, so why should we expect anything different now.

I would like to try to hit a middle road between those two poles and look at our violent past for the sake of understanding why we have had cycles of violence in the past. Why do we have one now? What are the factors that contribute to this, both past and present?

For the sake of trying to draw some lessons from history, I think we should recall that we have been through six previous cycles of violence. We are now in our seventh. The six previous cycles had to do with the revolt of the poor farmers right after the Revolutionary War, the Shay's Rebellion, which took place in 1786, and which occurred because the farmers felt they were being unfairly taxed by the legislature. So they rose up and seized the law courts and caused a great deal of disruption, very similar to the types of disruption that are going on now. The legislature finally got the message, as we now say, and passed fairer tax legislation.

There was another cycle of violence early in the nineteenth century, in the 1830's and 1840's. It had to do with the effort of Irish Catholic immigrants to get into the system and to be allowed to preserve their own religious forms and have something to say about their own communities. That occasioned a great deal of rioting, somewhat similar to what we see now. There were people in what was then the establishment who did not want the Irish Catholic movement legitimized.

Then there were the Civil War draft riots, which again had to do with justice vs. injustice. At that time, to avoid the draft one could pay $300. But there were many people who did not have $300 to get out of the draft. They felt this was unfair, and they began a great deal of rioting. The government got the message and passed fairer draft laws. There were finally the labor uprisings, which lasted from the 1870's until the 1940's. It took all that time for labor to establish its right to organize and to engage in negotiations with management.

Every single one of these cycles of the past has represented an instance in which a defined group of people was excluded from the system. They were excluded from the opportunity to have social and political equality with others in the American society.

In each of these past efforts an excluded group tried to gain entrance into the social system and to establish its rights. It succeeded only after a great deal of violence. We are now in our seventh cycle of violence, which has to do with the effort of black people to establish justice for themselves and the effort of young people to have something to say about their life style and their notions of what is just versus unjust. So I think we now have to ask: Have we learned enough from the past to be able to apply those lessons in such a fashion that *perhaps*, and this word is important, perhaps we can get through this particular cycle with a minimum of violence?

F.P.H.   At the moment I would say it does not look very hopeful, judging from recent events.

J.P.S.   We always are impressed with what is going on before our eyes and tend to exaggerate this in terms of what has happened in the past. The violence today gets a great deal of publicity; we see it on television and read about it in the newspapers, and therefore we are all very much aware of it. But it is by no means as extensive as the violence of the past.

Just recall that during the course of the Pullman railway strike, in the

1890's, 10,000 troops were called out to put down the strike all over the country, hundreds of people were injured and killed. We have seen nothing like that in our time. Comparatively few people have been killed and injured in our present cycle of violence.

F.P.H.   Perhaps we are learning how to deal with riots. Though television and the communication media have been blamed for escalating riots, I think in a way they have also spread knowledge of how to better deal with riots and prevent bloodshed. The knowledge of how to cope with riots, and prevent their escalation spreads as fast as the knowledge of how to incite riots. And prevention is the best method to deal with violence.

If we take as example the recent main areas of trouble, black riots and student riots, one of the chief factors responsible is the structure of our society. The difference between our democratic ideals and the authoritarian practices, which we often conceal, is one cause of constant trouble. Yet, practices of society continue to follow hierarchical lines.

J.P.S.   Students so often refer to it as hypocrisy. The gap between our democratic ideals and our authoritarian or elitist practices is huge. We are all taught in school and by the mass media about the democratic processes, about the importance of the individual, who should make his own decisions and be heard. We talk about participation in the political area pertaining to our own welfare. You might say the individual comes first.

Secondly, we are taught the importance of the group. The term "United States" implies that we are all united. The group principle, that we are all equal to each other, is extremely important. Insofar as decision making and social importance are concerned, we are taught that ranking, a lineal or hierarchical structure of who is above and who is below, is least important in our democratic society. But when we look at how our institutions actually operate, we see that this order of values is disregarded: The lineal, ranking elitist or hierarchical order of who is above and who is below is most important in many of our institutions—not only in the Army, where one would expect a command structure, but in our governmental and educational institutions. Almost every place where one looks, one sees that there is a ranking principle of who is in and who is out, who is making it, who is not making it, who is important, who is not important.

F.P.H.   Children are taught the democratic ideals from early childhood on, at home and in school. By the time young people get to the universities, they become conscious of how the world is really organized. Obviously this is a tremendous disappointment and letdown. In the process, the students try to find a scapegoat and try to blame who or what is closest at hand, and this usually is the university and its administration.

Besides, it is a fact that university systems particularly have not kept up with the times and don't practice the democracy they preach. Universities have grown rapidly since the war. Due to the GI Bill, they had to handle vast numbers of people very quickly without restructuring the basic organization, which was not designed for this.

So I think the students have much cause for their criticism. They also see no way of altering the authoritarian situation except by confrontation. Confrontations have occurred recently time and again on campuses all over the country.

J.P.S.   I would like to put this particular point back into historical context. As you say, we do so easily seize upon scapegoats and make them responsible for matters that are really a part of our social structure, and for which we should not blame individuals.

If we look at the social structure of the United States in the course of our history and try to correlate that with the past cycles of violence I described, then I think we see that there has always existed a set of principles that determined who was in and who was out. This set of principles for inclusion and exclusion I call the "WAMPAM structure" of the United States. And by that I do not mean a pun on the Indians. By WAMPAM I mean an acronym— W-A-M-P-A-M—which I shall explain.

In order to be included in the system as it was originally set up right after the revolution, you had to be White; you had to be an Anglo-Saxon, or some related Northern European; you had to be middle class or better (that is what the Shay's Rebellion was all about, or the Poor Revolt); you had to be Protestant, which means that all Catholics, Jews, Orientals, Buddhists, and so forth, were excluded; and finally you had to be Male; which means that women were excluded from the system.

If we look at the course of history, we see that the principles of inclusion and exclusion have been challenged in the past. The cycles of violence talked about had to do with the attempt in the past of one or another excluded group to challenge the WAMPAM structure. What we now see is the effort of black people, who have been excluded because of the white structure, and the effort of young people, who have been excluded because only adults are included, and the renewed effort by women to challenge male dominance.

From the point of view of escalation of violence, we know that if there is a conjunction of three challenges to the WAMPAM structure, there is likely to be more violence than if only one of the structural issues is being challenged at a particular time. So we have three sources of challenge to the structural principle of inclusion and exclusion: blacks, young people, and women.

F.P.H.   However, I think that especially the students want something quite different from the system they are challenging. They reject the whole structure. They don't want in; they don't want power in the system; they want to change the entire structure of power. They reject what is going on now; they reject our social organization as unjust and as incapable of delivering even the basic human needs, such as food, clothing, and shelter, let alone a secure job, education, or a basic income, which our affluent society could provide for everyone. They demand real social justice and equality, which are quite incompatible with the system. I see that this conflict is really different in that sense from what has happened in the past, because many of the young feel they cannot work within the existing framework at all. They ask for fundamental change in the existing framework. Unfortunately, they have not produced any kind of structure of their own or any goals to work for to achieve a new order. Therefore, it is extremely difficult to come to any sort of constructive compromise. You also characterize the position of the students as revolutionary in one of your own papers.

J.P.S.   Yes. I think it is important to try to get around our usual way of labeling political positions and political parties. For this reason I use a different terminology to describe the students and the attitudes of other people towards the current movement for change. I have designated three types of political attitudes that I think we can use to characterize and group people.

One is the *Nativist Pattern.* This includes people who in respect to change not only resist any movement of change, but would like to turn the whole country back to an earlier period, where it was "purer" and where it was "more American." The Daughters of the American Revolution, for example, are extremely dissatisfied with the way things are, to say nothing of the way things are going.

Second are the *Stand-Patters.* These are the people who would like the situation to change a little bit in the direction of something new, but they don't want it to go too far, and they certainly don't want it to go too fast. Many liberals take this point of view.

And finally there is the category of people I call *Revolutionaries.* These are the people who want fundamental change in terms of our prevailing system of values, and they really want America to live up to its ideals.

When I use the word revolutionary, I don't mean it in a political sense. I don't mean it to describe these people as seizing the government or taking over the White House, and so forth. I mean the word revolutionary in its value sense. That is why I group young people who are in "the movement" under this category. As you just said, they do want fundamental change and they are going to use any means necessary to try to get the country moving in

the direction of fundamental change. This means the realization of our democratic values in terms of our social structures. It means the overcoming of the
hypocritical gap between our ideals and our practices. It may require a certain
amount of violence the way the young people see it. Certainly it requires
militant resistance to establish these changes.

But on the whole these young revolutionaries are not trying to establish
themselves as a center of political power, because they don't want to run the
government. They merely want the whole society and its political representatives to move in the direction of justice and equality for all and to move away
from the excessive use of violence in our international relations.

F.P.H.   One of the difficulties that I see at the present time is that the
institutions charge that their attackers, the students and revolutionaries, just
don't know what they want, and they have no plan. On the other hand, the
revolutionaries charge that the institutions and the politicians don't listen,
that their demands for an open society are self-evident and perfectly clear.
They demand equal access by all people to the goods of the society, as well as
access to the power structure. They feel very strongly that this is being denied
to them now.

It is very difficult to reconcile these charges and countercharges. The institutions and the students talk past one another. They seemingly operate on
different wavelengths and are not able to communicate. Unless they do communicate, they are never going to be able to deal with the situation constructively, or settle anything.

J.P.S.   I think, however, that it is unfair to demand of the student movement and the young radicals a well worked-out program. It is true that when
they are asked, "What sort of society do you want? What is your political
program?" they are short of answers. But I think it must be realized that
what they are talking about is a life style; it is a way of living; it is a set of
attitudes that they would like to see govern social relations in our society.

It is also important to realize that, in terms of previous movements, there is
the movement for democracy versus tyranny and versus monarchistic government, the movement for social welfare versus an elitist, aristocratic society.
During the early stages of these movements a set of attitudes, a life style
could be articulated much earlier than any political program. After all, the
political program of the United States was worked out at the Constitutional
Convention by our founding fathers only after a great deal of labor and a
great deal of discussion. It was very hard for the founders of the American
Republic to work out their political program even though they were very
familiar with the underlying attitudes.

So it seems to me to be unfair to say to the young radicals, "What sort of a political reform do you want?" This is going to require a great deal of intellectual and political work. Right now they are in the phase of establishing the importance of new attitudes and new social relations. These are the chief items on the agenda of the movement for change.

F.P.H. In the last few years, I think we have seen a more fundamental, faster, and a more visible change in life styles than ever before. Certainly, the reaction of the establishment against this life style has been equally strong, though I think gradually people are getting used to it and are adopting at least some of the outward features.

But unfortunately many of the older generation lack openness. The generation gap of course is very strong where it comes to clothes, for instance, or hairstyles or other visible factors. This contributes to the differences. That is, the visible parts of the underlying attitude make their acceptance more difficult for many people. Many people simply don't accept or understand, or are unwilling to put up with what they see or to take it seriously.

J.P.S. Most people of the older generation are responding either as Stand-Patters or as Nativists. If they are Stand-Patters they simply say, "We will not permit this. We will not permit the use of pot, and we don't like the loud music and strange sounds or long hair or sexual freedom (all important items on the agenda of the young people's movement). We just don't like it." If they are Nativists they want to stamp it out, they want to crush it; they want to put all these young people in jail; they want to punish them severely: This is always the response of the Nativist.

Now, some people may have a certain amount of sympathy with what the young are trying to do in terms of changing life styles. In fact, some of that sympathy has commercial overtones. The new life styles tend to get co-opted by the establishment.

F.P.H. That has been severely criticized by the young people, too. They feel very strongly that the establishment is making commercial use of their ideas.

J.P.S. In this sense, the young try to remain revolutionaries. They don't want to allow the changes in style that they are promoting to be co-opted by the commercial establishment and turned into trivial matter.

Now it is long hair and rock music, but two years hence it will be something else. They are resisting that attempt to trivialize, one might say, the things that they feel are important. Whether they will succeed in their resistance one does not know.

F.P.H.   There are some contributing social factors that I think make social violence in the United States much greater than anywhere else in the world. One most frequently quoted is the plurality of our society. Many people from very different backgrounds, life styles, and attitudes conditioned by their traditional upbringing live closely together, especially in the cities. But they look at the world through very different eyes based on values that often are opposite.

Modern communication media, especially television, are also contributing factors to the present level of violence. Live news programs direct from the battlefields of Asia, are televised continuously, as well as upheavals occurring in United States cities. There are also numerous commercial programs that extol the frontier attitude of the gun. Finally, the fact that guns are readily available, as well as many kinds of weapons and explosives, allow people to carry out ideas much more violently than they otherwise would.

J.P.S.   Yes, all those things go together. In that way, the United States differs from most other countries. We are a pluralistic society; we are composed of people from so many different national, ethnic, and racial backgrounds, which are in the first instance incompatible with each other. So it is very difficult for people of an Anglo-Saxon background to understand people of a Latin or a Jewish or an Oriental background, and their lifestyles frequently are also incompatible.

We are still suffering from the frontier tradition, which was terribly important in the nineteenth century, when the country was being established. People, that is, mainly European immigrants, were finding ways of surviving in a difficult and hostile country. It was important for everyone on the frontier to carry a gun, when law enforcement procedures had not been established. We now suffer from the persistence of this tradition that each person has the right to defend himself with a gun, though it is not necessary.

F.P.H.   This tradition is particularly unfortunate, since we now live in an urban environment where the innocent bystander is as likely to be the victim as the people who take part in the struggle.

J.P.S.   It is in a way a tragedy that the mores, the social practices, of a frontier society have been imported to the city. The word "civilization" incorporates the term "civis," which means city. Cities are not a likely background for cowboys and Indians. Yet, many of the things that go on in cities are still in that tradition. This is something that the movement of the young and the students is trying to abolish. That is why they talk about flower-power and loving each other and understanding each other.

Certainly, one can see that an important aspect of the current movement is to overcome those elements of our tradition that rested upon the frontier. The young are trying to establish a life style in which the use of a gun and the use of violence in general to maintain dominance and exclusion are abolished.

F.P.H.   The United States is just about the only Western country where the police carry weapons at all times. Certainly the British police and the French police and the police in most democratic countries do not carry any guns or violent weapons.

J.P.S.   This is again a matter of cultural lag, of the survival of a practice that is no longer appropriate. The police in their bearing and their dress are like the sheriffs of Western frontier communities. Even the position in which the gun sling is carried is very much like that of the sheriff who had to have his gun ready to draw on any outlaw at any moment. It is extremely inappropriate that the police dress like this and persist in their frontier mannerisms, so to speak.

However, I do think that police are now beginning to listen to the recommendations of our various national commissions, of The Kerner Commission on civil disorders and The Eisenhower Commission on the Causes and Prevention of Violence. Police departments are now beginning to change their law enforcement customs and procedures to bring them more into tune with the times.

F.P.H.   We have talked about so many fundamental changes that are necessary to preserve peace and order, and that are required to build a new positive social structure. Much of the violence that we see now, especially in cities, is based on the social and physical deterioration in the cities, the very real deprivation in terms of housing, and the decay of the urban environment, but especially huge unemployment among the less-skilled inner-city inhabitants— many of them young and black.

Time and again recommendations have been made by high-level commissions, some going back more than twenty years, but nothing has been done. The goal of the housing legislation of 1949, of "a decent home and suitable living environment for every American," has not even been partially realized. Most recommendations have never been implemented, and the reports of all the commissions gather dust. Cities continue to deteriorate, with many more people from rural areas, mainly from the South, immigrating, as they have no other place to go. The quality of life in cities and the urban environment has gotten worse, especially for low-income people. The middle class are leaving the cities, which federal legislation through the FHA has enabled them to do. The lack of tax income in cities and their inability to render the services needed reinforce segregation and contribute to the violence in the deprived black areas.

J.P.S.   This is why the youth movement is so important, as the potential for change. Most of us older people have been brainwashed into accepting the very conditions that you just described. We have been brainwashed into accepting the ridiculous position of having made so many promises for change, for over twenty years, without having achieved any substantial results. Young people are saying that they are tired of promises, they are tired of rhetoric, they are tired of a system that does not intend to institute changes promised in political campaigns. They will not rest until that system is either changed or abolished and replaced by one that fulfills these real needs, which is possible in an age of plenty and technological power.

F.P.H.   To summarize, I would like to quote something from the Report of The National Commission on Causes and Prevention of Violence, or The Eisenhower Report as it is called, which you just mentioned. Again, this is one more report that is not heeded, though the advice and recommendations certainly are important and would alter the basic conditions so conducive to violence we have discussed.

It is the ghetto slum that is disproportionately responsible for violent crime, by far the most acute aspect of the problem of violence in the United States today. To be young, poor, and male, to be undereducated and without means of escape from an oppressive urban environment, to want what the society claims is available but mostly to others, to see around oneself illegitimate and often violent methods are being used to achieve material gain, and to observe others using these means and with impunity, all this is to be burdened with an enormous set of influences that pull many toward crime and delinquency. To be also a Negro, Puerto Rican, or Mexican-American and subject to discrimination and segregation adds considerably to the pull of these and other crimogenic forces.

Safety in our cities requires no less than progress in reconstructing urban life. We must meet the 1968 housing act's goal of a decent home for every American within a decade. We must take some effective steps to realize the goal first set in the employment act of 1946 of a useful job at a reasonable wage for all who are able to work. We must provide better education and opportunities for all our children. We must act on current recommendations that those American families who cannot care for themselves receive a basic annual income. We must restructure our local governments, restore their fiscal vitality, and accomplish a host of other major tasks of the kind discussed in the report.

This is an important prescription. If we follow it, we might be on the way to preventing violence, which probably is the best way of dealing with it.

Thank you, Dr. Spiegel.

BIBLIOGRAPHY

Spiegel, John P. "The Group Psychology of Campus Disorders—A Trans-actional Approach." Waltham, Mass.: Lemberg Center for the Study of Violence, Brandeis University.

———. "Theories of Violence—An Integrated Approach." Paper presented at the annual meeting of the American Association for the Advancement of Science, December 30, 1969.

———. "Toward a Theory of Collective Violence." Paper delivered at the American Psychiatric Association, Divisional Meeting, November 15-16, 1968.

For all three papers, write to the Lemberg Center for the Study of Violence, Brandeis University, Waltham, Mass.

BOOKS

Clark, Ramsey. *Crime in America.* New York: Simon and Schuster, 1970.
A pragmatic view of a former Attorney General of the U.S. crime problem and how to deal with it.

Demaris, Ovid. *America the Violent.* New York: Cowles Book Company, Inc., 1970.

Douglas, William O. *Points of Rebellion.* New York: Random House, Inc., A Vintage Book, 1970.
A very open, philosophical statement by a Chief Justice about the hypocrisy of our system.

Graham, Hugh Davis, and Greer, Ted Robert. *Violence in America.* New York: A Signet Special, 1969.

Hacker, Andrew. *The End of the American Era.* New York: Atheneum Publishers, 1968.
A devastating appraisal of the loss of moral fiber in the United States.

The Kerner Report. Report of The National Advisory Commission on Civil Disorders. New York: Bantam Books, 1969. Paperback.
The most comprehensive, honest survey of civil disorder, meticulously researched, and very informative.

The Politics of Protest. The Skolnick Report to The National Commission on the Causes and Prevention of Violence. New York: Ballantine Books, 1969.
Another excellent government-ordered survey which has been shelved like all others.

Reich, Charles A. *The Greening of America.* New York: Random House, 1970.
The most important book on understanding social change by and for the young.

Rights in Conflict. The Walter Report to The National Commission on the Causes and Prevention of Violence. New York: Bantam Books, 1968. Paperback.

Another opinion on the problems of violence by The National Commission on the Causes and Prevention of Violence.

Szent-Gyorgi, Albert. *The Crazy Ape.* New York: Philosophical Library, Inc., 1970.

A Nobel Prize-winning biologist with a very sane view of the irrational behavior of man.

13

URBAN DESIGN AND ARCHITECTURE

A discussion with IEOH MING PEI
Principal of the architectural firm I. M. Pei and Partners

INTRODUCTION

Architecture is a social art. Architecture is concerned with building a harmonious, useful, beautiful, and functional environment for people. Architectural form is the physical expression of all the social, economic, structural, and human requirements that shape a building.

Urban design is the relationship of buildings to each other and of people to buildings: Man is the measure of all things. Urban design is concerned with form and space and the larger architectural environment. It is expressed in the interaction of the many shapes of buildings and of streets, squares, and open areas between buildings.

Architecture, the art and technique of building, has vastly changed with new materials and new technology. Most contemporary highrise buildings are made of steel frame construction or of reinforced concrete. Both are quite new materials from a historic point of view. Steel and concrete have completely changed the form of buildings and have opened up totally new ways to build and shape the man-made environment. Highrise buildings and our modern cities are unthinkable without all the new building materials, without the transportation and communication technology that we are taking for granted now.

This new building technology has resulted in an extraordinary freedom to design in totally new ways almost anything we can imagine. The physical limitations of building materials which disciplined all architecture in the past no longer exist. Not even the sky is the limit—though, realistically speaking, economics usually is.

"Form follows function" has become the motto of modern architects after architecture first broke away from the formal dictates of design rules set by the Academy. Copying from classical models from the past and imitating different historic building styles was the goal of the architectural profession—building for wealthy clients or for the institutions in the rapidly growing cities of the nineteenth century. Today all our cities are still replete with public and institutional buildings copying the forms of Greek, Roman, Renaissance, or Gothic monuments, which have not the remotest social or historic base in the United States, but were the accepted official architecture until the 1930's. In fact, civic architecture in the United States often copied nineteenth-century European copies of historic building styles. To study in Europe, especially in Paris or Rome, to learn from the classical models, was the goal of every U.S. architect until the 1930's. Inherited architecture in the U.S. cities, with few exceptions, is devoid of any originality or any authentic design; at best it is an eclectic import; at worst a misunderstood mishmash in poor taste.

In the meantime, civil engineers had already begun in the nineteenth century to pioneer new building techniques and real innovation. But the advances in engineering and construction were at first ignored and rejected by architects. Only slowly after World War I a few pioneers in architecture began to chart a completely new course in architectural design, trying to find new forms expressing not only the new building materials, but also a very different and new society. LeCorbusier, Walter Gropius, Mies van der Rohe, and Frank Lloyd Wright, who all worked and built in Europe, as well as in the United States, are the architects credited with changing the basic concepts of architecture, indeed with initiating a new freedom of design and expression. The new functional architecture was accepted, but not without a struggle. After World War II, it was quickly adopted by corporations for their new office buildings, which have become the dominating buildings in cities everywhere. The same new highrise office towers of steel or concrete and glass can be found in cities all over the world. Frequently they are built for the same corporations by architects trained in similar ways. Architecture has become as international as the cities expressing the same values worldwide.

Certainly, architects today enjoy a freedom of expression that never existed before. Yet many of our new buildings suffer from dullness, monotony, and sameness; they are often poorly designed, thoughtlessly ugly, and without any architectural merit at all. The challenge to create truly new forms with the many new building materials and new technology that are available now, or to experiment to find new expressions for our different way of life is too seldom taken up. Instead, acres of cheap commercial construction are built everywhere, often without architects.

Urban design, the art of relating building and space into a harmonious, pleasing environment for the use and enjoyment of people, is almost totally absent in our cities in the United States and in most contemporary urban development all over the world. A different developer or owner builds on each piece of land, totally unmindful of what goes on next door or across the street. Adjoining buildings, instead of relating to create a unified street or area, compete with each other. Buildings try to outdo each other with cheap, blaring gimmicks to attract attention. Often the architecture is hardly visible behind huge advertisements and signs. Instead of creating a harmonious environment for people, our urban areas express brutal discord and harsh, strident competition in their design. The pollution of our man-made environment as a result of our unplanned, badly designed, thoughtless way of building is never mentioned; yet it thoroughly demeans our lives.

Architecture and urban design should express the positive values of a society and reflect the sum of its social and economic achievements. Architects should act as coordinators on behalf of the public interest and be the advocates for a harmonious, human environment.

DISCUSSION

F.P.H.　Mr. Pei, as architect, planner, and urban designer, you are planning as well as building whole urban areas. That is, you have much more control in shaping an urban environment than an individual architect. What do you think is missing now that historic cities, for instance in Europe, still have? What should we do to improve the quality of urban life, which is so much determined by what we build and how we shape the buildings which are our everyday environment?

I.M.P.　This question can only have one answer. That is, to improve the so-called "quality of life" requires the cooperation of all kinds of people. The architect-planner in this case is but a member of the team that must work together in order to make this possible.

F.P.H.　Other people of the team are certainly the owner of the building or the client who commissions the building. The city, with zoning and other regulations, is another member of the team. The infrastructure in terms of water supply, electricity, and other services is another important input, and most of all transportation, which connects the area or building as well as how you get in and out of the building—all these influence greatly what gets built and how. What should we add?

I.M.P.　As architect, we should not only be concerned with "what we build" but also with "for whom we build." When our interests shift from single buildings to a larger environment, it makes valid the "community as client" concept. Hence any attempt to improve the quality of urban life must take this into account.

F.P.H.　In the final analysis, it really depends on the people of the community, if an urban area turns out to be successful in its use or not. You can see this in our cities today. Even if the new buildings downtown are handsome and well planned and have all the qualities that we hope for and desire, come five o'clock, everybody leaves. Large parts of the city, particularly the office areas, are used only for some eight or nine hours a day, five days a week. In the evening and on weekends the plazas are empty. The most handsome urban spaces have no one to enjoy them.

It seems to me the most important criterion by which an urban area should be designed and judged is: What does it do for people, and how well do people use it?

I.M.P.   Single-use zoning is killing our cities and making bedroom communities out of our suburbs. I believe cities will have to regulate *uses* more intelligently in order to create the variety of life you are talking about.

F.P.H.   Often certain activities have been regulated out of certain areas. Different uses have been separated too much by zoning. For instance, we often have separated residential areas strictly from commercial ones. As a result, people often have to travel a good distance to get to stores for shopping, or else beautifully-built shopping plazas are empty except during business hours because they are too far away from where people live and don't provide for recreational use.

I.M.P.   I think you will find that mixed-use zoning is very much in the picture again. This is really nothing new. Paris, London, Rome—in fact, all European cities which we very much enjoy visiting—prove "variety of use—variety of life." We are coming back to that. The latest proposal for rezoning Fifth Avenue by the New York City Office of Midtown Planning and Development is a case in point.

F.P.H.   In some urban areas that you designed or redesigned, you have introduced many different uses and activities. For instance, Place Ville Marie, in Montreal, which is essentially an office area, also has a large shopping arcade underground which has a subway station and is connected underground with a hotel and other business buildings. In the cold climate of Montreal, it is especially pleasant to have a pedestrian mall uninterrupted by traffic and protected from the weather that connects a good part of the downtown area and buildings. It is a perfect example of multi-purpose use for people.

I.M.P.   Place Ville Marie is the result of successful collaboration of architects, planners, entrepreneurs, and municipal authorities. It stands astride

Montreal's retail center and Montreal's financial and transportation center. By weaving it into the existing fabric of the center city, Place Ville Marie draws a strength from all its parts. This assured the successful mixed-use development. Rockefeller Center is another such example.

F.P.H. Rockefeller Center, when it was built, was far uptown from the traditional commercial center. Now it has become a new center and certainly is one of the most successful urban areas that I know anywhere in the world. It is always full of people, day and night. Whenever you go there, something is going on. There are attractive flowers and all kinds of seasonal decorations. There are benches, there are all kinds of shops and restaurants, there is the skating rink in winter and outdoor eating in the summer. People have a place to be, and they also have something to see.

One great attraction everywhere is people watching: a place where one can see other people and meet informally. This has been sadly neglected in the design of cities today. Most cities have no such people centers. The idea of the city as a community for people is negated in this design because there are not enough places where people can get together, meet informally, and enjoy each other. I think a prime requirement for urban designers is to provide such places for people to meet and be, as you have done, for instance, in Place Ville Marie.

I.M.P. Well, I must make a point once again. Major activity centers such as Place Ville Marie and Rockefeller Center must possess certain locational requisites, such as intensity of surrounding developments, complementary uses, and ease of access in order to be successful.

F.P.H. You mentioned that people like to visit European cities which have handsome buildings and many open spaces that are attractive and well designed. The quality of the buildings and the quality of the environment provide something more than just a place for people to be. They provide architectural interest and harmony, something attractive to look at—a planned and cared-for environment. People, I think, react to that positively.

I.M.P. I agree. Once the development is woven into a healthy and lively fabric of the city, then the design and planning of physical and visual amenities such as you mentioned become important. The architect has the responsibility to make the physical environment attractive to encourage social intercourse. We have not appreciated the importance of public open space until recently. Of course, we have learned a good deal from Europe.

I think we have also learned that certain design approaches that are successful in Europe are not necessarily so here. We have a different life style and dissimilar climatic conditions. Consequently we have to make adaptations to suit our needs.

F.P.H.   Talking about European cities, one thinks of the pleasant outdoor cafes. Unfortunately, in most of the U.S. cities, particularly on the eastern seaboard, there are only rare occasions when it is pleasant to sit outside. It is either too hot or too cold, too windy, or too dusty. The climate is just one of the missing ingredients. Another is the quality of the environment, which lacks interest and amenity.

Recently, downtown streets in many cities have been turned into pedestrian shopping malls. Shopping arcades and malls actually are as old as many historic cities. But in U.S. cities the street is dominated by cars, while people are pushed aside. Cars are a means to get from here to there, but once you are there, you don't want the car any more.

I.M.P.   The automobile has done tremendous damage, in my opinion, to many of those attractive squares in Europe as well. In the United States, with but a few exceptions, we started with the automobile as a pre-condition. Europe created those attractive squares before cars were a major factor in urban design, and there lies an important difference. It is not that we must abandon cars altogether in order to have a successful urban place. Rather, we should design new kinds of urban space that can accept the intrusion of cars when they are necessary.

Europe now has to learn that too. Until they do, I think many of those beautiful places and squares will no longer be the same.

F.P.H.   What you are saying, I think, is that we should separate cars from people. There just is not room for both in the same space.

One example that comes to my mind is Harvard Square. In many ways it is quite an unusual place for people. But Harvard Square is mainly a traffic intersection. Cars take so much of the available space that people have very little room. There are all kinds of attractive and unusual shops in Harvard Square. A special street culture or people culture attracts many young people and students to "the Square"; they make it a gay and lively place of great diversity. The environment, that is, many of the buildings, certainly need to be renewed and even replanned. If we could only capture all the activity of Harvard Square and surround it with an attractive urban environment, I think we would have it made.

I.M.P.   This is precisely the point. I cannot remember Harvard Square ever being a quiet place, and I have known that area since the late 1930's. Even then, it was invaded by cars. So the problem has existed for some time.

The question then is: What to do with Harvard Square? If you cannot get cars to or near it, it will lose its advantages. There has to be access. While transit is an important means of access, it is not enough. We also have to bring cars to Harvard Square. We must find ways to park the cars before Harvard Square can be turned into a place for pedestrians.

And this must be solved in today's terms. I don't think we can just say, "Let's ban the cars and we shall make Harvard Square into an attractive place." By banning cars, you may be able to make it more quiet and restful, but you will also kill the very life that Harvard Square feeds on.

F.P.H.   You would also have to reorganize the regional traffic flow, replan and rebuild much of the larger surrounding area to divert the through traffic. There is too much long-distance, through traffic moving through the square. Forbes Plaza, the small, open space in front of Holyoke Center, Harvard University's Administration Building, is the only area specifically designed for people. Presently, as an experiment, part of Brattle Square next to Harvard Square has been closed to all traffic for six months and "given" to people. At the end of that time the results in terms of the effect on shopping will be evaluated to decide whether or not to make the area a pedestrian mall permanently.

I.M.P.   The Harvard Square problem is a very timely subject for discussion because I think the future of Harvard Square is now being decided. As a matter of fact, we should have attacked the problem five years ago.

F.P.H.   Since you are the architect of the Kennedy Library which will be next to Harvard Square, you have been directly concerned with this area. I understand it is anticipated that the Kennedy Library will bring much more traffic to Harvard Square.

I.M.P.   Having selected the M.T.A. (Metropolitan Transit Authority) yard right off Harvard Square as the site for the Kennedy Library, we have really posed the question to the community: What kind of place do you want Harvard Square to be? If you allow the economic forces to operate without controls, Harvard Square will become a very densely developed place and much of the charm will disappear with it.

I am sure you don't want to preserve Harvard Square the way it is. You would want to regulate its traffic, park the cars, and control its growth. The community must and should have a say in this.

F.P.H.   The University now attracts people from all over the country and all over the world. But if the Kennedy Library becomes as great an attraction as many people think, even more visitors will come to the Harvard Square area. Therefore, it is really important that the Kennedy Library should have a suitable environment. The Library is part of the university community, and is related to Harvard Yard and the whole campus.

Therefore, the community that should be considered in deciding the future of Harvard Square is really a very mixed kind of community including the academic community, the city of Cambridge community, and all the visitors who use the Square. It seems to me that from an urban design point of view this is a challenge that has fascinating possibilities.

I.M.P.   We were very much aware that the Kennedy Library would increase traffic to Harvard Square. Therefore, in 1965, we asked Barton-Aschman, Traffic Consultants, to evaluate its impact. Their study indicated that we could handle the increased traffic by reserving approximately two acres of land for new streets and for widening of existing streets. We would also need to provide necessary parking on the site. Incidentally, Cambridge together with Boston is already a major tourist center. The Kennedy Library would add to it particularly during summer months, but not as much as most people think.

One must also remember that Harvard Square has excellent rapid transit connections which we expect will service at least 25 per cent of the visitors to the Library.

F.P.H.   Another important area which you have planned and designed is Boston's new Government Center, which was recently finished. The City Hall Plaza is completed, and the City Hall is in use. Most of the surrounding buildings are completed. For the first time, one can see in reality the shape of the space that you created more than ten years ago. The fountain on the plaza is operating and is a great attraction in that very handsome new space; but so far it is not used enough by people, unfortunately.

I.M.P.   I think you will find that conditions will improve with time. Included in our master plan is a very large residential development towards the waterfront that is now under construction. In addition, we have also projected a very sizeable hotel for the area, south of New Congress Street.

The construction of more residential units will bring more people to live downtown. The kind of activities which a hotel can provide and attract will add a great deal of liveliness to the place. We can also look forward to more intensive development around the Government Center area.

F.P.H.   The Quincy Market area next to Government Center is going to be renovated and rehabilitated under the B.R.A. (Boston Redevelopment Authority). The redevelopment of the Market area certainly will add a lot of interest and attract many people, quite aside from the residential area you mentioned. At present there are very few people living around Government Center. That also reflects on its use, in particular in the evening.

You also planned and designed the Mile High Center in Denver, which includes a large hotel, shopping facilities, and more. Society Hill in Philadelphia is another important redevelopment project which has been under construction for some time. Or is it finished by now?

I.M.P.   As far as new construction is concerned, Society Hill is almost complete. But rehabilitation of the area will continue.

F.P.H.   Cities are always in the process of building and rehabilitation and urban design is never really completed.

In the introduction I mentioned that the form of buildings is no longer limited by structural materials as it was in the past. What are the limitations that are imposed on the architectural imagination today?

I.M.P.   You mentioned the economic factor as being one limitation that shapes architecture. That certainly is true. Technically speaking, we now have far less constraints than architects of the past. But constraints are not necessarily detrimental. For example, cities like London and Paris have great unity in the urban design sense largely because there were constraints of materials and techniques.

F.P.H.   The limitation of height of old cities was caused by materials. This establishes a unity of scale. Today there are two scales in a city, the first being the traditional scale you mentioned due to building materials. Now many of the cities superimpose on this another scale, the highrise scale. There is always the period of transition which is very difficult. Until, as in New York, a completely new highrise urban scale is established.

What is the architect's contribution to this new highrise scale? Where are we going in the future? Is all building going to become higher or are we going to keep certain areas at a residendial or walk-up scale?

I.M.P.   I think the future of our cities very definitely points toward greater intensity, that is, higher buildings. I have no doubt of that. Intensity in itself is not a bad thing if the infrastructure of a city is properly planned. Unfortunately most of our cities cannot accommodate even their present levels of development.

I would venture an optimistic prediction that our future cities will be better planned from the infrastructure on up. Of particular importance is the need for a coordinated transportation plan. Figuratively speaking, the governors and the mayors should be the planners of tomorrow. *Ad hoc* planning in response to private development is out.

The Government Center in Boston is in a way a good example. The B.R.A. directed the design and development of the infrastructure such as circulation, parking, and land use as the framework for urban design. This makes possible a coordinated development, such as we now see.

F.P.H.   The B.R.A. has devised and enforced strict design control review procedures which many other redevelopment authorities have not done. This was one of Edward Logue's contributions; he was the first administrator of the B.R.A. and is very interested in design. He insisted from the beginning that certain urban design and quality standards be observed.

These design standards assure harmony and scale and coordination between building forms in a given area, but otherwise they don't limit the work of the individual architect. As architect you have built a number of buildings in urban renewal areas, some in areas you have also planned, for instance, the Arena Theater in the Southeast Washington urban renewal area. Do you think you have enough freedom to express yourself as an architect in an urban renewal area?

I.M.P.   Never enough, of course. There are other successful developments; for instance, Society Hill in Philadelphia would not have been possible without an intelligent program outlined by the Philadelphia City Planning Commission. It takes a very positive position on planning, much as the B.R.A. does in Boston.

F.P.H.   We have not really taken seriously the idea of rebuilding our cities until quite recently. The entire Urban Renewal legislation only dates back to 1949. Up to that time, there was absolutely no way to coordinate anything that was built in a city. The planning commissions of cities exist purely in an advisory capacity and have no real power to make decisions. I hope in the future more people will take an interest in their cities and their environment, including expressing their ideas of what should be done and *how* it should be built. I am sure that you, as an architect, feel strongly about the support and interest of people in what you build. The quality of architecture can only be improved if more people are interested in their environment, in building, and in their cities.

I.M.P.   That is unquestionably true. The concern on the part of the citizenry for the visual environment, I think, is paramount. You will find that cities that have been able to make something out of the 1949 National

Housing Act that launched the Urban Renewal Program really are the ones that had strong civic support. Planners like Ed Bacon in Philadelphia and Logue in Boston had the support of strong mayors, civic leaders, and the community. This is why Philadelphia and Boston are successful examples of urban redevelopment of the 1960's.

F.P.H.   I think we must begin by teaching young people about the visual values of the urban environment in which they will spend most of their time. The greatest polluter of our life is *how* we build our man-made environment and cities; our physical surroundings influence our well being and how we react to the world: that is, the quality of life directly relates to the quality of architecture and urban design.

Thank you Mr. Pei.

BIBLIOGRAPHY

BOOKS

Bacon, Edmund N. *Design of Cities.* New York: The Viking Press, Inc., 1967.
Excellent, profusely illustrated history of urban design by the man behind Philadelphia's urban renewal plan.

Blake, Peter. *The Master Builders: LeCorbusier, Mies van der Rohe, Frank Lloyd Wright.* New York: Alfred Knopf, 1961.

Crosby, Theo. *Architecture: City Sense.* New York: Reinhold Publishing Corp., 1965. Paperback.

Danby, Miles. *Grammer of Architectural Design.* London: Oxford University Press, 1963.

Doxiadis, Constantinos A. *Architecture in Transition.* New York: Oxford University Press, 1963. Paperback.

Fitch. James Marston. *Walter Gropius.* New York: George Braziller, Inc., 1960.

Giedion, Sigfried. *Space, Time and Architecture.* Cambridge, Mass.: Harvard University Press, 1967.
A "classic" book, explaining the development of contemporary architecture by its foremost historian.

———.*Mechanization Takes Command.* New York: A Norton Paperback, 1967.

Heyer, Paul. *Architect on Architecture: New Dimensions in America.* New York: Walker and Company, 1966.
A beautifully illustrated book, giving a view of contemporary architecture by its foremost practitioners.

Hosken, Fran P. *The Language of Cities.* 2nd ed. Cambridge, Mass.: Schenk-man Publishing Company, 1972.
A visual approach to understanding the urban functions.

Moholy-Nagy, Sibyl. *Matrix of Man: An Illustrated History of Urban Environment.* New York: Frederick A. Praeger, 1968.
An excellent historic view of city design, with new insights, many new examples, and excellent illustrations.
Rasmussen, Steen Eiler. *Experiencing Architecture.* Cambridge, Mass.: The MIT Press, 1959.
How to "see" architecture.
Rudofsky, Bernard. *Streets for People: A Primer for Americans.* Garden City, New York: Doubleday and Company, Inc., 1964.
A visual evaluation of the street scene, beautifully illustrated.
Spreiregan, Paul D. *Urban Design: The Architecture of Towns and Cities.* New York: McGraw-Hill Book Co., 1965.
An explanation of urban design criteria with many sketches and examples.
Zevi, Bruno. *Architecture as Space.* New York: Horizon Press, 1957.
The form of a building as a "container" of space: a new approach to understanding architecture.

PERIODICALS

Architectural Record. New York: Mc-Graw Hill, Inc.
Forum (The Architectural Forum). New York: Whitney Publications, Inc.
Progressive Architecture. Stamford, Conn.: Reinhold Publishing Corporation.

14

INDUSTRIALIZED BUILDING SYSTEMS

A discussion with LAURENCE S. CUTLER
Professor of Urban Design, Graduate School of Design, Harvard University;
Principal of ECODESIGN, Cambridge, Mass.

INTRODUCTION

First, we should define the term "industrialized building systems" because there has been a great deal of confusion as to what industrialized building really means and how building systems are used.

Basically, it simply means applying industrialized methods, much like those employed to manufacture cars or trailers, to produce building components and even whole buildings.

At the International Systems Building Round Table Conference at the Boston Architectural Center in November 1971, systems building was defined as the process of producing a man-made environment: the planning, organization, financing, component coordination, timing, and administration of building production by industrial methods. Design is an integral part of each activity and the product of this process is the building, or sometimes a complete environment.

Most of the time when we talk about industrialized building we are concerned with the hardware or the actual construction of the physical building.

Traditionally, buildings have been made up of many different materials which are brought onto the building site and then put together, creating a building according to a specific design by architects and engineers. The general contractor and each of his subcontractors on the project gets a set of plans, detailed instructions, and specifications by the architect as to what to do and how.

The initial act is to dig the foundations and prepare the general site utilities. The actual building operations are divided up according to trades, such as bricklayers, plumbers, electricians, and many other specialties. The entire building process, controlled by the craft unions, has not changed substantially since antiquity. To erect a building by putting together thousands of separate pieces is a long and laborious process and was always done by different trades. Though many buildings today are highrise and much more complicated, incorporating all kinds of standardized mechanical systems and new sophisticated materials, the methods used on the building site still follow the inefficient craft approach.

The use of industrialized building systems instead of a craft approach means to rationalize the whole building process and change it from what is virtually a piecemeal operation to a highly mechanized process, integrating trades, materials, and production techniques on a controlled basis, usually applying systems analysis to the composition of the building. This may mean factory production or using on-site special construction techniques. For instance, large sections of wall and floor panels are poured of precast concrete, including the electrical conduits, mechanical, and utility systems; or complete kitchen and bathroom units can be factory produced. The components are designed in such a way that they can be easily erected on the site without the many different trades whose work is for the most part done in the factory.

Bad weather is still a serious problem on the building site and costs construction workers many days of work and income, as well as delaying occupancy for the owners. Therefore, the wages of building workers must be high enough to compensate them for the time lost by poor weather, which, in turn, increases all building costs. Industrial production processes, carried out under cover in a factory, increase the productivity of each worker, provide good working conditions, efficient use of materials, and also make it much easier to control quality. Besides, it reduces the often hard, dangerous, exposed work on the site to a minimum.

Basically, a building system can produce more square feet of building of better quality in a shorter time than the traditional approach. A large item in the production of a building is the cost of the money. Therefore, a saving of time of construction is especially important as a means of reducing overall costs. Building systems, by employing unskilled help, can also open up much employment to minority groups, which the highly skilled craft unions have not been willing to do.

New systematized construction methods and techniques are especially important when we consider that in the next thirty years we shall have to build as much as in the entire history of the country: to replace what has become obsolete and to accommodate our growing population. Without a rationalized, systematized approach to building, it is impossible to build what we need of good quality and at a price that a majority of people can afford.

At present the cost of building is steadily increasing, while the quality of what is built by traditional methods is getting poorer everywhere. For instance, fewer people now can afford well-built new housing, while what is built or rehabilitated often does not even last the life of the mortgage. Industrial production techniques have been used in all consumer industries to reduce costs and increase production, but building methods still continue in traditional ways, reinforced by the craft unions and by building codes that support the craft approach and perpetuate the status quo.

The many different structural building systems, which are at present mainly used in Europe, are known under their trade names. They can be broken down into "open systems" and "closed systems." An open system can be combined with a variety of different subsystems made by different manufacturers, such as mechanical or electrical systems, windows, etc. Closed systems can be combined only with specially made subsystems.

Another classification method of building systems is according to construction method used. There is a box system, such as mobile homes. There are load-bearing panel systems; most concrete panel systems work that way. Then there is a frame and panel system where the load is carried by a structural frame and a non-bearing panel encloses the space. Finally, there is a performance standard system where different manufacturers are invited to bid for X number of square feet of exterior wall, or roof, or floor, which they can manufacture any way they wish, as long as they fulfill certain performance specifications of insulation, structural strength, acoustic qualities, and more, fulfilling given measurable requirements at the lowest price.

DISCUSSION

F.P.H.   Systems building, considering the very long history of building, is very new and still developing.

Mr. Cutler, how would you elaborate on my explanation of the meaning of industrialized building techniques?

L.S.C.   I think I should first clarify an important point that is misunderstood among most people, including architects, as to what actually is an industrialized building system. HUD (Department of Housing and Urban Development) itself is incorrect in its definition of industrialized building systems, as expressed in the "Operation Breakthrough" program. The misunderstanding lies in the fact that most people consider industrialized building systems to involve solely the manufacture of self-contained units in a plant, that is, factory-fabricated buildings.

Here is a definition that I have put together: "Industrialized building systems may be defined as the total integration of all subsystems and components into an overall process fully utilizing industrialized production, transportation, and assembly techniques. This integration is achieved through the exploitation of the underlying organizational principles, rather than the external forms of industrialization, including mechanization and programming, to structure the entire building process."

Now, this implies that industrialization can also take place on the site, that the building itself can become the plant, that industrialized building systems dont necessarily mean mobile homes built in a factory and shipped to the site, as implied by the federal government's definition.

F.P.H.   You mentioned mobile homes, and I think we should begin by discussing the basic generic types of systems in terms of the structural systems used. First of all, there are the panel systems, which are used most frequently. One type consists of load-bearing wall panels usually fabricated of precast concrete produced in a plant or on the site.

Then there are the frame systems, where a frame which bears the loads, is constructed first, and then non-bearing panels are filled into the frame.

Finally, there is the box system, for which a mobile home is probably the best illustration. The problem here is that when you transport a box, you are shipping around a lot of empty space, which is a very expensive proposition.

L.S.C.   Well, I would like to refine your definitions. Taking the box system first, though I prefer to call a box a monolithic unit, there are two classifications: there are heavyweight boxes and lightweight boxes. I think the one that is most familiar to everyone is the box system of "Habitat" at Expo '67 in Canada. Habitat, the experimental apartment block designed by Moshe Safdie, is an example of a heavyweight concrete box, manufactured on the site.

A typical lightweight box is the one you referred to earlier, the mobile home. This is not very flexible in terms of architectural expression or in the relationship of the factory to the site. Mobile homes require a close proximity between the plant and the building site; in most cases, the economic distance cannot exceed two or three hundred miles, a fact which also holds for panel systems.

F.P.H.   There is a definite economic radius for all industrialized building systems, as well as all building parts and components that have to be shipped from a plant.

But I think there is another differentiation that we should make as far as systems are concerned. That is between highrise buildings and lowrise buildings because they require quite a different structural approach. A load-bearing-wall panel system can be used for a highrise building, as can a frame system. But very few box systems are efficient for highrise housing, due to the redundant nature of putting one box on top of another or inserting it in a steel or concrete structural frame. Examples are the Jones and Laughlin mobile home box unit with steel frame, and "Habitat" at Expo '67.

L.S.C. There are, however, some box systems developed in Europe, one in Switzerland in particular, that can adapt to highrise housing. The Israelis have experimented with something they call the Modified Disken System, which Conrad on the West Coast is attempting to utilize in this country these are examples of box systems.

F.P.H. Before we discuss the foreign experience—and many countries in Europe have done far more in terms of industrialized building than the United States—we should first briefly discuss the history of the United States industrialization efforts. After World War II, "prefabrication" was the magic word among architects, builders, and engineers, and the idea gained much consumer support. There was a tremendous housing shortage after a hiatus of more than five years when very little housing was built. The GI's were coming back, all wanting to have homes. As a result, the construction industry attempted to speed up the building of housing. An effort was also made by the government to support firms that had developed some ideas and methods to build housing quickly, i.e., by prefabrication.

A number of different prefab houses were introduced. The Lustron House, a small metal house which the public did not accept, was one of the early government-supported efforts. Borg-Warner created a "mechanical core," a bathroom-kitchen unit that could fit into any kind of house and saved a lot of assembly time on the job. There were also numerous panel systems: one of the best, the General Panel System, designed by Gropius and Waxman, was made out of wood and was a very attractive and flexible unit, from which a variety of very different houses could be built. But it ran into difficulty with the FHA. There was Buckminster Fuller's Dymaxion House, which was a unique circular house made out of aluminum. A model house was built and on display in an airplane hangar in Wichita, Kansas, and a number of orders were taken, but it was never produced. In different parts of the country there were many more systems developed by local builders, but the effort to introduce prefabrication and new methods on a large scale failed for the most part. Instead, individual builders stepped up their production, and more entered this field. They built millions of little houses by traditional methods, one-by-one in different metropolitan areas, and these subdivisions finally supplied most of the market.

The idea of industrialized building had been welcomed, and everyone thought it would change existing, obsolete building methods; but in practice it failed. I think the main reason it failed was a lack of substantial government support. There are other related reasons which we all know, for instance, the multiplicity of building codes, the resistance of labor unions to adapt to any new construction methods and materials. If we manufactured automobiles according to different rules and safety standards of each city, county, or state, we would have to build them one-by-one just as we build houses. The building code regulations and union rules simply make no sense in today's industrial world.

L.S.C.   A good example of the difference between the European experience and the American situation you described is exemplified in an analysis of the concrete-panel systems. In Europe when the war ended, there was not only a demand for housing, but there was a shortage of labor. At the same time in this country, we had a demand for housing and a tremendous labor force that needed civilian jobs, while highly sophisticated building techniques by trades were already developed.

In Europe, what is essentially an American strategy in industry was adopted, that is, mass production. The first true panel system was developed in France just after the war, giving great flexibility in terms of low- and highrise dwelling units and in architectural expression. In fact, some of the first buildings using this panel system were built for the SHAPE Command (Superior Headquarters of Allied Personnel in Europe) near Paris.

The overall criteria for building housing in Europe were: limited labor, no union problems, no code problems, and a tremendous demand, as housing had been destroyed all over the continent.

F.P.H.   One other reason why the European experience differs and has succeeded is that it is massively supported by the public sector. It was a political imperative to governmentally support building after the war, because the private sector simply could not cope with the housing emergency. But even now the National Building Agency in London carefully tests and evaluates all building systems and makes recommendations to local housing authorities as to what systems are suitable for their purpose. Only accredited systems are subsidized. This, of course, makes a great difference, as the vast majority of all housing built in the United Kingdom is publicly subsidized. Therefore, most of the housing built is industrialized housing.

L.S.C.   In England, close to 85 per cent of all the multi-family housing is built with industrialized building systems. It is interesting, as you said, that the government not only supports but also accredits systems. When the British government, following the war, decided to promote building systems in order to solve the housing problem, there appeared overnight on the market some three hundred building systems. Today we note that in the United Kingdom there are only between twelve and fifteen building systems of the original three hundred that still operate. And of the twelve to fifteen, perhaps four are being utilized by one company.

We are going to have a similar kind of experience here in this country, I believe. When you look at the results of some of the recent government programs, the In-Cities Program of HUD (1967-1968) and the current Operation Breakthrough program, they have generated a great excitement and a tremendous response in volume from producers who have never before been on the housing scene, as well as from small contractors, small developers, and architects, working together in consortium. The government in this country does need an accrediting agency similar to the United Kingdom's National Building Agency or the French Agreement, or the kind of structuring that the Danish government gives to the housing market. I think we really need an agency in this country that can accredit, rate, and classify building systems for use on both federal and private projects.

F.P.H.   Thamesmead, the latest new town that is being built inside greater London, is utilizing building systems. The Balency system, a structural concrete panel system, won the first part of the contract, whereby 4,000 housing units are being produced by the fabricating plant located on-site. Later, more contracts will be awarded, again on a competitive basis between accredited systems firms, until a total of 16,000 units are built-or the whole planned town. The first 4,000 units under construction now by Balency are proceeding just as fast as people can be settled, which is one critical limitation. Another limitation of the operation is that the production of the panels is way ahead of the on-site assembly. They can produce many more than they can assemble, and on-the-site operations are holding back the progress.

L.S.C.   The Thamesmead experience should be closely watched by the American market. We know that panel systems such as Balency require approximately 4,000 units in order to pay for and amortize the expense of equipment and the setting up of a factory.

The goal of 16,000 units at Thamesmead, or 20,000 units at Lysander, near Syracuse, as Edward Logue, President of the New York Urban Development Corporation, is planning, really is a tremendous number when you look at the present American market.

We talk about large-scale entries into the market, we talk about industrialization, and we talk about a comparison with the European experience; but we find that in our free and open enterprise system, with the huge demand for housing, the country is not generating enough housing or enough factory power or production facilities to meet even the minimum national demands.

F.P.H.   We mentioned before the constraints on the market from building codes and labor unions. This is one reason why we have been so unsuccessful in producing housing. Complicated financing methods are another reason.

The market is split up further by individual demands and great economic insecurity. It requires a considerable investment in money and time to build housing. There are other more attractive investment possibilities for the same money. It seems to me that housing is not an attractive investment in our capitalist system. We should finally recognize this fact and reorganize the financial end of the housing market. The introduction of building systems certainly could become a means to that end.

Building systems have been successfully used in the United States in school building. In California, Ezra Ehrenkrantz, an architect, started a very different systems approach to produce schools. First, he aggregated the demand of various fast-growing communities in the San Francisco area. He designed a user or performance standard that was then sent out for bids to different manufacturers. That is, he wrote a set of specifications for the requirements of the school buildings. The manufacturers could meet these user specifications any way they desired, using any materials or methods any way they chose, as long as they satisfied the requirements at the lowest price. This is a totally different approach to producing a building or producing an enclosed space. Usually you go about it exactly the opposite way.

L.S.C.   The idea which Ezra Ehrenkrantz developed on the West Coast should really be termed a fourth generic systems classification; I would call it "performance standards." The method which you just described is indeed another very important approach to industrialized building techniques, and one which I think industry can really benefit from in this country. It certainly proves that we can get manufacturers working together in concert to produce bids based on the performance criteiria and the user-needs of a building, or complex of buildings.

F.P.H.   In California, this particular experience has been very successful. Contrary to many of the scruples voiced by many people, it has also produced very different schools. In fact, each school can be designed in any way the community or its architect wishes. There is an enormous amount of flexibility available in terms of space arrangements, window and door openings, finishing materials, in almost everything.

These SCSD (Southern California School District) schools have another immense advantage: they simply supply a covered space; all the partitions inside are readily moveable. Everything that goes on in the school or within a given space can be changed around to meet specific needs for classrooms or meeting space. In fact, the rooms can be altered overnight quite easily with little labor and no damage. All the partitions can be moved in response to different educational programs. Knowing the changes that have been made in education and the constant demands for new methods and ideas, this flexibility is particularly important, because the investment on the part of a community in a new school building is considerable. They want to have the school for the next fifty years. But nobody knows how education will change in that time. Unless you provide a flexible school building, your investment may well be lost.

L.S.C.   I think you bring up another very important aspect of building systems. There is a general misconception among the public that a building system implies that all buildings are the same, that they are box-like structures looking like prisons, and so on. As you point out, the same system can produce some very different looking buildings, but its qualities such as fire resistance, acoustics, or insulation are the same.

This brings us to the issue of "open systems" versus "closed systems." An "open system" is something like what you just described with respect to the SCSD system. An example of an open system under one of our generic classifications would be a panel system that permits the panels to be shaped and formed according to a particular architect's design for the needs of a particular community.

Then there are "closed systems," where, again using a panel type as classification, you could have perhaps thirty-seven different panel shapes that could be put together from a kit. It could produce a building that always looked the same, or had a limited number of variations on a theme. A "closed system" in this country is not as acceptable, because we have a wide range of environmental conditions and a wide range of tastes and styles. We need to describe the user's requirements in the architecture. Only an "open system" can answer these needs.

F.P.H.   As you mentioned, we have a wide range of climates. While California offers an ideal climate in which to experiment with new building methods, the SCSD system has now been adapted for cold climates and also for highrise buildings. Toronto is just now involved in a major program to build its schools by systems methods adapted to their needs from the SCSD system. Boston also is very seriously working on this idea. In fact, the Public Facilities Department, which is in charge of all school building in Boston, got a grant from the Ford Foundation to help Boston schools adopt a systems-building approach. It is a matter of accommodating existing building regulations to new methods and vice versa, which is enormously difficult.

Boston fell very far behind in terms of building schools. Therefore, many more schools are now becoming obsolete all at once, so that the idea to build a system is very appealing indeed, because of the time and money-saving factor.

Perhaps now having defined systems, we should really discuss the advantages and disadvantages of systems building. What are the pros and cons in practice of using systems?

L.S.C.   The major advantages to systems construction, I think, would fall into two or three categories. The first category is in terms of time saving. Systems construction, such as an on-site technique developed in France, can save up to 50 per cent of the time over more traditional construction techniques. Any savings incurred beyond that are progressive savings, in that money is saved at each step in the project. By completing units six months earlier, they can be rented earlier. The developer is saving money from the construction loans, and in addition, he is collecting rent through early occupancy.

F.P.H.   Is this a net saving, or is it time saved at the building site which is now spent in the plant? That is, is it an all-over saving, which means a considerable cost saving also in terms of labor?

L.S.C.   The labor saving is where the real money savings come from. Using less skilled labor on the site reduces costs most of all. In view of the fact that today in New England carpenters are getting $8 or $9 an hour, and steel workers are getting around $10 an hour, the fewer skilled laborers that we use on the site, the more money we save.

One point I would like to add here is that there is too much emphasis on the amount of money saved through industrialized building systems. A lot of it is done at the expense of good architecture, of a good quality environment. We really need a cost-benefit study to see what we can do with the monies we are saving by going into industrialization. How can we provide more amenities for the family, for instance, by building a balcony for each apartment or creating a nursery school and attractive open space? You can provide better landscaping, you can use better materials, larger apartment units, more acoustical privacy; you can provide a whole range of elements that make for a better total life by going to industrialized building systems. This is really the crucial area where we are saving: We are saving people.

F.P.H.   The importance of systems is not only the price, as you point out, but the quality of the environment that can be achieved. The prejudice has always been that a system will create a mechanical, ugly environment of sameness and dullness, especially in housing. The average suburban development today, built by the average builder, really is dull. Most houses are the same on the same small lots. Systems well used can create much more variety. A system is a tool, it is a means to an end, and it will be whatever the architect makes out of it. The quality of a building or environment depends largely on the skill of the architect and the designer, not on the building methods used.

L.S.C.   The best example of this can be found by looking at the East European experience. In Czechoslovakia, the most frequently used panel system gave a very drab, box-like appearance to all the buildings, which were always set down at right angles to each other. Recently in Czechoslovakia, using the same system, architects in a more enlightened atmosphere have created buildings that articulate with the site conditions, that follow contours, that provide all kinds of amenities. The same system expresses a whole new quality of life. It really is in the hands of the designers to mold the kind of environment that we all need and require to live a happy life.

F.P.H.   Perhaps now we should summarize. It seems to me that with the predicted population growth, we must produce more and better buildings, and especially housing, and we must do it faster and more efficiently, and that is what systems building is all about.

L.S.C.   I would like to say that we have the talent, the enthusiasm, the idealism which produces good design and good building with industrialized building systems. The monies which we accrue through time savings, through training unskilled labor, offer us a chance to build a better environment. I would simply make a plea for the correct usage of industrialized building systems techniques to produce a better environment for everyone.

F.P.H.   Thank you, Mr. Cutler.

BIBLIOGRAPHY

BOOKS

Cutler, L.S., and Cutler, S.S. *Housing Systems for Designers and Developers.* New York: Van Nostrand-Reinhold, 1972.

Diament, R.M.E. *Industrialized Building,* Volumes I, II, and III, *The Architect and Building News.* London: Lifte Books, 1968.

Dietz, A.G.H., and Cutler, L.S. *Industrialized Building Systems for Housing.* Cambridge, Mass.: The M.I.T. Press, 1971.

Educational Facilities Laboratories, 477 Madison Avenue, New York, N.Y. 10020. Write for information and pamphlets on School Construction Systems Development and other types of school construction.

International Systems Building Round Table Conference. 1971. Boston Architectural Center, 320 Newbury Street, Boston, Mass. 02115. Write for conference summary.

The latest information on systems building gathered at an international conference of experts from all over the world discussing the "process" rather than the product.

Jeanneret, Charles E. (Le Corbusier). *The Modulor: A Harmonious Measure to the Human Scale Universally Applicable to Architecture and Mechanics.* Cambridge, Mass.: Harvard University Press, 1948.

Kelly, Burnham, *The Prefabrication of Houses.* Cambridge, Mass.: Technology Press of M. I. T., and New York: John Wiley and Sons, Inc.,1951.

Kettaneh, Anthony, ed. *Project Romulus: An Adaptable High-Density Urban Prototype.* Cambridge, Mass.: The MIT Press, 1968.

Operation Breakthrough. For information write to: Department of Housing and Urban Development, HUD Library, Washington, D. C. 20410.

Safdie, Moshe. *Beyond Habitat* (John Kettle, ed.). Cambridge, Mass.: The MIT Press, 1970.

The creator of Habitat looks into the future and explains his far-reaching ideas.

Schmid, Thomas, and Testa, Carlo. *Systems Building: An International Survey of Methods.* New York: Frederick A. Praeger, 1969.

An excellent illustrated (photos and drawings) explanation of building systems showing actual examples.

School Construction Systems Development, 120 Broadway, San Francisco, Calif. 94111. Write for information on this system (SCSD) of school construction.

PERIODICAL

Progressive Architecture. A Reinhold publication. Write for all issues and articles on industrialized building, modular housing, etc., which they produce on a continuing basis.

ARTICLES

Hosken, Fran P. "How Can We Solve the Housing Shortage?" *Boston Sunday Herald Magazine,* February 9, 1969.

———. "A New Town Within London." *St. Louis Post-Dispatch,* March 1, 1970.

———. "A New Way to Build Boston's Schools." *Boston Herald,*

———. "Our Cities of Tomorrow." *Boston Sunday Herald Magazine,* January 7, 1968.

———. "Systems building touted as only way to go." *Christian Science Monitor,* date?

———. "Well, what's new? Systems building for instance." *Christian Science Monitor,* April 9, 1971, p. B11.

15

THE UNIVERSITY AND THE CITY

A discussion with RICHARD P. DOBER
Principal, Dober, Paddock, Upton Planning Consultants, Cambridge, Mass.

INTRODUCTION

The university's mission traditionally has been defined as teaching, research, and service. All three areas are under attack at present by students, frequently joined by faculty. Change is a fact of life at all universities now. The only question that remains is how fast can it be accomplished. The constantly growing and changing student populations are becoming increasingly politicized, and this is having its effect on the structure of the universities. The very concept and tradition of academic life and of education is under attack. Universities as institutions are changing under student pressures, while recently very serious economic constraints have been added to the difficulties universities face.

In turn, the relationship of universities to their surrounding city and community is beset with severe problems. In the traditional "town-gown" controversy, the students are often playing a new role as advocates for the less affluent members of the community. Where universities have taken over housing and other facilities to expand their own plant, students have demanded redress from the university administrations. To provide housing for the community, for instance, has been one of the student demands at Columbia and Harvard Universities. The wrath of students against the establishment has often been vented by attacking the symbols of the establishment in the university communities, such as local banks, for instance, in Santa Barbara, California.

After several years of turmoil and escalating protest universities seemed ominously quiet in 1971. But to any observer it is clear that their troubles are not over: many institutions are fighting for survival in a deteriorating economic climate while trying to defend their purposes and relevance.

Since the present problems that engulf universities seem utterly overwhelming, it may be useful first to define some limitations for the present discussion and then to look at recent history.

The topic "The University and the City" should take its direction mainly from the definition of "Service" as a responsibility of the university. Service in this context has been interpreted as service to the surrounding, frequently urban, community: that is, to open the university's resources, teaching, and cultural facilities to the citizens of the community, as well as to assist with advice, information, and skills in the many different functions of the city. In turn, many students have become involved in all kinds of social service activities in the city, such as teaching and tutoring children, working in hospitals, and doing other community work.

The university faculty and administration frequently are involved in national service functions, working under government contracts of all kinds. Many universities can no longer support their research programs and have become dependent on federal monies of all kinds while their faculties have become more interested in these government- or foundation-sponsored research activities instead of teaching. The students, in turn, have charged that they are being neglected by professors who are more interested in obtaining grants, money, and political influence. Many of the grants, especially at technical institutions, serve the defense or war effort, or in other ways support U.S. domination over third world countries—so the students charge. Therefore, some of these research activities have been repeatedly and severely attacked. In the students' view, service at a university must be for all mankind. In relation to the city, it must help the urban underprivileged, the poor, and the minorities.

The administration of the university is frequently viewed with hostility: it is seen as ruling the institution, without any concern for the surrounding community, in what seem to the students as totally arbitrary self- and establishment-serving ways, bent on perpetuating the past. Participation in the decision making is demanded by the students, especially in the decisions affecting the surrounding community.

As outlined earlier, recent history should be examined, as the past constantly intrudes on the present in terms of outmoded rules and regulations. It must be clear that present-day universities no longer resemble in any way the elitist or alternatively competitive-sports-directed institutions of the recent past. It is for these kinds of institutions that the rules and administrative structures of most universities were designed. The GI-education bill opened the universities as exclusive organizations and changed them into inclusive ones.

As recently as 1955, the number of college students was 2.6 million: ten years later it had more than doubled, and by now it is over 8 million and still growing. The number of people attached to the academic enterprise as teachers, professors, researchers, administrators, and staff, as well as employees, adds more millions, and is constantly growing as a percentage of the population. The fact that both students and professors are very vocal increases their political influence.

The growth of students and of universities has resulted in an even greater growth of university-connected institutes, research organizations, and foundations, as well as university-connected consulting and business establishments of all kinds in the vicinity of the institutions. The surrounding city and community frequently does not appreciate this growth, as it often takes place at the expense of the community, without their prior knowledge or consent. Though the university in many cases serves as a major employer and creator of jobs, especially in college towns, there has been and continues to be considerable friction between university administrations and city fathers, and between students and citizens.

Universities are tax-free institutions. This puts a great financial burden on the surrounding communities which depend on the property tax to finance city services. Universities use the city services, for instance, fire and police protection, water supply, street lighting, and more, but don't pay for them. Some private universities, for instance, Harvard, are making contributions in lieu of taxes to help pay for the costs of the city services they use. Yet it is a fact that the payments of the institutions don't begin to cover expenses which also have increased very much recently. Universities also have grown very much in size and therefore are removing more and more land from the city's tax rolls.

As a result, for instance, in Cambridge every tax payer whose average income is only just above the poverty line subsidizes Harvard University which has an endowment of over two billion dollars. Similar conditions prevail in many university communities and do not improve the town-gown relationship, especially when universities expand and conceal their plans from the community.

Campus planning as an organized activity—since the campus can be viewed as a city within the city—was initiated by many universities only in the late 1950's. Until then, even major universities enlarged their plants, mostly without long-range plans by buying any available piece of land. Universities now have to consult with the city about all their expansion plans. It also became apparent that community-university communication could not be limited soothing citizens, protesting noisy student activities, or the takeover by students of citizens' parking lots. "Community relations" has become one of the most sensitive offices on every major campus, presided over frequently by a vice president. University officials who in the past had remained aloof from the dirty politics of the surrounding city are finding themselves very much involved as active participants in city and community affairs.

Change is evident everywhere on the campus. Most of all, the strict lines of division between city and university, especially on the urban campus, can no longer be drawn.

DISCUSSION

F.P.H.   Mr. Dober, you have studied the university-city relationship for a long time. In your book, *Campus Planning,*[1] you have made one of the most comprehensive surveys of universities and colleges all over the United States. Do you think that the present politicizing of campuses, the fundamental changes in student attitudes that we see, will alter the way of life at universities even more, as well as their education and physical form?

R.P.D.   You have touched upon some of the most critical issues that our urban society faces. But I am not sure that the issues are as clear as you have described them. For instance, I think there is a real danger in suggesting that what happens at some universities is a pattern for all universities. I think much of the conflict and questioning that is occurring is still limited to a small number of colleges and universities, mostly in urban areas, which happen to be the scene of the urban problems. Since students tend to come and go, quite often the "politicizing" of the campus may only be a temporary phenomenon.

F.P.H.   In your opinion, what is the relationship between urban problems and the urban universities?

R.P.D.   I think part of the problem is that the urban university as an institution has failed, much as the city has failed, to create a satisfying environment. I recently visited some student housing on urban campuses, and I have noticed several things. First of all, the students do not want to live there. From fall to spring, the vacancy rate increases in the dormitories and in on-campus student accommodations. Students are voting with their feet: they are leaving these restrictive, domineering physical environments. In some places, you can hardly see any difference between highrise public housing projects and a highrise student dormitory. The chief difference is that the students have some degree of mobility and of choice and can reject this environment.

F.P.H.   Yet, so many of the universities are urged by the city fathers to build more student housing, because they say that students impinge on the housing facilities of the surrounding city and push people out of their living quarters.

R.P.D.   The reason why university housing has failed is that it perpetuates a housing system that goes back to the nineteenth century. The university

---

[1] Richard P. Dober, *Campus Planning* (New York: Reinhold Publishing Corp., 1963).

then came to the conclusion that the answer was to build "shelter" as opposed to an environment with a sense of community. Another aspect of this question is that those who live in dormitories in urban areas live in fear. Students, for example, when they leave for the weekend take with them all their belongings, everything they can.

F.P.H.   Why is there no longer safety in the dormitories?

R.P.D.   In some urban areas security is quite limited. It is not only security from external forces, it is security from inside. This suggests to me that one kind of change that may occur is a total recasting of the physical form of the university in the city. I think you are right to describe it as a campus surrounded by the city, as opposed to a campus in the city. What the eventual emerging physical form of this might be I am not sure.

Another aspect of what you mentioned is the real-life attitudes of students and their demand for attention to the problems of the surrounding community. But I would not simply see this as a student issue. I would add to the constituency that is asking for change, the younger faculty, certain alumni groups, and some of those who finance the institutions in various ways. I think urban communities are asking for help with their problems, and there is a growing university administration leadership body which intends to respond to these problems.

F.P.H.   In the past, students stayed a maximum of four years at a university. Now some of them spend eight to ten years there. They get married, they raise families, and they still go to school. They should take a far greater interest in the surrounding community to which they actually belong.

R.P.D.   This is another manifestation of change of the university. If I understand history correctly, one of the community-supporting aspects of university growth in the nineteenth century was that it did tend to create and stabilize a local community around the campus. Today you will rarely find faculty living in a walk-to-work situation. Part of this is due to the failure of the community to provide a physical pattern that is satisfying to the faculty. For example, we have done a couple of in-depth studies on how to reconstitute a real university community. We established as a model that it should be a comprehensive community, with a variety of age groups, a variety of income groups and social groups.

F.P.H.   In fact, a mixed urban community rather than a one-sided community.

R.P.D.   Yes. A utopian dream of a new-town-in-town, if you will, with many kinds of people and many kinds of activities. One of the important parts of the community would have to be a large faculty community that would be visible, that would participate in local affairs, that would make itself available in formal and informal ways to the people in the area surrounding the university.

The difficulties of creating this utopian state are understandable. Faculties as a group are not much different in their habits and preferences from other middle-class professionals and managers. Our recent studies indicate that the older, tenured faculty, especially those married and with school-age children, follow the typical middle-class pattern of wanting to live in the suburbs. An important reason for this choice is the quality of the local urban schools, or rather the lack of quality. Younger faculty at first, even those with children, seem willing to stay in town and fight for better schools. But over time we notice that they, too, tend to move out of the core city. They see visible evidence that the local school system is demeaning and destructive.

F.P.H.   You mean they don't wish to sacrifice their own children to set an example of social integration?

R.P.D.   The problem is not just social integration; in fact, the urban schools are really very bad.

F.P.H.   The city that surrounds the university neither spends enough money on schools nor is it interested in innovative education programs that university faculty and students want for their children.

R.P.D.   There are a number of two-way streets in this discussion. To point fingers at the university and at the community, and vice-versa, does not explain the problems. In developing a new community around a university, the school problem is a real one and has to be addressed. It cannot be solved by establishing a simple laboratory school or a private school, which some universities do. It is going to require a major effort to bring the urban school systems up to a satisfactory level of opportunity and achievement.

F.P.H.   Do you feel that the universities could play a positive part in that?

R.P.D.   There is no question that it could, though their participation in this process to date has not been satisfactory and has often been a source of local town-gown conflicts. People often take the point of view that any problem today has to be solved immediately. Not enough time is given to creating the network of communication and participation that can really achieve fundamental changes in school systems.

F.P.H.   Also recently, the school-age children of students as well as faculty have become involved in the local school problems.

R.P.D.   People are marrying younger and having children younger than in the past, although since 1970, trends show a dramatic change in the demographic profiles: fewer children. However, the presence of sizeable numbers of student families with children could have a strong influence on a local school system. Unfortunately, my own observations suggest that this group, too, tends to abandon the campus neighborhood when and if their children reach ages seven, eight, and nine. The public schools are thus deprived of parents who care about education and a child group whose presence, again, would have beneficial effect both on teachers and other children.

To turn to another area of conflict and a physically demonstrable campus-community problem: the condition of the parking and circulation system that feeds, erodes, and clearly demeans the physical environment around a so-called "campus." As more people drive longer distances to reach the campus, there are more cars and the net effect is to push automobiles and parking lots into the surrounding community.

F.P.H.   I understand that often student parking is the number one concern for the citizens living around universities. Many people react angrily when they find a strange car parked in front of their door when they come home at night and want "their" parking space.

R.P.D.   This is a source of constant antagonism. I know of one community that in response to that problem passed a law forbidding overnight parking on the street. The university failed to provide an instrument to develop proper parking facilities on campus. The net result is that a once lovely street, with trees and lawns, is now a connected series of black-topped parking lots. The trees were cut down and the lawns paved. The effect was to further push out people who had wanted to live in the neighborhood. Finally, what were some very handsome-looking residences in the past became boarding houses. These, in turn, needed additional parking. The remaining landscape was then paved. The people who owned the property began to lose interest in maintaining the physical facilities. Density increased. The cycle continued. A very pleasant place to live is now ten acres of parking lots with boarding houses in between cars.

F.P.H.   At many urban universities such as Harvard, Northeastern, M.I.T., N.Y.U., the University of Pennsylvania, and others, the parking problem now has begun to be a major concern in terms of planning new facilities. Cars and parking are not only a problem for the surrounding community and the police, who hand out enormous numbers of parking tickets; but I understand that in planning a new building the university has to consider most of all where it is going to put the additional cars. The cost of the building and the ability to accommodate new students are directly influenced by parking space.

R.P.D.   One measure of this—I will use the word "insanity"—that afflicts us all is that the parking problem becomes number one on an agenda of things to discuss when planning university facilities. There are more fundamental issues than parking in campus planning and in university development. Nonetheless, it is symptomatic of our automobile culture. Technically, I think there are some resolutions to this.

With some of the new building technologies there are ways to construct large-scale parking facilities, and to use them for many different purposes. For example, with the new artificial grass and turfs, the tops of parking decks can be used for playfields or for recreation space. The cost of parking can be shared by those who park and those who play. Of course, any kind of fee system for parking has always been resisted by faculty and students. But that too is changing. Parking is a small issue that grows and erodes the community-university relationship and obscures more fundamental issues.

F.P.H.   What are some of these fundamental issues besides the ones we have already discussed? What does the future hold for urban universities?

Since we are concerned with urban problems here, the relationship of the institution to the surrounding city needs to be examined in much greater depth. What does the university have to offer to the city? What should their future relationship be? Urban problems are becoming a more and more important matter to all of us because of the complexity of urban life. The university as the seat of the production and dissemination of knowledge about urban problems should therefore take a special place; most of all this applies to the urban university.

R.P.D.   Perhaps we can pose this question in another way. For example, if we speak about the immediate interaction between people and problems, between campuses and social and technical action, then I am not sure that the university itself, as an educational institution, ought to be the first point of intervention. I think the community colleges, as a group, may be able to respond more quickly to some of these questions.

The community college is, in a sense, a micro-university, more "egalitarian," if you will, in which technical, vocational, and service programs have a very special kind of central role. They are also institutions involved in continuing education and have relatively great freedom in setting up and running their programs. They are free of traditional views of how to apply resources and skills to solve local problems. Some most interesting things are occurring in these community colleges, which perhaps are the intellectual centers where poor cities and communities can redevelop themselves. Places like Cleveland State or Manhattan Community College are rooting themselves into the whole issue much more effectively than any of the universities that are nearby.

Universities take on a more national role. Community colleges, by the very word community, take on a local role. This is not to say that a university should not be involved in its community. I am just suggesting that there may be more opportunities at the community college level than is presently appreciated or understood.

F.P.H.   Community colleges also draw their students from the surrounding community. That means they don't have to put up dormitories, they don't really develop any kind of community of their own, but they naturally are a part of the surrounding community.

R.P.D.   Very much so. It is a kind of walk-in environment. It also happens to be an environment that can work twenty-four hours a day, seven days a week, twelve months of the year. Universities are not presently constituted to operate their calendars that way, though there are one or two exceptions such as M.I.T.

Community participation in the educational programs of community colleges can be very effective. Community colleges can respond to needs much faster than the traditional route that universities have to take with committees, reviews, board actions, fundings, always taking a national posture. I don't find universities as a group as sensitive to change as community colleges, especially towards their immediate environment. On the other hand community colleges are not as aggressive as they could be—perhaps because they are overly sensitive to local politics.

F.P.H.   For a university, tradition may be a handicap rather than an asset. Perhaps institutions that are not burdened with a lot of traditions and rules have an advantage. A university also is defined in terms of its buildings, which stand out from the surrounding community. A community college has a certain advantage in being literally submerged in the community.

R.P.D.   It can be an advantage, but this remains to be proven. I think a community college can fit into the urban fabric much easier than a university. By university, I must again generalize and think of a comprehensive set of physical facilities ranging from nuclear reactors to large theaters, lecture halls, dormitories, and so forth.

F.P.H.   In the introduction I suggested that the fact that universities have grown so much in the last twenty years certainly accounts for many of their problems. From experience with cities we have learned that rapid growth in relation to the rest of the environment is bound to create problems. It was hoped that universities, by virtue of their intellectual endowment, might be able to cope with this without creating disruptions in their environment. However, it has been found that this is not very often the case. Universities have tried to perpetuate their nineteenth-century postures, structures, and organization at any price and have not modernized. This is creating great difficulties for themselves, for the students, who have changed, and for their urban environment, which also has changed.

R.P.D.   Universities have directed their attention to the problems of scale. They have experimented with ideas for making large and diverse campuses more comprehensible and comfortable for the people who use them. A campus of 20,000 to 30,000 students means a total population of 50,000 to 70,000 people when one includes faculty, staff, and visitors. The traditional physical forms of university design are not sufficient, so we see several things happening. For example, the so-called "cluster college" concept is used to organize the student population into smaller social groups. Housing is decentralized. Sometimes satellite campuses are set up.

F.P.H.   That is, the students are divided up into a number of colleges to give them a chance to get to know each other, to communicate, to have a sense of belonging.

R.P.D.   It is a response to the anonymity created by too large a group to have effective personal contact.

F.P.H.   Still, students have charged that they are nothing but numbers on IBM cards as far as the university is concerned, that nobody pays any attention to them, least of all the faculty.

R.P.D.   This, I think, is only partly true. For example, large numbers of faculty of every age are teachers in the true sense of the word. I do not think we have really stepped back far enough to look at that particular charge to see whether it is correct.

In the ten years between 1955 and 1965, institutions of higher education were asked—they did not request it—to *double* their enrollment. The result was a number of unfortunate sociological and technological distortions brought about by scale. But I think the goodwill and dedication of faculty are ameliorating what I think are short-term difficulties.

F.P.H.   You said that universities are being physically subdivided into smaller residential colleges within one campus to deal with the unfortunate results of bigness.

R.P.D.   I mentioned satellite campuses as well as workshop activities carried on in the city, outside the campus itself. For example, Cornell has a program in architecture and planning which includes a workshop in New York City. This is a very interesting indicator of how other campuses may eventually work.

F.P.H.   Many universities, particularly those located in rural areas, are isolated, and some of their students don't like this. Originally, the concept of a university was to be away from the distractions of the city: a scholar had to be apart from the world. Now, we feel that an urban environment stimulates education and instills social purpose, just the opposite from the past opinion.

Students today want to be "involved," and many of them have organized internships or work-sessions like the one you mentioned in New York. Many universities and colleges offer students the opportunity to spend a certain amount of their academic year in a practical work environment of their choice—in some activity relating to their main interest or intended profession.

R.P.D.   The interest and involvement in the city is an international phenomenon. I recently looked at six of the new universities in Great Britain which were built to enlarge educational facilities to accommodate more students. All of these universities are, to my mind, delightfully designed. They have very alert and real-world educational programs. They have a varied faculty, and a varied student body. They are all located within a radius of sixty to one hundred miles from London. But the students do not find them a satisfactory environment for twenty-four hours, seven days a week. As a result, after twelve noon Friday at a place like Colchester, England, when the afternoon train for London pulls out, most of the students go with it. They come back again Monday morning. The attraction of the central city, both in an educating sense and a social sense, is very strong.

We shall have to be very watchful of the next phase of university development. Beginning now, we should examine some of the basic principles, the substance as to what university development is all about. If I were to forecast what the future might be like, I think we are going to see an extension of one of the oldest American traditions in higher education: Alternative physical forms of higher education are on the horizon. One of the strengths of higher education has been its diversity and its ability to respond to new problems. In effect, we seem to create a new institution of higher education every time there is a new need.

Supporting this view is a crisis in higher education as serious as anything we spoke about—the cost of maintaining a higher educational system. Expenses have grown beyond what private institutions can fund on their own. The Carnegie Foundation Study[2] of the future of higher education found many private universities in very serious financial troubles.

We will see new forms of public aid to private education in the coming decade, and I expect this aid will come with some conditions attached so that the line between "private" and "public" will be blurred. As a result, further sensitivity and response to the urban problems are likely to occur, perhaps even some form of public service (now voluntarily given by some students) will be demanded, and become part of the "requirements" for a degree. I think this would be beneficial as long as the universities can control the educational aspects of this service, and the quality of the work performed.

The economic pressure is going to have some interesting chain reactions. For example, a private university that has in effect ignored its local government no longer can turn its back on its city or state when it needs money. It will have to trade off some aspects of its independence for cooperation and involvement. Neighborhood determination and local control of the community will result in a transfer of political power from City Hall and State House to the people who live in the environs of the campus. This transfer of power is going to have dramatic effect on the ways universities make decisions and in turn will affect the form of the campus.

F.P.H.   Perhaps some of the solutions in Europe in the past might be helpful here. The traditional university cities within larger cities, for instance, in Paris, or in Vienna, or certainly in the German university centers like Heidelberg, have become a definite part of the urban structure. From what you said before, you seem to visualize that this might be one viable answer.

I think we are going to be forced in the near future to seriously consider the building of new communities, new cities, and new towns away from existing ones for any number of reasons including pollution, population growth, and economic development. It seems to me that no better city centers could be found than universities. Cities have always needed some kind of physical center, such as the palace or cathedral of the past. With the central role that education plays in our society, a university could be the center of the life of a new city or town.

R.P.D.   This is a good possibility. Especially as higher education becomes increasingly a cultural phenomenon, a continuing activity that affects a per-

[2] Carnegie Commission on the Future of Higher Education. Carnegie Commission for Higher Education, 1947 Center Street, Berkeley, Calif. 94704 [14 volumes to date].

son, not just from eighteen to twenty-four, but for his entire life. In that case, some serious thought has to be given to reorganizing what we call a university.

If we look to a university as it is presently structured, programmed, and designed as the core activity for a city or town, that form will not be enough. However, if attached, there is a vibrant, exciting, changing responsive community education and recreation program, a university may become a real center of activity. In that case, there is some hope that higher education can play a central role in a new settlement or town.

F.P.H.   To build new cities and new towns, with a university as intellectual center and physical focus, is a real challenge. This creates a completely new prospect for the university-city relationship.

Thank you, Mr. Dober.

BIBLIOGRAPHY

BOOKS

Dober, Richard P. *Campus Planning.* New York: Reinhold Publishing Corp., 1963.
An excellent illustrated study of all the major campuses of the United States and their history and physical development.
———. *Environmental Design.* New York: Van Nostrand Reinhold Publishing Corp., 1969.

Editors of *The Atlantic: The Troubled Campus.* Boston: Little, Brown and Company (an Atlantic Monthly Press Book), 1965. Paperback.
Barzun, Jacques. *The American University.* New York: Harper and Row, 1968.
Bell, Daniel. *The Reforming of General Education.* New York: Columbia University Press, 1966.
Brubacher, John S., and Willis, Rudy. *Higher Education in Transition: A History of American Colleges and Universities, 1936-1956.* New York: Harper & Row, 1958.
"Carnegie Commission on the Future of Higher Education." Published 1970-1971 by the Carnegie Commission on Higher Education, 1947 Center Street, Berkeley, California, 94704. Over 14 individual volumes on different topics of higher education.
Gardner, John W. *Excellence: Can We be Equal and Excellent Too?* New York: Harper Colophon Books, Harper & Row, 1961.
A most important book, concerned with social and academic attitudes.
———. *The Recovery of Confidence.* New York: W.W. Norton and Company, Inc., 1970.

The Godkin Lectures given at Harvard by the former Secretary of Health, Education and Welfare, who summarizes his concern about the development of U.S. society and its attitudes.

Jencks, Christopher, and Riesman, David. *The Academic Revolution.* Garden City, New York: Doubleday and Company, 1968.

Kerr, Clark. *The Uses of the University.* Cambridge, Mass.: Harvard University Press, 1963.

The Godkin Lectures of 1963 at Harvard by the then President of the University of California, the "Multiversity." A classic.

Klotsche, J. Martin. *The Urban University and the Future of our Cities.* New York: Harper & Row, 1966.

The President of the University of Milwaukee is the exceptional university president, genuinely concerned about urban problems.

Metrocenter Seminars, "The Urban University and the Urban Community." Six seminars held in April and May 1966 at Boston University.

Perkins, James A. *The University in Transition.* Princeton: Princeton University Press, 1966.

Pusey, Nathan M. *The Age of the Scholar: Observations on Education in a Troubled Decade.* Cambridge, Mass.: The Belknap Press of the Harvard University Press, 1963.

Society of College and University Planning, c/o Columbia University, 616 West 114th Street, New York, N.Y. 10025. Write for information and publications.

ARTICLES

"The Contemporary University, U.S.A." *Daedalus* 93:4 (Fall 1964).

A series of articles by the foremost academics knowledgable on university affairs.

Hosken, Fran P. "Topics: The Future of the Urban University," *The New York Times,* September 10, 1966, editorial page.

———. "Urban Community." *Christian Science Monitor,* November 3, 1971.

———. "The Urban University and the Urban Environment." *Architecture Canada* (November 1966), pp. 48-50.

———. "Students and Public Housing." *Sunday Post Dispatch,* May 11, 1969.

Meyerson, Martin. "The American College Student." *Daedalus.* 95:3 (summer 1966).

"Students and Politics." *Daedalus* 97:I (Winter 1968).

16

URBANIZATION AND ECONOMIC GROWTH
IN DEVELOPING COUNTRIES

A discussion with RICHARD M. WESTEBBE*
Chief, Economics of Urbanization Division, International Bank of
Reconstruction (1968-70); Senior Economist, Western Africa
Department, IBRD, Washington

INTRODUCTION

Two-thirds of the world population live in developing countries. While the majority of their inhabitants still live on the land, large-scale migration to cities and towns, which began recently, is becoming a growing problem, both for the people and the cities involved. The larger the city, the more attractive it is to immigrants who come there in hope of finding work and a better life. But the cities are not able to produce enough jobs, basic services or housing for the ever-growing flood of immigrants.

Urbanization is a world-wide phenomenon, but it is most drastic in developing countries, where the cities have neither the resources nor the institutions to absorb the unskilled, often illiterate immigrants. The most critical issue, however, is work or some sort of gainful employment on which the rural immigrant, who no longer can grow his own food, totally depends. Yet cities everywhere produce a growing share of the GNP (Gross National Product) and the national tax income, while their own finances and services deteriorate.

In the cities of the developed world, notably Europe and the United States, industrialization preceded urbanization; indeed the reason for the growth of cities, starting in the nineteenth century, was the need for workers. Technology and transportation developed simultaneously, enabling more people to live in greater densities, or an urban way of life. The newly established factories were located right in the cities near transportation, that is, rivers, harbors,

*Disclaimer: The views expressed in this discussion may not be attributed to the International Bank of Reconstruction and Development and its affiliated organizations and may not be quoted as representing their views.

or the newly-established railroad lines. The nineteenth-century industrial city was incredibly densely populated, had bad and frequently unsanitary housing, poor health conditions, and little open space or recreation; but there was work and therefore hope for improvement for the immigrant.

The presently very rapid urban growth in developing countries is not due to industrialization or the creation of jobs in cities or towns. Indeed, the completely uncontrolled growth of cities throughout the developing world is causing severe social and economic problems and threatens peaceful development and social stability. But most of all it creates enormous hardships for the immigrants, who have no experience with urban living, who have no marketable skills, and who leave their only security, their families, when they move into town.

Cities have always depended on trade and specialization, on the production and the movement of goods and services. People traditionally have come into cities to find gainful employment, a better life, and personal security. But in developing countries, many more people are moving into cities than cities can sustain economically. Most cities cannot produce the infrastructure for planned economic growth, let alone organized physical settlement patterns and housing. The large, haphazard squatter settlements, some observers believe, are really extended villages that gradually become more and more densely inhabited. The economic costs of these unplanned and uncoordinated settlement patterns are enormous both to the city administrations and the immigrants, quite aside from the social costs, the increasing pollution, and often the very great physical difficulties in supplying basic services, transportation, and roads.

The move to the city is caused by many factors that vary from country to country with the state of economic development of each country. The most important reasons are rapid population growth due to health improvements, while agricultural land is no longer able to support the additional families. Mechanization of agriculture makes small farms uncompetitive in a market economy. Land owners prefer tractors and mechanical tools; therefore, many agricultural workers are pushed off the land. The "Green revolution," or miracle seeds that are very much needed to improve agricultural production, often result in making even more agricultural laborers surplus. Land reform, or the distribution of land to those who work it, which could keep more people on the land, has only been marginally carried out in some developing countries. Better transportation and communication than in the past, combined with what seems a better life in the city, is a most powerful stimulus for urban immigration. Finally, the all-important fact is that all over the world, but especially in developing countries, farm incomes are declining, while incomes of urban inhabitants steadily increase.

As a result, cities in all developing countries grow, many by more than 5 per cent per year. In many developing countries, the natural population growth rate is as high as 3 per cent per year, to which immigration must be added in the cities. Population control programs, though actively supported by many governments, have proved to be relatively ineffective, especially where large rural populations are involved. While to have many children is a prime need and desire of all agricultural families, once they move into the cities large numbers of children become an economic burden. Therefore urbanization has always resulted in population control.

Strong efforts must be made by government-supported population control programs to stem excessive population growth if economic development is to succeed. The economic growth rate has to double or materially exceed the population growth rate in order to have any noticeable effect on the standard of living. Urban living patterns support the dissemination of population control, which is beginning to be effective in some urban centers, though it is still offset by immigration.

Most capitals have doubled their population in the last fifteen to twenty years, which has upset any rationally planned economic and physical growth patterns and created chaos in transportation. City administrations, created years ago when they were small towns, cannot cope with this growth, nor can new institutions be created fast enough in the absence of money or technical help. At present, urban living conditions are worsening everywhere, with serious air pollution added to the hardships of the immigrant. Yet most immigrants claim they live better than they did in the villages and on the land.

Large squatter settlements and shanty towns, with ever-increasing populations, grow uncontrolled in and at the edges of all cities in developing countries. Yet very few cities have been able to develop any rational solutions to the immigration problem, which is still on the increase almost everywhere. Singapore and Hong Kong are the two exceptional cities which have successfully combined economic growth with planned physical development and housing.

Without the commitment to rationally plan and organize growth to benefit the majority of the citizens, as well as help the immigrants gain economic independence, the cities will never be able to improve or control their future. Yet despite their difficulties, cities in the developing world are still the economic engines of their countries in terms of economic growth.

DISCUSSION

F.P.H.   Mr. Westebbe, how do you see the relationship between economic growth and urbanization—which I believe is a key factor in all developing countries, as all cities in developing countries are rapidly gaining population, and immigration is still increasing everywhere?

R.M.W.   The phenomena of urbanization and economic development are intimately related. I think one important fact which should be kept in mind is that the rates of urbanization of the larger cities are not uniform throughout the less-developed world. For example, in India, the larger cities, Bombay and Calcutta, are growing considerably less rapidly than, for example, Sao Paulo in Brazil, or Dakar in Senegal, or Mexico City. The reasons for the disparity are mainly due to the fact that the economic development of the countries differs. India has a very slow rate of economic growth, and cities are also growing more slowly. Brazil, on the other hand, particularly Sao Paulo, has a very rapid economic growth rate, with a corresponding ability to create jobs and incomes. The creation of modern sector jobs leads to a growing demand for services, and in turn leads to large-scale employment of migrants in what is called marginal service occupations. The whole economy is of course benefitting by the taxes Sao Paulo pays, by the capital exports to other regions, by the efficient markets and goods it creates, and finally by the work it provides for the surplus labor of the country.

Urbanization and economic development are really parts of the whole process of social and economic change. Urban centers, urban agglomerations, are the mechanisms by which modernization takes place. This has been historically true of the Western world, particularly in Europe in the nineteenth century and the United States later in that century. Modern industrial processing—related service activities, the development of markets (particularly the development of mass transportation), have all changed the economics of location markedly so that large cities become favored, while small isolated production units are no longer economic. This phenomenon is increasingly apparent in the less-developed countries, particularly as transportation facilities are improved. We find, for example, in West Africa that the colonial pattern of cities is changing quite rapidly as rail lines and roads are built. Old commercial, old administrative or religious centers are declining because they are no longer on the main routes for moving goods and people efficiently.

F.P.H.   Larger cities are growing faster than smaller ones everywhere. One major reason for this snowball effect of growth of cities is that the urban income, as compared to agricultural income, is substantially larger. In turn, the average income in large cities, and especially capital cities, is materially greater than in small towns. This income discrepancy is very great, and this contributes to the rapid growth of what has been called the primate cities. Bangkok, for instance, has grown much faster than any other city in Thailand, though Thailand has several urban centers. The same is true of Caracas, Venezuela, and of capitals generally, especially in South America.

R.M.W.   The primate cities throughout much of the less-developed world are growing far more rapidly. In turn, larger cities are growing faster than smaller ones. There is a certain agglomeration of economic forces which thrive in large centers and which build upon each other. Economies of scale and external economies are fundamentally related to the fact that industries have to have supplier and complementary industries, nearby markets, a pool of trained labor, cheap transportation, and such services as banking, research, and government. There is a great advantage from the economic point of view of being located in the same area or city. This is the essence of development. It is a phenomenon not to be discouraged but one upon which to plan future economic development.

The second factor which leads to the growth of cities is the fact that in many countries agricultural incomes are not rising at all. Therefore, the attraction of the city, the growing modern sector, becomes rather overwhelming in comparison to the lack of agricultural income growth, and the very bad living conditions found on the land. Many people who deplore urban slums often fail to look at similar or even worse conditions in rural areas. But the immigrants to the cities know the difference. The immigrants don't go back although they have the option of doing so.

F.P.H.   I recently talked to one of the professionals in the Planning Department of New Delhi who is concerned with relocating squatters on urbanized city plots. Though from his point of view he felt that the squatters were leading a really miserable existence, all of them told him that they were much better off than the rest of their families who were still living in the villages. One persuasive example is Calcutta. Though Calcutta is certainly, from every point of view, one of the worst cities in the world and does not even have a viable water supply, nevertheless the people who are there prefer to be there rather than to go back to their villages. They are able to eke out some kind of living, while in their villages they have nothing at all.

R.M.W.   I think one should distinguish between a place like Calcutta, which is notorious for its terrible living conditions, and other cities in India, like New Delhi or Bombay. The difference, I think, is certainly in large part the efficiency of the management of cities. I think in Calcutta there is administrative and political chaos. Therefore, the performance of Calcutta, its ability to provide services, to organize itself, to meet the demands of people, is accordingly much lower.

Another question is the differences in migration patterns. In Calcutta, and also in Bombay, much immigration is temporary. There are a substantial number of single males who come and stay to earn a living. They are not terribly concerned with where they live or even the conditions in the city. They are only concerned with income. They earn their incomes and send the money back to the interior villages to their families. You will find the phenomenon in India that the purchasing power in many villages is often far higher than expected, knowing what incomes are being generated in those particular rural areas. This is because of income transfers. A similar phenomenon occurs in many African cities, where a large part of migration is temporary. People from tribal areas have a very strong desire to go back home. They even send savings back to build houses in rural areas. Nevertheless, while the patterns differ, immigration to cities still is substantial and continuous, and cities are growing rapidly everywhere.

F.P.H.   One problem that has been also confirmed in the technical literature is that industrialization in this century is no longer able to create the large number of jobs that originally attracted the immigrants to the European cities in the nineteenth centry. While the establishment of industry preceded immigration in the nineteenth-century cities, in the developing countries immigration now precedes industry and the job-creating capacity of the cities, in terms of producing a stable viable income for growing numbers of families.

Furthermore, industry is already capital intensive. Sophisticated manufacturing methods and machinery are being exported by Western countries to the developing world. While the manufacturing requirements of the developing world are very highly labor intensive, that is they must create as many jobs as possible, Western industry has developed beyond this and is increasingly automated or capital intensive and doing away with as many jobs as possible. The dilemma for developing countries is that in order to manufacture competitively with the West, they must use Western production methods, which means importing Western machines and technology. Alternatively, they can create import barriers—but the experience has been that industry, economically protected, becomes increasingly inefficient and expensive, while the developing countries need large amounts of cheap consumer and other products.

R.M.W.   You raise a number of issues that are very important. Let us begin with urbanization in nineteenth-century Europe, where there was some correspondence between growth of industry and urbanization. The cities were able to absorb people who had lost their livelihood on the land because the same technological developments which transformed the cities were also transforming agriculture. Consequently, there was some balance in the movement of people. There were many ups and downs of course; certainly living conditions in the cities were often horrible. Little was known and done about water, sewers, or health, and suffering was great.

In contrast, in the less developed countries now, health conditions are comparatively better than was the case in nineteenth-century Europe because we know how to deal with epidemics, with hunger and starvation, and with most of the major ills which beset a population. So the death rates are considerably lower in these cities than they were in Europe at a comparable state of development. The cities, therefore, have natural rates of increase which are quite high, whereas European cities in the nineteenth century were not reproducing themselves from their natural populations, but were dependent on immigration. Many of the less developed countries have both high natural rates of increase, as well as very high rates of immigration. We estimate, for example, that in Africa in the next three decades there will be a 5 per cent annual increase in population in all urban areas, not just the large cities, whereas rural areas will only be growing by 2 per cent. And we expect this disparity to continue.

Now to the question of the technology. It is quite true, and I think inevitable in the way economic development is proceeding, that many more people are coming into the cities than can be employed under any reasonable expectation of job creation through industrial growth. I will give you a fact. In the decade after 1955, according to UNIDO (United Nations Industrial Development Organization), industrial output rose by something like 7 per cent a year in the less developed countries, while employment rose less than half that amount. That gives an idea of how much industrial output would have to grow to increase employment to where it could even approach the increase in the labor force. This leaves aside the question of how much employment would have to be provided in order to employ the currently underemployed labor force.

Another fact is that people who come to cities are rarely unemployed in the Western sense of the word. People have marginal service occupations. They find something to do. It may be extremely inefficient. It may be very low paying, but they are always occupied in some way or another; they survive. Some, according to research over a generation, emerge quite nicely into lower-middle-class and middle-class occupations as they learn their way about. But basically there is an excess number of people in relation to available job opportunities.

Another point which you touched upon is the question of development policies. Many countries which are importing Western technologies and are establishing conditions of investment both for foreigners and at home are making the mistake of emphasizing capital intensive investments. For example, these countries set up development banks, which give low interest, long-term loans for industrial projects. Most often they do not ask, when giving these loans, will the industry emphasize employment, will it use to the maximum the available labor force? They usually base the loan on what is called efficiency criteria: what rate of return can be made on the capital invested, regardless of how many people are employed. In the cost calculation, no social costs are taken into account, such as people who do not have enough to eat, enough housing, enough clothing and no future for their children, as a result of policies. Countries can correct this by having policies which do not subsidize capital intensive uses, but emphasize instead that capital is scarce and labor is plentiful. Therefore, the technology issue is important: by changing the incentives, in many cases one can change the technologies. It is of course true that the now available technology is based on Western scarcities of labor in relation to capital, while the reverse condition exists in the less developed countries.

F.P.H.   We also ought to consider in this discussion the economic differences between different countries or areas of the world which are in very different stages of development, though they may be neighbors. For instance, one talks about Latin America. But Latin America is made up of numerous different countries who all are in very different stages of development. Bolivia is still an agrarian society which is largely dependent upon a subsistence farming economy, while certainly Argentina or Brazil are highly urbanized and industrialized or in a different stage of development. Venezuela, which is an oil-producing country and highly industrialized, has a very sophisticated, comprehensive urbanization and economic plan.

In turn, Southeast Asia, probably Thailand, and certainly the city-states of Singapore and Hong Kong, are far ahead of agricultural countries like Burma or Indonesia. One should not lump countries together economically, even if they are in the same region. Certainly Israel is vastly different in its economy and standard of living from all its neighbors.

I would generalize by saying that Latin America is ahead in urban development, generally speaking, from most countries of Asia. In turn, Africa seems to be generally least developed and also least urbanized. Mr. Westebbe, you have been working with numerous countries in Africa, I understand. It would be very interesting to hear about some of your experiences there.

R.M.W.   The urbanization process in Africa is different from elsewhere. First of all, these countries are at a lower economic stage of development, with some exceptions of course. The urbanization levels are also quite low in Africa. For example, the average rate of urbanization today is less than 25 per cent and somewhat lower south of the Sahara. It is much higher in Latin America, probably closer to 40 per cent and somewhere in between in most of Asia. These very diverse patterns reflect the different stages of development, the different cultural conditions, and the different historical traditions. Africa has the opportunity to plan its urbanization, or foresee what is likely to occur if it is not planned in some better fashion than was the case in many other parts of the world. By looking ahead, urban services can be planned at lower cost, thus freeing savings for growth and job creation.

The development process first of all inevitably requires urbanization. It does not, however, require urbanization to proceed at the extremely rapid rate we have had. In order to avoid the very rapid rate of immigration, rural opportunities should be developed where they exist. Also, policies can be redirected to make better use of labor and more intelligent use of scarce capital. Why use a tractor when you can use several hundred men who otherwise would be unemployed?

The problem remains that no matter what we do, it is almost inevitable that the number of people arriving in cities will continue to exceed our abilities to employ them. This, I think, is a problem that we have to face. There is no effective way known, there are no social or economic mechanisms for controlling or stopping migration. We can try to divert some of the immigrants. We may be able to reduce their numbers. But in general we have no way of keeping people from coming to the cities.

F.P.H.   In your article, "Urbanization Problems and Prospect" in *Finance and Development,*[1] you suggest some approaches to controlling urbanization or improving the present haphazard urban growth. One suggestion is to establish some alternate growth poles to keep people from all migrating into the same city. The other is to improve the allocation of resources, with the objective to create better services and to achieve maximum efficiency of urban space, that is, better land-use patterns to reduce costs of infrastructure.

The idea of establishing alternate-growth poles in terms of locating new economic enterprise in smaller towns in the region of the large cities to reduce immigration to the capital or primate city, has been widely used in a number of regional development plans. For instance, Bombay and New Delhi and Madras in India have such regional plans. Teheran recently made such a plan; Cairo years ago started such a plan and is continuing to implement it in Nassar City. Singapore is implementing such a plan, and so are several South American cities, especially Caracas. Venezuela has a national plan for coordinated urban growth.

But in fact, or in terms of stemming immigration into these cities, I would say these plans are total failures: because immigration is as great as before, or even greater—though of course there are many other advantages to having a plan or some means of rationally directing growth.

Perhaps here we should mention that one method—by far the most effective one long range—is population control. Without effective population control, or rather with continuing population growth rates at around 3 per cent, the hope for improved economic and living conditions for that many more people fades. I mentioned in the introduction effective population control must be the goal of every government that hopes to improve the life of its citizens or

---

[1] A publication of the International Monetary Fund and the World Bank group.

generate enough economic growth so that people can support themselves. Population control and urbanization are linked historically, and hopefully this will become effective also in the developing countries. Population control really is the *sine qua non* if you are concerned with effective economic development or controlled urbanization.

R.M.W.   With excessive population growth rates, no amount of resource creation that we can feasibly imagine can be sufficient to absorb the increasing standards of living of all the people who will be coming into the world and therefore into urban areas. So population control remains the pre-condition of much of what we are talking about and will determine to a large extent how the future will look in the developing world. I don't think the situation is entirely bleak. History has shown populations have responded to resource constraints, to the social conditions of overcrowding, and I think with the techniques we now have, together with those pressures, we have some hope.

Certainly none of the measures to reduce immigration can succeed in the long run under ever-increasing population pressures. The establishment of alternate-growth poles which produce less growth than the main cities means the nation has given up something. There are natural economic forces with which you have to contend, and if they are violated, you pay for it in terms of reduced growth, reduced creation of resources which are needed to feed, house, and provide health services. For example, the challenge in Caracas, as elsewhere, is to find alternatives in and around the core region to keep people out of the main city, which usually is already too large and difficult to manage. One of the solutions frequently is to develop satellite cities in the region of the capital or to make regional development plans. On the other hand, the creation of new centers in areas with limited growth potential will not divert migration and will be quite costly.

Now to the question which we touched on earlier. What to do about cities? We have limited resources for development; therefore, we have to use these resources economically. We know that cities are going to contine to grow. It may be 5 per cent a year, or 7, or 8. We know from all projections that there is no way to stop the growth, particularly of the large cities. Why don't we look ahead and plan the use of land which will have to be urbanized, plan the infrastructure, and plan the location of facilities in the most economic way? Cities now are growing incrementally without any relationship between the various functions they perform. The public authorities have to provide the services after the demand for them has arisen. Why not plan ahead to make sure people and industry move where they can be efficiently served and where transportation facilities exist?

There are other questions related to planning for cities in an economic way.

In most of economic development the decisions are made at the central level. Most developing countries have national economic development plans. These plans have very often failed to take account of economic land-use factors which make cities essentially the crucible where development takes place. Investments are allocated without much regard for location constraints because they are not well understood by economists concerned with national development plans. Decision makers and central planners must be made aware of the role of cities in the economic and social development of the nation.

Within the cities themselves, looking at the administrations, what can be done about growth? The administrations of these cities need to be reformed drastically. There is no sense trying to manage a city of seven million people with an administration designed for ten thousand, a situation which is common in many of the former colonial or medieval capitals in Asia and Africa, and even to some extent, Latin America. Administration, in other words, management, is a very critical factor. I don't mean centralized municipal governments which control every function. I do mean an administration which at least is able to coordinate vital functions and decisions. Investment planning, for example, has to be coordinated, as do such general services as water, sewerage, telephone, and police. The planning of roads, the planning of housing, and industrial estates, have to be related.

Cities cry continuously for money to finance their growth and their needed facilities. This money is really necessary if the cities are to perform their role as engines of economic development. If the cities don't grow, the nation won't grow. The cities generally contribute more than they receive, since they are the primary sources of incomes and taxes in each country. Yet often you find that the cities are undercollecting taxes and making inefficient use of their resources. They are not doing a good job with their own money and with their own budgeting. I think this can be corrected from within the cities. It is a solution which is in the hands of the existing governments.

F.P.H.   You pointed out the lack of attention that is being given to spatial location of facilities and investments in the national economic development plans of most developing countries. Yet most of the cities in these countries have physical development plans which are rarely coordinated with economic development and usually entirely ignored. The physical development plans of cities and regions, particularly in terms of land use and location of the economic development, should work hand in hand with the economic plans for most efficient use of resources. The economic-development plans of many developing countries are reasonably effective documents, establishing goals and also means to reach those goals. However, they have by and large neglected any kind of provision for the physical location of the planned facilities and investments or any planned land use which is needed for the most economic use of resources. Furthermore, social development has been entirely neglected, both by physical and economic planners. In fact, what is needed are comprehensive plans.

Planning of urbanization of new land has also been neglected, as you point out. Services are provided in hindsight in the most inefficient manner virtually by political pressure on the part of the immigrants. Instead of growing by rationally planned, coordinated location-development policies, cities grow piecemeal, by the decisions of individual squatters who settle wherever they can find a suitable piece of land. In turn, industrial location takes place according to what each industry considers best for itself, while services often are supplied after the fact and after political pressure is applied. These development patterns obviously make no sense from an economic or any other point of view.

Yet land values, which I believe are a most important economic factor, are so far entirely neglected. Land value, or the cost of the land, increases manyfold through urbanization. That is, agricultural or rural land is worth a fraction of urbanized land: by providing infrastructure and services, that is, building roads, a water supply, sewers, electricity, etc., a piece of land multiplies its value in the market place. This economic fact has been neglected as a source for public income, because land is mostly in private hands. The city, though it provides the services and pays for the road building and urbanization, cannot make good on those investments, while private land speculators make enormous profits.

In developing countries, due to population pressures and rapid growth, land values are increasing very rapidly, and cities could finance a major part of urbanization costs from valorization or the increased values of the land. Often the decisions where to locate a new road or build infrastructure are made with political pressure by the land owners in the vicinity who reap enormous profits from these public decisions, while the majority of the people are unable to get basic services or even a piped water supply.

In Seoul, Korea, for instance, the ratio between building and land is 1:10, or the land is on the average worth ten times more than the buildings built upon it. This ratio is the opposite of land values in the developed countries, which in turn is due to the enormously rapid growth of Seoul, as well as inflation and population pressures.

A recent mayor of Seoul, in order to increase his very inadequate city budget, developed the following land-development scheme. He got the approval of the majority of a group of contiguous land owners on the outskirts of the city and took, with their consent, 35 per cent of their land holdings. The owners were more than compensated by the increased value of their land, while the city built roads and intensively developed the 35 per cent of property they had acquired. After building roads, schools, public facilities, and infrastructure, about 6 to 8 per cent of the original 35 per cent of the land appropriated by the city was left, which was sold to the highest bidder. While the raw land had served as collateral for the city to borrow enough to pay for development, the profit of the sale of the urbanized land not only enabled the city to pay back all the loans, but in fact to add large sums to the meager city budget.

Similar development programs could of course be carried out in most cities of developing countries. For instance, there is a development plan for a satellite town of Bangkok that is financed by a similar principle. Valorization could be a most useful development tool for cities everywhere. Unfortunately, land speculation and large private land interests have prevented most land development in the public interest. But in fact valorization could finance most urbanization and city services and could materially contribute to the solution of the urban problems in developing countries and especially help in settling urban immigrants.

The same principles apply of course to the developed world, particularly as far as new towns or satellite towns or the development of new areas are concerned. The first generation of new towns in Great Britain are built on this same principle. All land acquisition, infrastructure, and services were publicly financed. Due to the fact that the land is being held by the new town corporations, which are public agencies, now, twenty years later, all the new towns are financially solvent economic enterprises. This despite enormous front-load investmentw which were all publicly financed.

R.M.W.   What you describe is to a large extent a neglected area of potential resource mobilization for urban growth. It relates very much to what I said about the necessity for land-use planning before the land comes under urban use. The public authorities themselves can determine and to a certain extent are responsible for land value increases. If, for instance, you build a road to an otherwise unoccupied land area near a city, the land will go up in value because it now has access to other uses. It is well known that the land costs near subway stops built by public authorities go up more rapidly in value than land which is not so served. Consequently, there is an increase in value which can be predicted when building urban public services and when the city has control over its future pattern of growth. These increases of value can be acquired by the public authorities for further development of the city. The authority can either acquire ownership of the land or a proportion of the increased value, which may be through the tax mechanisms. This is an area which ought to be looked at very carefully.

In India, a similar proposal was made and was put into effect last year. A national agency of the Ministry of Housing was organized and given a certain amount of money. With this capital, they help cities acquire land to be used in the next step of urbanization. This land then is developed by local authorities in conjunction with the central authority, by putting in water, sewers, roads, and other services. Then the land is sold to the various users, to industries, for example. Provision is also made for low-income housing. The increased value so obtained then is used to develop the next piece of land, and so on. This makes eminently good sense. The public authority then becomes a partner or the main agent of land development. The private sector makes use of the developed land and pays for the increased value of the land after it has been developed. Perhaps the Indian scheme is too vast. It cannot possibly be carried out on the entire sub-continent, given the limited resources available to the government and the vast sums which would be needed to buy up all land lying close to growing cities. But in principle it makes sense to buy land in the path of urbanization or tax it in some appropriate manner. This is one way in which we can make the course of urbanization manageable.

It is often said that housing cannot be built because of the cost of land. For instance, if a public authority builds a housing development on unimproved land, all the surrounding land acquires the value of the developed land immediately. As a result a second housing development has to go further out. You keep leapfrogging. To avoid this, it seems to me you need a much more comprehensive approach to land development and to land planning and therefore to city and urban planning.

As for the point you raised about the physical planner and the economist: better communication and coordination between them is needed. It is very clear that physical planners rarely think about economic constraints and potential. They are thinking in terms of the physical location, the esthetic appeal, and the relationship between physical functions. The economists, on the other hand, tend to ignore the fact that the location in itself is a critical economic variable and the physical placement of facilities, buildings, and roads is an important economic factor.

F.P.H.   We have touched on many problems here pertaining to urbanization and urban development in relation to economic development. We have discussed numerous problems and some solutions. Can you give us some examples of problems that international agencies are concerned with?

R.M.W.   I cannot of course speak officially for the World Bank. But I can say that the problems of urbanization have come to our attention. In fact, they have occupied a good deal of staff time and management time, particularly in the last couple of years. Progress is difficult at best because of the very complex nature of the issues discussed. They reach into social problems about which agencies, such as a Development Bank, are relatively inexperienced. However, there is a tremendous amount of interest in doing more.

At present, for example, we are looking very carefully, with a view to possible ultimate financing, into a scheme in Dakar which would resettle people who are now living in squatter shanty towns outside the main city. The land would be laid out with water, sewers, schools, and roads, on which squatters could build their own dwellings with what savings they have and can generate. The public authorities in Senegal cannot afford to provide any housing, and the way the squatters are living now is chaotic and completely unacceptable from a social point of view.

This solution is one to which people in other areas have responded very well. It gives people the opportunity to own land which in turn provides the incentive to build and invest their limited savings in better housing which they themselves then own and occupy. I have seen in Dakar an early version of this scheme which has worked very well.

In other areas, international agencies such as the World Bank are looking at mass transportation systems to see how and what we might do to make the growth and operation of some of the major cities of the less developed world more efficient. There is a considerable amount of money continuing to go into water and sewer works, which are essential public services. I would say that in the future much more attention will be given to the urban impacts of these investments to see that they are made in relation to a plan for the whole urban area which takes into account the requirements of a growing economy, as well as the social needs of a growing population.

F.P.H.   Several United Nations agencies have done a great deal in terms of extending technical aid to various developing countries under the UNDP (United States Development Program).

R.M.W.   The UNDP also finances institution building and studies which tell us a good deal about what needs to be done. They also do what we might call pre-investment planning. The World Bank works closely with them in devising and executing studies in urban areas, as well as other aspects of development. The UN Centre for Housing, Building and Planning does a good deal in the way of technical assistance with respect to such studies and assisting countries with their urban problems. The Organization of American States has an extensive program in Latin America of technical aid for education for people who work in urban areas. Then the Interamerican Development Bank has had an active interest in urban development problems in Latin America and is moving now from what was formerly an exclusive concern with housing into the field of wider urban development and planning.

F.P.H.   Finally, from all of what we have said, what do you think about the future in terms of the problems we discussed? Do you think there is some hope that in the future at least some solutions can be found for the many difficult problems and dilemmas of the cities in the developing world? Many observers and professionals with long experience, for instance, Dr. Gunnar Myrdal, an authority in economic and social development, are very pessimistic. I must admit my own direct experience worldwide does not permit me to take a very optimistic view, especially concerning the continued population growth.

R.M.W.   The future, I think, is not entirely hopeless, but as I first said there is a dilemma. For some time to come we will have far more people in the cities than can easily be accommodated. Yet there is hope through better management, through better use of our resources, that we can do a better job for people. Next, the rates of economic development themselves can be kept at high levels, high enough to provide the resources to give people the kinds of standards of living they aspire to. I think this is a function both of international agencies, but mainly of the countries themselves; they must plan their own futures and carry out these plans.

Finally, this must be said again: with excessive population growth rates, all economic plans are doomed to failure. Effective population control is really the pre-condition for the changes we have discussed.

F.P.H.   Thank you, Mr. Westebbe.

BIBLIOGRAPHY

Westebbe, Richard M. *The Economy of Mauritania.* New York: Praeger Publishers, 1971.

———. "Urbanization Problems and Prospects." *Finance and Development* Quarterly). A Publication of the International Monetary Fund and the World Bank Group. (Volume 4), 1970, pp. 44 ff.

———, and Wingo, Lowden. *The Use of Cities in Economic Development.* (In preparation.) Sponsored by Resources for the Future. Publication date, 1973.

BOOKS

Abrams, Charles. *Man's Struggle for Shelter.* Cambridge, Mass.: The MIT Press, 1966.

Hosken, Fran P. "Urban Development and Housing in Asia." Unpublished report, 1970. (Available at MIT Roach Library and Harvard Graduate School of Design library.)

Lewis, David, ed. *The Growth of Cities.* London: Paul Elek, 1971.

Meier, Richard L. *Developmental Planning.* New York: McGraw-Hill Book Co., 1965. Myrdal, Gunnar. *Asian Drama.* New York: Pantheon Books, A Division of Random House, 1970.

Myrdal, Gunnar. *Asian Drama.* New York: Pantheon Books, A Division of Random House, 1968.

―――. *The Challenge of World Poverty: A World Anti-Poverty Program in Outline.* New York: Pantheon Books, a Division of Random House, 1970.

Pearson, Lester B. *Partners in Development: Report of the Commission on International Development.* New York: Praeger Publishers, 1970.

Rodwin, Lloyd. *Planning Urban Growth and Regional Development.* Cambridge, Mass.: The MIT Press, 1969.

Turnham, David, *The Employment Problem in Less Developed Countries: A Review of the Evidence.* Paris: Development Centre of the Organization for Economic Co-Operation and Development, 1971.

"Urbanization: Development Policies and Planning." *International Social Development Review* (No. 1). New York: United Nations, 1968.

Ward, Barbara. *The Rich Nations and the Poor Nations.* New York: W.W. Norton & Company, Inc., 1962.

PAMPHLETS

Interamerican Development Bank, 1118 Sarmiento, Buenos Aires, Argentina. Write for information on South American countries.

United Nations Information Services, ECAFE, Sala Santitham, Bangkok, Thailand. Write for information on Asian countries.

UN Publications, United Nations, Sales Section, New York, N. Y. 10017. Write for general information, worldwide.

World Bank, 1818 H Street, N. W., Washington, D. C. 20437. Write for Annual Reports, especially 1970 report, "Urbanization," pp. 57-63.

ARTICLES

Hosken, Fran P. "Too Many People Too Fast." *St. Louis Post-Dispatch,* January 18, 1970.

17

URBANIZATION AND HOUSING
IN DEVELOPING COUNTRIES

A discussion with JOHN F. C. TURNER
Association of NETWORK, Cambridge; Lecturer, Department of
Urban Studies and Planning, Massachusetts Institute of Technology

INTRODUCTION

Urbanization, the move of rural populations into the cities, is seen as one of the critical international phenomena of our time. This immigration, added to the already rapid natural increase of the urban populations, is doubling many cities' inhabitants about every fifteen years.

The populations of all developing countries have been rapidly growing due to improved health conditions. Rural-urban migration is inevitable in countries with rapid population growth rates and limited areas of agricultural land. Mechanization of agriculture further increases migration to the cities by reducing the need for agricultural labor. While improved agricultural methods and miracle seeds, "the Green revolution," are very much needed for improvement of agricultural yields, they often contribute to more people leaving the land, as their work no longer is needed.

Industrial prices have increased all over the world since World War II. But agricultural prices and wages have been decreasing. This substantially supports the move into cities, especially in developing countries which have large rural populations. Better communication and transportation and the hope for a better life have motivated large numbers of peasants all over the world to leave their hard, isolated village life and the land which often cannot support them. By comparison, life in the city, though beset with many problems, seems to many urban immigrants better than what they left behind.

Social change, the dissolution of a rigid class society and of the traditional family patterns, is the result of urbanization: but it also results in the loss of the only social security most people have. While in the past the scattered peasants were easily controlled by the landlords, who virtually owned them, the urban inhabitants, who live closely together, can organize political action for joint demands. Upward mobility and social change, especially for young people, is one of the promises of urban life.

The usual young urban immigrant first tries to live with relatives or friends or anyone he knows in the city center, close to the jobs and the central markets where food is cheap. Often groups of squatters occupy any available space in the city and build squatter huts from scraps, old tin cans, cardboard boxes, sticks, rush mats, or anything they can find. Many inner-city squatter settlements are built on valuable land and are densely inhabited by large numbers of people who spend little effort improving their miserable shacks, as they may be driven off the illegally occupied plots at any time.

Once the initial squatter immigrants find some sort of employment, their families usually follow them, and they need more room. They build on the outskirts of the cities dispersed settlements of one-story houses, much like their villages at home. In time, if some of the family members succeed in finding some regular employment, the houses are improved by the inhabitants and are rebuilt with more permanent materials.

These sprawling squatter settlements on the outskirts of many cities and towns, though growing steadily, are built entirely without any plans; they frequently lack viable access streets and have no transportation. Many of them are fire hazards and frequently burn down. To supply services to these squatter areas is often difficult as they have very poor roads. Many squatter settlements on the outskirts of the cities are becoming larger than the city itself, for instance, in Lima, Peru. Though the land is often illegally occupied by the immigrants, the numbers of squatters are so large that it is politically unfeasible to remove them, especially in many cities in Latin America. Where squatters continue to occupy publicly-owned land and are able to obtain water, roads, and other public services through political action, they begin to improve their shacks, and some are able to gradually build better houses.

In some cities, squatters are ruthlessly driven out by police, and their huts are burned down, as in Taipei, Manila, or Rio de Janeiro. Djakarta tried to "forbid" all urban immigration—with little success.

Other city governments have recently started to settle squatters on urbanized plots of city-owned land. That is, the city builds roads and provides services such as water, sewers, and electricity to urbanize rural or undeveloped land to permanently settle immigrants. The immigrants are encouraged with technical help and credit to build better houses, and they are given legal title to their plots. Surrounding Brasilia, the new capital of Brazil, large areas are being urbanized for immigrants who build their own houses on plots of land subdivided according to plan. Similar programs can be found in Venezuela, Chile, and also in some Indian cities, especially New Delhi, where a vast resettlement program has been initiated recently with most squatters building their own houses with technical help.

During the last ten years, Hong Kong resettled most of its two million Chinese refugees into huge, fireproof, concrete, highrise buildings, after a terrible fire that wiped out one of the largest squatter settlements. There simply is no room on the very limited land areas surrounding the harbor of Hong Kong to settle the two-million immigrants any other way. Singapore has made the building of housing the first priority of the government. This policy has greatly increased the standard of living, created many thousands of jobs, and supports the social stability and economic well-being of all the people of Singapore.

DISCUSSION

F.P.H.   Urbanization is in progress in all cities in developing countries. New settlement patterns are spontaneously developing in many areas with quite a different social and economic base from the traditional city. These urbanization patterns probably are the key to the future of all developing countries, as the cities are growing very rapidly and producing most of the economic growth.

J.F.C.T.   Yes, the world is often referred to as an urbanizing world. As you said, urbanization is essentially the transfer of people from rural and farming areas into the city. But of course it is not just a geographic phenomenon; it is an economic, social, and political phenomenon as well. In fact, some of the most urbanized countries in the world are not what we would call the most urban in the physical sense. Argentina and Uruguay, for instance, are much more highly urbanized geographically than either Sweden or the United States. Among these Latin American countries, 70 to 80 per cent of the people live in the largest cities. However, one could not say that Argentina is more urban than the United States socially or economically speaking. Probably most of the farmers and people in the small towns in the United States are in fact very urban in the political and cultural sense.

F.P.H.   It depends, as you say, entirely on what one considers urban. In this country we consider the sometimes very dispersed living patterns of the suburbs "urban," simply because suburbanites don't derive their livelihood from farming, even if they live outside the city. Due to mechanization of agricultural production, fewer and fewer people live on farms as farmers, and this is where we must draw the distinction.

The other problem that speeds urban growth in all developing countries is the natural population increase. Together with immigration this increases the population of the cities entirely out of proportion. In most of South America and the Near East and in most of Southeast Asia, the natural population growth is about 3 per cent. That means that the populations double in less than twenty-five years.

The immigration patterns, of course, are different from one city to another. But certainly the largest immigration is in the largest cities, particularly in the capitals where the total growth, that is, immigration plus natural increase, is sometimes as high as 8 to 10 per cent.

The largest cities are not only the largest population centers, but they offer the most jobs. Work or opportunities for a better life is what attract the people from the land, so that immigration in one sense is really an economic proposition.

J.F.C.T.　It is very important to note the differences between different countries. There is an enormous difference, for instance, between countries like Bolivia and Peru. Bolivia is still a rural country where a small proportion of the population lives in towns and the national population growth rate is relatively slow.

Contrast this with a country like Peru, its neighbor, whose population is growing twice as fast, and which has a much higher proportion of its population in towns and cities. Naturally, there is a much higher rate of movement away from the countryside, which is becoming rapidly over-populated in relation to its capacity to hold people and give them employment. This surplus population really has no alternative. Sooner or later these people must move to the major cities, or to the cities where they have the best opportunity of getting jobs. Usually, the larger the city the better the opportunity; therefore, more people go to the largest cities.

F.P.H.　In the U.A.R., or Egypt, the land problem that you mention is acute, as only so much land can be irrigated. Even with the new dams of the Nile, which increase the water supply, the acreage per person is now less than it was some thirty or forty years ago because of the population growth. The people have absolutely no alternative but to move into the cities, mainly Cairo and Alexandria. But there are many more immigrants than regular jobs.

One of the main problems in all developing countries, certainly, is the economic growth rate, which simply does not keep up with the population growth rate. On top of this, most people want to improve their way of life. Consequently, the rate of economic growth should be considerably greater than the rate of population increase. To make any visible improvement it should be at least double and, of course, be broadly distributed. Both of these conditions are hard to meet.

The percentage of the younger population is far too great, and children are unable to earn. In many countries half the population is under fifteen. That means each wage earner has to provide for many extra people, in the face of the fact that it is extremely hard to get and hold regularly-paying jobs. Underemployment or unemployment is rampant in all cities in developing countries. I think this is one of the fundamental problems; it is a structural problem of the economy of all developing countries. The question is how to deal with the people who are moving into the cities if they cannot find jobs.

J.F.C.T.   I think one has to be careful about seeing urbanization itself as a problem. Because if you look at it from the point of view of the people who live through this process—and it is a very large number of people in many cities—they are better off than before when living in the countryside or the small towns.

For instance, in Lima, Peru, about two out of every three adults were born in small towns or villages, and most of their grandparents were born in villages or rural areas. From their point of view, they are better off than they were before. There are many studies to support this. For surveys that ask, "Would you rather go home to your town or village?," the answer is almost always, "No, I am better off here in the city."

In fact, the people are appreciably better off than they would have been if they had stayed in the country. They do have more opportunities in the bigger cities despite the unemployment problems or the under-employment. In Peru, for instance, about two-thirds of the people who migrated in the 1940's and 1950's had made quite considerable advances by the late 1960's, even though the economic growth rate barely kept pace with the population growth rate.

This can be explained by the fact that average working-class incomes are generally three or four times higher in the cities than in the country, and that enough of the newly-acquired national wealth is distributed to this sector for it to absorb much of the growing population. Those who migrate from the poorer countryside or small towns or who are born to families at the lowest income levels, may move up, therefore, from lower and poorer levels of living. The median income may not change but, as long as the newcomers are poorer and as long as the people with average incomes grow faster, there will be a fair amount of upward mobility in the cities.

F.P.H.   These facts show why people in the cities prefer to be there. In the country, they have been poor for generations and nobody has paid any attention to it. Probably the fact that in the city you see the poverty provides an incentive towards improvement of the living conditions.

Again, conditions vary very much from city to city. For instance, Sao Paulo in Brazil was, and continues to be, built largely by immigrants. Though it is growing faster than any other major city in South America—it is adding something like 300,000 people per year—it is also able to provide an extraordinary number of jobs. The first job that an unskilled immigrant can find is often in the building industry. The immigrant learns new skills in the building trades and becomes acceptable for industrial employment and better-paid work. A good deal of the industrial production of the whole country is located in and around Sao Paulo, and so there is a ladder of improvement available for its immigrants.

It is extraordinary that in a space of a few years people coming from a very primitive rural environment move into the city and begin to do relatively well. Despite the fact that there is a constant stream of newcomers all the time, they get absorbed into the economy at a very high rate. But I think that Sao Paulo is probably not characteristic of most cities in developing countries.

J.F.C.T.   Certainly it is one of the most fortunate. There are only a few other towns like it. For instance, Seoul, Korea. Seoul has an economic-growth rate which is in fact double the population-growth rate. The gross city product is growing at about 15 per cent per year, which is nearly twice the city population-growth rate. As in Sao Paulo, people establish themselves as modern citizens remarkably quickly.

Squatter settlements in Seoul are of a high standard. Immigrants will build in a very short period of time one- or two-room houses. They are substantially built with walls of brick or block, and with tiled roofs, which the people need, as their climate is very harsh. These are the equivalent of the tar-paper shacks or the straw shacks that you find in a city like Lima, which has a much slower economic growth rate.

It is quite important to note that there are no major cities in the world where the growth rate and the opportunities are not appreciably better than in the countryside. Even in Calcutta, where the most deplorable living conditions exist, people who have the option of returning home to the villages don't go. They go home once a year to see their families, but there is no way for them to earn a living in the countryside. They have to stay in the city, where though the physical conditions are terrible, they can at least earn a living for themselves and their dependents.

F.P.H.   India is another country where the land is running out in proportion to the number of people. There is just not enough agricultural land available; yet the population continues to grow.

I also would like to stress that all developing countries are different. For instance, we cannot lump together the countries of Southeast Asia or South America, or of any given area. Each country has reached a different stage of development in terms of industrialization and job creation, and they offer different kinds of jobs. The climate frequently makes a major difference and materially affects the housing situation or the ability of immigrants to build their own shelters.

Sao Paulo, which I mentioned before, is largely built by immigrants, who frequently find their first jobs in building which uses unskilled labor. In Brazil, the government provides a great deal of money to build housing. In order to create jobs, the government supports public programs, such as road building, housing, the building of much needed infrastructure, and services, which can be built by unskilled workers.

But, each country has a unique population base and a different demographic situation, its own history, and specific, often-changing political institutions. A city may already be capital-intensive in its economic development or may still be labor-intensive. In many developing countries, machinery is beginning to replace people, while there are still millions of people looking for unskilled jobs. This is another great problem for the unskilled immigrant. Instead of providing more jobs for the immigrant to the city, many industries import machinery that costs the country a great deal of capital and foreign exchange. It is often cheaper for an industrial enterprise to mechanize than to train workers.

J.F.C.T.   Loughlin Currie, in a book called *Accelerating Development,*[1] makes the very plausible argument that a basis for a viable development policy would be to employ the urban immigrants to build what they themselves need. However, there are some difficulties that I don't think Currie faces up to, and which I hear the government of Brazil is facing now. The first problem is that governments of developing countries simply don't have enough capital. They don't have the money to build housing or finance infrastructure on a significant scale.

Brazil is now building a very large number of housing units, but it is also a very large country. It has a rapidly growing population of ninety million people. The housing they build is financed through social security deposits. Every registered worker in Brazil deposits 4 per cent of his salary, and his employer is required to deposit a matching amount of 4 per cent to a national housing bank, which uses that money for building housing for lower-income people. Brazil is building a great deal as a result. The problem is that they are not getting their money back. In many projects, some of which I visited myself, at least 60 per cent of the beneficiaries or tenants of the houses were delinquent in their payments. So, much of this money is not being returned. If this goes on, one can imagine that in fifteen or twenty years, when the workers want to retire on their social security payments, there is not going to be any money.

Another case is that of Colombia. In the recent past, the government of Colombia has spent much more of the national budget on housing than

[1] Loughlin Currie, *Accelerating Development* (New York: McGraw-Hill, 1966).

economists generally regard to be wise. But they have not even been able to stabilize the housing deficit. That is, there is a greater shortage of dwelling units now, even though much housing was built, than when the building programs were started.

F.P.H.   It has been said by both economists and housing experts that housing is a luxury that a developing country cannot afford. However, as you mentioned in the case of Brazil and other South American countries housing is being used by governments as a means of creating employment. Of course, the fact that people may become delinquent in their rent or mortgage payments has not been considered.

On the other hand, don't you expect that if the people manage to improve themselves and earn enough, they will eventually keep up with their payments, and that there is some hope that this program will succeed over time when the economic situation of the immigrants improves. I see in building housing the beginning of a positive economic cycle for the immigrants. That is, if the government provides the first job and initial income, the immigrant will continue to improve himself.

J.F.C.T.   Well, perhaps if Loughlin Currie's ideas were carried out, and a much higher proportion of all the people in the city were employed in building, the principle might work. At the moment, only about 20 per cent of the blue-collar labor force in a typical city of a rapidly urbanizing country is employed in construction. In other words, if the employment could be more permanent, and the wages earned would be high enough so that the workers could pay their rent, then, theoretically, this could be a solution. But it has not been proven in practice.

What actually happens, in Brazil for instance, is that a great majority of the recipients or beneficiaries of the houses or housing simply cannot afford to pay. They are not delinquent because they don't want to pay, but because the houses that are built for them are very far out on the periphery of town and a great distance from their jobs. Consequently, they have to spend a lot of their income on commuting and much time and energy as well. Their wives cannot get any secondary jobs such as laundry or domestic service, because they cannot afford to commute or leave the children. So, while their new homes cost them much more than their old inner-city homes, which were often squatter shacks, they earn less and they simply don't have enough left over to pay for the rent or for the mortgage payments on the house.

This is a universal phenomenon and is not peculiar to Brazil. It also happens in Chile, in Pakistan, and in the Philippines and in many other countries. Nevertheless, it is absurd to say that people must have jobs before housing. Nobody can live without some kind of shelter.

F.P.H.   You mentioned that a government of a developing country should not spend its money on building housing; rather, that the people should be encouraged or helped to build the housing themselves. There are many different programs, particularly in South America, that have encouraged low-income people to build their own housing by providing technical help and services. The government is building the needed infrastructure of urbanization and makes available lots or urbanized land where people can build their own houses.

J.F.C.T.   Yes, this is a very much more sensible approach. There are two sides to it. First of all, people should be provided with land and services, that is, basic utilities such as electricity, water, and so on, technical assistance, and, perhaps, some credit. This is not only a way of capitalizing on the efforts that people will make for themselves, but it also indicates a rather more realistic definition of what housing is. One problem is that the international agencies and also national governments generally concentrate their attention on the actual structure of the house.

It is not only the house, but everything that goes along with it, that makes family life possible. There are the schools, transportation to work, shopping, health facilities, and the like. In tropical and sub-tropical climates—and the great majority of the countries we are talking about are in those climates—the actual structure of a house is not so important. Even a shack or a half-built house can be used as long as the density is not too high, and the family has a decent plot of land with water, as long as the sidewalks and main roads are paved so pedestrians and buses don't get bogged down in the mud.

Public utilities and community facilities are much cheaper on a per capita basis than housing units. The government can serve many more people with these greatly needed services, and this is a very much more practical approach. Governments can make a really substantial contribution to the housing problem by providing the infrastructure that the people cannot provide for themselves.

F.P.H.   That is, the governments should concentrate on providing the public services, roads, and community facilities, and give each family a piece of land on which to build their own house.

I understand that you spent about eight years in Peru, mainly Lima, and also a good deal of time in Colombia to study the sociology of squatter settlements, and how they grow. It would be very interesting to hear your views.

J.F.C.T.   This is very difficult to summarize in a few words. First, you cannot generalize about squatter settlements. In some areas, what one might call "the bleeding-heart view" of the squatter settlements is fully justified. But you could be completely wrong if you are referring to other settlements. Take the squatter settlements in the city of Lima, which I know very well. There you get the full range. There are some shanty towns that are almost as poor as the bustees in Calcutta. But other squatter settlements are much more like some of the lower-middle-class suburban neighborhoods of Lima.

There are some reasonably well-built squatter settlements on the outskirts of Lima. They are built by the ex-migrants who have steady jobs and who move out from the tenements or the inner-city shanty towns to a reasonable plot on the edge of the city. Over time, that squatter and his family will build quite a good house.

F.P.H.   You described the spontaneous improvements that go on in many squatter settlements, particularly in Lima. Again, I should think this is not a universal pattern and, as you mentioned first, that conditions differ from one settlement to another. The question is: Why do the people in one settlement have the strength, the capacity, and the ability to improve their environment and create some kind of community life, while others don't?

J.F.C.T.   Perhaps we should reframe that question. There are enormous differences between the poor and the very poor. The inner-city shanty towns, along with a lot of the very overcrowded tenements in the central areas, house the poorest of the poor—those who cannot afford to spend time and money commuting to the edge of the city, or who can't find a regular job. These, when they are not working, have to be in the city looking for work. They cannot afford to live on the periphery.

Now, those who no longer are the very poorest, but who have more or less regular jobs and a small savings margin, can afford to commute, since public transport in the kind of cities we are talking about is usually very cheap. These are the people who create the large self-improving squatter settlements you very often find in the outlying suburbs, the *barriadas* of Lima or the *gecekondu* of Ankara.

The solution we are talking about just now, the sites-and-services solution, may be very applicable to the squatter of the self-improving type, the suburban squatter. But it would be quite inappropriate for the very poorest people, who don't have steady jobs. If you give them a plot of land and services out on the edge of the city they simply will not be able to find a better job or get themselves out of the poverty situation. They may be better off in a shanty or a shack in the central city than in the improved housing on the edge of town. Location is a very important factor, which a lot of housing agencies and housing policy-makers in these countries fail to recognize.

F.P.H.   One solution that has been much discussed is that the villages and small towns where the immigrants originally lived should be improved, in order to discourage emigration. Do you believe this is a possibility?

J.F.C.T.   No. That point of view I find impossible to support. The facts of population growth point to the impracticality of rural development as a way of preventing migration. Unless you have the kind of situation that existed in the United States in the nineteenth century with a rapidly expanding frontier, where all the newcomers could become homesteaders and would have land. This does not occur in a great majority of developing countries, where the land is already overpopulated, and there are, with few exceptions, no frontiers that could possibly absorb the new and growing population.

F.P.H.   You mentioned that you have advised some U.S.-based agencies. There are a number of housing programs in South America, sponsored by the Inter-American Development Bank and U.S.A.I.D., mainly housing-investment programs. Do you think they are at all effective?

J.F.C.T.   These housing programs are not effective for low-income people. If we are talking about housing programs for middle-income people, particularly those programs that are based on the development of savings and loan associations, then I think they are effective, and that they do a good job as long as they support small and labor-intensive construction firms and technologies. These middle-income housing programs cannot solve the problems we have discussed, and there is always the danger that, as in the U.S.A., they are subsidized at the expense of the poor.

F.P.H.   What do you think about the future of the urbanizing, developing world? Considering the population increases that we discussed before, the scarcity of jobs, the continuing immigration to the cities, what should we expect?
    The initial move to the city is a great improvement for every family. But after they are there for a while, what then? With electronic communication, people quickly learn about urban living and they want to continue to improve their lives rapidly. Living at great densities is often said to be a strain on the immigrant, and, if the opportunities for improvement are lacking, this may provide a basis for political upheaval.

J.F.C.T.   Clearly, if the economic development and industrialization does not continue to increase and keep ahead of population growth, then, indeed, the outlook is bad. But urbanization, the actual fact of concentrating people in the cities and especially the large cities in the poorest countries, may be an essential step toward stimulating industrialization. There also is a high correlation between falling birth rates and rising urbanization. Therefore, urbanization does three things: it helps to keep the birth rate down, it helps to stimulate industry, and, very importantly, it is the essential means for democratization of what often was a feudal or colonial society.

F.P.H.   Thank you, Mr. Turner.

BIBLIOGRAPHY

BOOKS

Abrams, Charles. *Man's Struggle for Shelter.* Cambridge, Mass.: The MIT Press, 1966.

Breeze, Gerald. *The City in the Newly Developing Countries.* London: Prentice-Hall, 1969.

Currie, Loughlin. *Accelerating Development.* New York: McGraw-Hill Book Company, Inc., 1966.

"Improvement of Slums and Uncontrolled Settlements: Report of the International Seminar on the Improvement of Slums and Uncontrolled Settlements." New York: United Nations, 1971.

Lewis, David, ed. *The Growth of Cities.* London: Paul Elek, 1971.

Mangin, William P. *Peasants in Cities.* Boston: Houghton-Mifflin, 1970.

Oliver, Paul, ed. *Shelter and Society.* New York: Frederick A. Praeger; London: Cresset Press, 1969.

Peattie, Lisa Redfield. *The View from the Barrio.* Ann Arbor, Mich.: University of Michigan Press, 1968.

Rodwin, Lloyd, ed. *Planning Urban Growth and Regional Development.* Cambridge, Mass.: The MIT Press, 1969.

"Urbanization: Development Policies and Planning." *United Nations International Social Development Review 1.*

PAMPHLETS

Interamerican Development Bank, 1118 Sarmiento, Buenos Aires, Argentina. Write for information on South America.

UN Information Services, ECAFE, Sala Santitham, Bangkok, Thailand. Write for information on Asia.

UN Publications, United Nations, Sales Section, New York, N.Y. 10017. Write for general information, worldwide.

18

NEW CITIES AND NEW TOWNS

I. THE CONTEXT AND NEED
II. A COMMITMENT
III. THE EXPERIENCE: UNITED STATES AND INTERNATIONAL
IV. THE NEW TOWN LEGISLATION AND GOVERNMENT SUPPORT
V. A PROPOSAL FOR A COMPREHENSIVE NEW TOWN POLICY

I. THE CONTEXT AND NEED

The pragmatic discussions of this book show the scope and pervasiveness of urban problems, as well as our failure to relate them into a manageable pattern. Each city "function" is dealt with in isolation by a separate set of institutions and administrative bodies which jealously guard their "domain." The city is a system of services that must relate in order to efficiently perform.

Specialization is both cause and result of urban life: but decision-making is far too important to be left to specialists.

The complexity of the urban systems is ever increasing, especially with the growth of our urban agglomerations. But the relationships between the functions and the systems are neglected. They must mesh and support each other to achieve results. The urban citizen, the user of the city functions, too often is voiceless and overwhelmed by the complexity, by the cacophany of experts and politicians who mostly defend their own special interests.

City Hall, the city's administration, is supposed to ride herd over the multiplicity of special agencies, needs, and economic imperatives: but City Hall has neither the power nor the money to effectively relate and monitor the multiplicity of services, let alone be a guide towards a better life for all citizens. City Hall, in turn, depends on money and decisions from the state government and the federal government, quite aside from the powerful influence of the surrounding suburbs and special agencies that operate quite outside any jurisdiction, such as the Port Authority. It must also be said that leadership of City Hall is tightly circumscribed by political considerations, such as the need to collect enough voters for the next election, while long-range commitments are neglected: to achieve better housing, better public services, and to improve the quality of city life often just takes too much time.

If nothing else the discussions of this book show in a very pragmatic way the fragmentation of the city, which in turn fragments the lives of all citizens. Isolation is one of the greatest modern ills, for individuals and for our urban society. Despite continuous attempts to improve communications on every level, this fragmentation has become a national affliction of ever-greater proportion, which is threatening to tear the whole country apart.

Since nearly 80 percent of the U.S. population now live an urban way of life, it would seem only reasonable that a politician who is seriously interested in creating better understanding and constructive cooperation should begin by restructuring the cities and metropolitan areas, where most of the people live. What is needed is to reorganize urban life by establishing better face-to-face communication and broadly organized citizen participation through decentralization, starting with the many systems that operate in the urban areas that administer the lives of almost all citizens.

For example, it has been shown in implementing the urban renewal program that most city service agencies (and the same is true on the state level) operate in splendid isolation without any knowledge of each other's plans and sometimes pursuing conflicting goals. As always, the urban citizen is not only the victim of all disagreement, but his taxes finance the agencies. Modern technology and especially computers could be of real service here; we most certainly have all the technical tools to better organize and relate the ever-growing number of systems and subsystems of increased complexity that confuse and bedevil the urban citizen's life.

Each "function" or system has its own experts and specialists. In this book the topics discussed can only outline some of the broadest concerns. In the real-life city some of the special interests not only conflict, but are further subdivided according to political jurisdictions. For instance, the metropolitan area of Boston is made up of 101 cities and towns, each with its own administrative service system and series of subsystems, such as housing, street cleaning, police and fire protection, and many more. The same is true of all cities—in metropolitan New York the jurisdictions are so numerous that it has been said that results of decisions are entirely unpredictable.

In turn, the administrators and politicians, faced with decisions that affect their constituents who are more vocal than informed, have to meet deadlines continuously and are seldom able to consider long-range results. Add to this the continuously changing base from which all decisions have to be made. The process that animates urban life can best be compared to a river which presently is flowing ever faster through some very rough territory. The stable moorings along this river, the institutions, at this stage are hopelessly obsolete, antiquated, and unresponsive to the tide that threatens to swamp them into total submersion. The fact is that our mainly nineteenth-century institutions simply are not able to cope with today's urban life and rapid change. These institutions were designed for a much slower past. Their system of checks and balances obstructs modernization, creates havoc and constant danger, much like the rocks in a turbulent, ever-faster flowing stream.

It is important that the urban citizen on this perilous voyage keeps his direction and purposes firmly in mind. But it is essential that, in order to steer his own boat, he must understand the obstacles, the reasons, see cause and effect, and most of all, relationships.

Those of us who have had the occasion to observe, from many directions and points of view and worldwide, cities and urban life and the very fragile organization that holds together their network of services, often wonder how much longer it can hold. Being in the center it is hard to gain the distance essential to observe the whole. Yet that is what is needed most. Only then the isolation of all the parts becomes apparent—and the need for cooperation based on better communication.

Indeed, the greatest need of our complex life today is to achieve better communication, a better understanding from which to judge each other and therefore become more tolerant. This is true both nationally and internationally, as urban life is becoming more alike all over the world.

What is needed is not just reportage of problems—this every city paper and TV news program does comprehensively every day. But what is needed is to show relationships, to establish connections, to explain and interpret causes and effects: to ask and answer why and wherefore, to analyze, to follow up and learn. Communication, pragmatic and firsthand, is the way towards better answers and to create a more viable organization of human affairs. Better communication is needed if we want to build more efficiently related urban-service systems and therefore more viable living patterns for all citizens.

The series of discussions of this book are trying to establish better communications through a pragmatic look at what goes on. This final chapter on new towns tries to outline a direction and commitment for doing something new a process that could be made to work.

II. A COMMITMENT

The one most serious national failure of the United States is and has been to create a decent life-supporting, man-made environment—cities and towns. This failure is becoming an overwhelming problem, as it is beginning to affect and destroy everything else that has been achieved. As yet, too many people do not recognize the causes of this failure that are so grotesquely evident in the distortions of our urban life. Pollution of the environment for the first time has forced many more people to stop and look and listen and to account for what is happening all around them in their own neighborhoods and towns: the result of actions motivated solely by the most selfish gain. Pollution and uncontrolled growth, if allowed to continue on the present scale, will obliterate also those who pollute.

To rebuild our environment, it is not only necessary to create new forms, but we must change the institutions, our direction, and, most of all, our values and priorities. There are those who predict doom. I believe there still are viable choices, and these choices are all related to how we structure and direct growth. Even though the birth rate is now dramatically declining, demographers predict a substantial increase in population. Besides, much of the dysfunctional environment in which we live is rapidly deteriorating and must be replaced. The large metropolitan areas will continue to grow, creating more problems for more people unless we institute some alternatives and controls. The decisions *how* we build new cities and towns are as vital and important a commitment to the future as any decisions that have ever been made affecting our environment and life.

The building of a new environment, new cities and new towns, has been the most important achievement of all mature societies. It represents a positive commitment to the future, based on the experiences of the past. How do we define a new town or new city? It is a "self-contained, planned environment that offers employment, housing, and a system of life-supporting facilities and integrated services to all citizens."

New communities can be classified as "satellite" towns, located contiguous to existing cities and therefore able to draw on the cities' resources, especially during their development. Most of the new towns built in the twentieth century have developed this way. For instance, the planned new towns built in Great Britain after the war around London and outside Glasgow; the new towns presently under construction in the Paris region, the new communities in Scandinavia and Northern Europe, and many more.

New communities can also be "free standing." This means they have to first develop their own economic, employment, and industrial base. Examples here are new capitals: for instance, Brasilia, the new capital of Brazil built in the middle of the country to develop that area, Chandigarh in India, the capital of Punjab, and Canberra in Australia.

Finally, new communities can be built next to or in conjunction with existing small communities, to focus the growth of a region and concentrate it into one urban center instead of creating indiscriminate sprawl. Some of the second generation new towns in Great Britain are planned that way, for instance, one in Lancashire or Senri Tew Town in Japan in the Tokyo-Kyoto megalopolis. Several new towns in France and Venezuela are planned that way, and many such regional development projects are planned in India and other developing countries.

The definition of new community or new town usually implies a community of more than fifty thousand people, though some well-known ones, for instance, Tapiola in Finland and the new communities surrounding Stockholm, are considerably smaller. The definition implies self-sufficiency in terms of services and institutions, as well as an employment base able to eventually produce jobs for at least half of the inhabitants.

New towns have been discussed in the United States for some twenty years, while other countries have gone ahead and built them. Perhaps this failure can become an advantage by learning from the experiences gained around the world.

However, the time has come to consider new-town building as a serious option in coping with our urban problems, especially pollution, which are a result of uncontrolled development. The building of a new environment is a pragmatic enterprise and must be undertaken in a variety of ways, building not a few but many very different new towns; nothing else will satisfy the needs and aspirations of our plural society.

Urbanization in the United States has been progressing at a furious pace, especially during the past twenty five years or since the end of World War II. Pushed by both economic and population growth, the formerly green countryside around most cities has become an unrecognizable jungle of commercial enterprise. Growth seems to have become an end in itself, creating in its wake ever-mounting pollution of every kind: not least of which is the indiscriminate building of an appallingly ugly, uncoordinated, man-made environment.

Bos-Wash (Boston Washington), San-San (San Francisco-San Diego), and Chi-Pitts (Chicago-Pittsburgh), the three megalopolitan regional developments, are sucking in people, business, and industry from the whole country, while many regions are losing population and dying economically. The eastern seaboard alone will grow by fifteen million people in the next ten years. Metropolitan New York threatens to double its present population by the year 2000. All this growth is taking place at present without any plan, without coordination, and from the very limited point of view of maximizing individual private gain.

Land and real estate speculation—which is the name of the game—is euphemistically called "development." This is still one of the best means of making a large profit fast—and getting out before any adverse results show. Since nothing is built to last, living conditions, or what is called the "quality of life" are deteriorating ever faster for rich and poor alike.

Cities throughout history have been built as communities for people. Cities are communal enterprises organized by many for the use of all. Cities must be planned, designed, and built for human needs in full recognition of the public interest. But most city building and urban development in the United States was and is undertaken purely from a business point of view for the profit of the investors and developers. The problems cities face today—a deteriorating environment, collapsing services, skyrocketing taxes, housing abandonment, insecurity, crime, and a whole range of social pathologies, quite aside from ever-increasing pollution and traffic problems—can be attributed largely to the basic misdirection of city building: the perversion of purposes and the absence of any public responsibility, the lack of concern for the most elemental human needs. The urban citizens and taxpayers have to make up over and over the profits the developers and speculators take out. But the absence of planning in the public interest and the absence of any provisions for social services or communal and human needs—which are not profitable for the developer—can seldom be restored or added after the fact—or only at enormous additional expense in a patchwork way.

During a period of rapid expansion, as has existed over the past twenty years, the real costs of haphazard speculative development are deferred, and individual upward mobility is accelerated. This temporarily conceals the structural faults, the basic lack of planning and long-range goals. However, these mistakes of omission are now beginning to bear their terrible fruits.

While in the past it has been possible to shift the burdens incurred by this type of development onto the poor, the newcomers to the cities, the helpless, the blacks and other minorities, this will no longer be possible in the future. One reason is that the disadvantaged groups are now inheriting the cities; the other is pollution. Besides, growth, in the absence of planning and coordination, is having more and more unpleasant side effects, such as large-scale power failures, breakdowns in transportation, mounting inefficiency of services resulting in increasingly expensive operating costs. But the social costs are beginning to affect everyone's life, no matter where or how they live: the rising crime rate, accompanied by mounting insecurity and fear; an escalating drug problem, ever-increasing human isolation, and segregation of racial and economic groups; a growing distrust by the public of all institutions and decision makers; ever-greater corruption in literally every area of urban administration and politics. All these are telling symptoms that something is terribly wrong.

Nearly 80 per cent of the U.S. population now lives in an urban, man-made environment; people come to the cities in hope of finding a better life. Rural living conditions are worse—the notion of a bucolic existence in the beautiful countryside has always been a myth and untrue for all but a fraction of the wealthiest farmers. But the concentration of more and more people in urban areas which are increasingly dysfunctional, deteriorating, and unequipped to hold the growing masses is a danger to everyone and to a civilized and free way of life.

I don't suggest abandoning the existing cities; our investments in cities are far too great. But in order to replan and rebuild them as decent places to live and work, the people who live there now first must have the choice of a better place to go, some viable alternatives and help to rebuild their lives. New cities and towns can offer such alternatives, new choices, and new ways to live.

Building new cities, furthermore, will create millions of new jobs. It can mean a new economic future for the country and a positive commitment that can involve constructively many of those presently left out. It can be instrumental in solving the problems of poverty, unemployment, mobility, and, most of all, segregation. The building of new cities can become a national commitment and a positive goal that can solve many of the urban problems. For the disenchanted young, it offers means to create a new environment and a new way of life of their own.

The building of new towns and a new environment requires very large investments and continuing government support. But in contrast to the investments made for armaments and defense, new towns make a return that grows with time. For instance, the new towns in Great Britain, after twenty years, have not only amortized their costs, but are making a return. They are financially sound public investments that continue to improve. These new towns have been built by public new town corporations which own and control all the land in and around the towns and operate in the public interest.

There are many financing mechanisms available also in the United States to build new towns as long-range, stable, public investments that are profitable financially, as well as socially, if they are planned from a public-interest point of view. The gains made will benefit millions more people than can live in new towns by creating a chain reaction of jobs. A new direction can be established away from pollution by initiating viable priorities and new values that replace growth and competition with quality and community.

There are solutions to the urban problems; technology can cope with pollution, given the proper directions and support. To create a better physical environment for people to support human potentialities is entirely possible here and now. Urbanization and land development must be redirected to safeguard the public interest and to benefit the people who live in new communities—as has been done abroad—instead of maximizing profits for the private entrepreneur, investor, and developer.

"There is nothing as persuasive as the real thing." It is difficult to imagine a new man-made environment, the physical reality of a new town. But it is even harder to visualize a new town that is based on new institutions that are truly responsive to the citizens and invite people to participate in the decision-making process: a new town that has job opportunities nearby and eliminates the wasteful commuters' ride; a new town that offers an open-education system which enhances the natural curiosity of all children and encourages imagination and diversity; a new town that provides continuing health care to every citizen and supports health education and preventive medicine; a new town that provides social services and individual counselling, all kinds of training, and adult education programs in many areas; a town that not only has a variety of houses, apartments, and many different living arrangements for individuals and families, but all kinds of community facilities and programs, including recreation and sports, music, art, and cultural programs; a new town with a variety of supportive services planned from the start and built into a handsomely-designed and soundly-constructed, flexible environment with a potential for change.

It is not only difficult to imagine such an environment, but indeed many very different such environments can and should be built in response to different tastes, different life styles, and different needs. Technology and software development at this stage make it quite feasible to provide not only variety, but continuous change from a properly designed or programmed base. Rigidity is not an inherent feature of institutional systems, but resistance to change or "checks and balances" were built into most institutions that were designed during the nineteenth century and before. The same is true of buildings: construction technology offers much more variety and flexibility than what is in actual use today.

There are all kinds of new building techniques to build new kinds of environments expressing different life styles that, because of institutional resistance, are never explored. In turn, new living patterns can be expressed and supported by new environmental and building forms that are technically and economically available now. For instance, our family living patterns and social customs have vastly changed. But housing is planned pretty much the same as hundreds of years ago, except for the new mechanical additions such as plumbing, central heating, air conditioning, and kitchen equipment.

Richard Buckminster Fuller, the engineer, philosopher, and inventor, is one man who has concerned himself with creating new forms (for instance, his geodesic domes) expressing new concepts of resource utilization and new ideas of human cooperation. His philosophy is based on worldwide cooperation in utilizing resources to create a life-supporting environment. He recognizes the finite nature of what he calls "Our Spaceship Earth,"[1] but at the same time he states his belief that resources and energy are constantly recycled and not lost. Our philosophy of scarcity that has created tne political and economic barriers is wrong, he claims, but we are able to build a life-supporting environment that can constructively function for all mankind.

---

[1] R. Buckminster Fuller, *Operating Manual for Spaceship Earth* (Carbondale and Edwardsville, Ill.: Southern Illinois University Press, 1969).

While for many years Buckminster Fuller has been regarded by many as a visionary, time and change have caught up by now with his ideas. His approach to problem solving uses the gaming technique. "World Game" is the name of a gaming-teaching program created by Fuller to reorder and redesign the environment and the uses of resources on a worldwide basis. Fuller does not believe he can change man. The whole emphasis of his work is on reforming the environment and thus creating new options and different living patterns based on a comprehensive view. Our man-made environment is built expressing the notions of scarcity and survival of the fittest—the ideas of Malthus and Darwin—which Fuller claims do not apply today as our scientific knowledge enables us to establish a balance against entropy, the dissipation of energy. Fuller's ingenious engineering ideas, as well as his philosophy, should be studied by anyone concerned with building a new environment, new cities and towns.

The architect Walter Gropius, the creator of the Bauhaus School and philosophy, many years ago concerned himself with devising new urban forms for new cooperative life styles. But his ideas and teaching were considered subversive in the Germany of the 1930's, and only now some of the work in this area will be published in a forthcoming book.[2]

Le Corbusier, the very influential French architect, has occupied himself for many years with creating new city forms that are documented in his many drawings and books and have been in part realized, for instance, in Chandigarh in India.

The CIAM group (Congrès Internationaux d'Architecture Moderne), made up of the most noted European architects and planners, met regularly and carried out many urban studies in the 1930's and 1940's in Europe. Several books have been published documenting their work.

The Ekistics group (Science of Human Settlements) in Athens, for the past ten years under the leadership of Constantinos Doxiadis, has carried on diversified research studies of settlements and has sponsored regular annual interdisciplinary meetings of the most creative people working in environmental and allied fields. The Ekistics magazine, the graduate education program, and the library at the Ekistics Institute in Athens, as well as the worldwide influence of the Ekistics members, testify to the validity of their work.

Many contemporary architects have been concerned about creating new urban forms. Among the best known are Moshe Safdie, the creator of "Habitat," the experimental housing development built for the Montreal World's Fair.

A major new city study, "Holopolis, Systemic Sketches of a New Whole

[2] Reginald Isaacs, *Gropius and the City* (tentative title), (New York: New York Graphic Society, first volume to be published in 1973).

World," by Clive Entwistle, a British architect, will be published in 1973 and may well initiate a whole new approach to environmental problem solving.

Throughout history, architects have concerned themselves with creating new urban forms, but the opportunities to actually build new physical environments expressing new social, organizational, and economic concepts have been very rare. While new governmental and political concepts or the description of social innovations have given rise to the special literary form of utopias—starting with Plato's *Republic*—almost none of these ideas were ever related to new physical urban forms.

Even the great modern behaviorist, B. F. Skinner, in his remarkable utopia *Walden Two*[3] does not attempt to translate his ideas into reality in terms of suggesting a new physical environment to serve and support his new ideas. In his latest book, *Beyond Freedom and Dignity*,[4] Skinner discusses the history of the utopian literature—in terms of redirecting human behavior before setting forth his own ideas. Certainly from the point of view of building a new physical environment, *Beyond Freedom and Dignity*, and all of Skinner's work should be studied, though he has made no attempt to relate it to the physical man-made world.

Communitas,[5] a remarkable utopian critique is the only book that backs up new social ideas with new plans and architectural forms. It was jointly written by the brothers Paul and Percival Goodman, one a sociologist and critic, the other an architect. However, they make no attempt to deal with the political and administrative organization and reality.

At no other time in history has technology offered the possibility to create and realize not only entirely new social and administrative systems, but to correlate them with entirely new environmental forms—and vice versa—because the building of new physical environmental forms influences behavioral, political, and administrative systems.

To really explore some of the new ideas of building cities, the new environments must be planned for actual sites and pragmatically developed with the participation of people who will live in the new towns. One possible approach or organizational framework is outlined in the proposal for a new town policy which follows. Many others are possible; variety is an asset in designing a new environment.

But new towns cannot really be created on paper. A process that extends over a long period of time cannot be accurately forecast in a time of rapid change. True, it is possible to make models or simulations, to test responses and gain experience before actually building. Computers have many useful

---

[3] B.F. Skinner, *Walden Two* (New York: The Macmillan Co., 1967).

[4] B.F. Skinner, *Beyond Freedom and Dignity* (New York: Alfred Knopf, 1971).

[5] Paul and Percival Goodman, *Communitas* (New York: Vintage Books, 1947). Paperback.

applications here, especially when coordinating the complexity of systems and the multiplicity of information that make up a new environment, based on a new social and economic approach.

Technology is no longer the barrier; experimentation and simulation exercises have been successfully applied in many areas and can be used here. The technical know-how is not the limitation. The limitation is the political will and most of all the commitment to use a new approach to experiment and to try something new.

III. THE EXPERIENCE: UNITED STATES AND INTERNATIONAL

The first generation of new towns in Britain and Scandinavia has produced sound alternatives to the congested old cities: a new way of life and steady employment for people who formerly lived in slums. A whole new generation of healthy and happy children is growing up under conditions very different from those of their parents: a visit to any new town in Great Britain or Scandinavia is a convincing experience.

These quotations are from *The New City:*

> New communities are an essential element of a strategy to shape growth. .... The European experience demonstrates that new communities can be, from the beginning, places of openness and diversity. They ... show just how pleasant an urban environment can be if the full talents of planning and design professionals are brought to bear. They can bring man, buildings, and nature once again into proper balance. ...
>
> New communities should result in socially and economically adjusted communities. Special account should be taken of the needs of low- and moderate-income families. Special opportunities should be provided to afford gainful, varied and satisfying employment to such families. ... New Towns should be attractive to all classes, creeds and races; to all types of businesses and industries; to a mix of citizen talent that will insure new town success.[6]

Several new towns are now under construction in the United States. The best-known ones, all undertaken by private developers, are Reston, Virginia, eighteen miles south of Washington, and Columbia, Maryland, near Baltimore. Irvine Ranch, built around a new campus of the University of California in Orange County, south of Los Angeles, is generally cited as the major new town development in the West. Many more are planned or have been recently

[6] The National Committee on Urban Growth Policy, including The National Association of Counties, The National League of Cities, The United States Conference of Mayors, and Urban America, Inc. (Donald Canty, ed.), *The New City.* (New York: Frederick A. Praeger, 1969).

started, most of them in metropolitan areas, for instance, of Chicago, Minneapolis, in the Los Angeles area, and several in Texas. HUD (The Department of Housing and Urban Development) has a complete list of all private developers who have submitted new town projects in order to obtain bank-loan guarantees and to make use of other federal programs.

There is only one new-town-in-town—Cedar-Riverside in Minneapolis, Minnesota, which differs from all the rest of the new town developments. Cedar-Riverside was started from a social service point of view. The commitment of its developers is to create a better environment for the people—mostly poor—who live there, and not to push anyone out. Other new-towns-in-town, which were undertaken by real estate developers primarily as profitable ventures, have all failed by now, because of resistance by the contiguous community and by the people in the area who refused to be pushed out.

The New York State Urban Development Corp., a public body, is sponsoring several new towns. They are Lysander in upstate New York, which is still in the planning stage; Amherst in the metropolitan area of Buffalo, which includes a new campus of SUNY (State University of New York); and Welfare Island in New York City. While both state and federal housing programs will be extensively used in the new towns sponsored by NYUDC, the fact is that all programs combined are at present unable to provide adequate responses to the real needs of housing, especially for low-income people, let alone accomplish the considerable economic and social advances that the new towns in Great Britain, Scandinavia, and many other European countries represent.

It must be said here that all new towns undertaken by private developers in the United States are nothing so much as glorified suburbias with some recreational features. It would be totally misleading to assume that what is presently being built in the United States under the new town label can solve any of the urban problems. Most of the new towns again are built to maximize private profits. This became entirely clear even to those who might have been misled by the excessive rhetoric in the past, at a three-day new-town conference sponsored in November 1971 by the AIA (American Institute of Architects).[7]

It is true that in Columbia, due to the devotion of its developer James Rouse, some middle-income housing was and continues to be built, and many more blacks than in most other suburban communities are attracted. Besides, some serious effort is being made in Columbia to create some community coherence around a carefully-planned social structure of neighborhoods and community facilities. This resulted in more variety and a more interesting

---

[7] New Communities Conference, Washington Hilton, Washington, D.C., November 13-16, 1971. For papers, write American Institute of Architects, 1785 Massachusetts Avenue, N.W., Washington, D.C. 20036.

social environment for the mostly professional and upper-class inhabitants. But there are also some problems by now, as community facilities are available only to those who pay membership fees and not to people who do not live in the town but in the area. It must be clear, however, that in terms of solving any of the terrible problems of cities, the experience of Columbia, or for that matter any new town development in the United States, is so far entirely irrelevant. Because these new towns are speculative developments that only cater to upper-income groups, where a profit can be made, social programming is entirely neglected, and the vast majority of the people living in the cities could never afford to live in any new town built for the profit of the developer.

The fact is that even the much-hailed Urban Growth and New Community Development Act of December 1970 simply does not provide the legislation needed to create the kinds of new towns that could conceivably help the cities. Up to a point, this is being done in the new towns of Great Britain: to decant the cities to offer the low-income people in the crowded old deteriorating slums viable alternatives at a price they can afford to pay. The new town inhabitants in Great Britain pay rent of about 20 per cent of their income. They live in a variety of houses or apartments that are well designed, substantially built, and properly maintained, and that will outlast the financing. Social programming is an integral part of all housing. Schools are built before families move in and at public expense, instead of in hindsight at the taxpayers' expense. All services are provided from the start, instead of residents having to raise additional taxes for sewers and other service needs. Community facilities are planned into the towns, as well as commercial facilities of great variety.

The new towns in Great Britain and Scandinavia do not provide all the answers, and there are too few as yet; but they are a start. The new towns offer a new direction and represent a public commitment to create a decent living environment for a vast and growing number of people who are at present entirely left out in the United States, as far as decent housing, adequate city services, and good schools are concerned.

The new towns in Great Britain, furthermore, have been able to influence and structure growth and direct it away from London. There are those who say the new towns have not succeeded or done enough. But if all the new town growth in Great Britain were spread in haphazard fashion throughout the countryside, as is happening in the United States, pollution would be completely overwhelming, and the natural environment around London completely spoiled. Instead, London has managed by steady effort to clear up its appalling air pollution. One can actually see the sun again even in winter. Only a few miles outside the city, one can enjoy some of the loveliest unspoiled, carefully conserved and tended parks, and natural scenery.

Thamesmead, a planned new town inside London for sixty thousand people, is presently under construction, planned and built by the Greater London Council for people who presently are living in substandard housing in the London slums.

France, after years of doing nothing, has embarked on a nationwide program of decentralization and new town building that has been in the planning stage for well over ten years. Currently, a number of new towns are under construction.

A new office with ministerial power is part of the central government—L'Aménagement du Territoire, the office for land management—and was created in 1963. A national plan was developed according to which France is divided into eight economic and geographic areas, plus the Paris region. Each of these regions has several existing cities which are to be strengthened and are to become growth poles by decentralizing certain service functions away from Paris. Industrial- and job-creating business development is publicly supported in these urban centers designated for development.

Different degrees of public support, depending on the development policy of the region, are given to industries and enterprises moving into the locations designated for growth. This support consists in outright payments for each job created, tax incentives of all kinds, low cost of land, and the like. Depending on the demographic, economic, and social studies undertaken by the new regional development offices and approved by the central office in Paris, each region offers different financial incentives, while the Paris region offers no tax incentives at all. In fact, the thrust of national planning is to create balanced development throughout France. The greatest growth by far has always been in and around Paris. Without control and proper guidance, that is, planning, Paris and its surroundings would become totally polluted and would be strangled in congestion and traffic.

Much new construction, indeed whole new towns, are planned for the eight different regions of France to strengthen this decentralization plan. The only thing these new towns have in common is that they are all quite different in concept, in design, and in the approach to solving the problems indigenous to the different localities, including their geography. The physical plan of the new towns consists not in designing a land-use development plan, but rather in establishing development priorities and growth poles. Areas for specific land use are identified by economic studies and research. New activity centers, for instance, for intensive commercial development, are designated to flexibly guide rather than physically fix growth. The growth poles are supported by public decisions, such as the construction of roads and transportation networks, infrastructure, and public buildings of all kinds.

All services, roads, schools, and social centers of the towns are not only planned concomitantly with the housing, but they are publicly financed and built before the first inhabitants move in. Most of the housing, furthermore, is publicly subsidized in one form or another. Private developers are encouraged to participate on every level and given a town outside Toulouse, and Hérouville outside Caen, are well under to the new towns through all kinds of incentives in order to make the towns economically independent and create as many jobs as possible.

It is of course debatable where a satellite development ends and a "new town" starts; professionals use different definitions. Le Mirail, a town outside Toulouse, and Hérouville, outside Caen, are well under way and are considered by many to be in the process of becoming new towns. There are more and larger ones in various stages of planning outside many older cities, including whole new vacation towns in the south of France.

But without doubt the most interesting new town project is the one at Vaudreuil outside of Rouen. Vaudreuil is an experimental town in every sense of the word. A new approach to planning is being used whereby the town has different options to grow, instead of along one predetermined line as has been the traditional way. To start with, a "seed" town for about fifteen thousand people will be built. This seed town is to the developed city what the child is to the man. Experiments of all kinds will be initiated, carefully studied, and evaluated in terms of town building in the rest of France and other countries. Vaudreuil is also trying to evolve planning and development methods that are adaptable to rapid change. Innovations are planned in site development, circulation and transportation, industrial development, and housing. For a start, four thousand housing units will be built.

The Ministry in charge is working with a group of developers and industrialists who are interested in experimenting. They want to try out new ideas in every area of town building to study the economic feasibility of new methods and experiments.

But the guiding and most innovative factor for the development is to create a pollution-free environment from the start; or, stating it realistically, an environment that will minimize water, noise, and environmental pollution of every kind by building in safeguards and recycling methods in all services, industries, and permanent installations. Each decision as to what is built in the new town, where and how, will be considered from this point of view: How does it affect the quality of the environment, what are its sociological and psychological effects, and what are the costs? Feedback mechanisms are built in, and the effects of the new experiments on the environment and people will be carefully studied.

Vaudreuil is right outside Rouen, which is a highly polluted industrial city. Rouen will serve as comparison for Vaudreuil's new pollution-free environment.

HUD has joined the French government in some experimental programs in

Vaudreuil, in the area of pollution control. Because in the United States we still lack the basic planning legislation and the financial support that would make it possible to carry out such experiments, Vaudreuil should be watched with care by all those who are truly concerned about how to create a better way of life in our industrialized world without ruining our natural environment. Vaudreuil is the only planned new town taking this experimental approach and trying to make it into an economic reality with the cooperation of business and industry.

Demographers predict that the Paris region will grow from eight million to some fourteen million people in the next thirty years; this kind of growth must be organized and channeled into viable urban centers, or it will kill its heart: that is, the city of Paris itself. The Paris region, which is much larger than any U.S. metropolitan area, has been growing more rapidly than any other area of France. To control and organize this growth, the government has designated areas of concentrated development. Five new towns in the Paris region are progressing very rapidly now.

According to the national decentralization plan of France, new industry locating in the Paris region gets no subsidies or tax advantages. For businesses that still wish or have to locate in the area, new urban centers have been designated, around which new intensive development is being organized. The new towns are built near or in conjunction with existing older settlements utilizing existing transportation routes by modernizing and strengthening them.

The towns or areas going ahead most rapidly now, vigorously supported by the government, are Cergy-Pontoise, Evry, Trappes, Valée de la Marne—an urban region that as yet has no named center—and Melun-Senart. The double names connote old, existing towns on the outskirts of which the new planned towns will grow, eventually to form a whole.

These towns, or centers for concentrated urban development, follow a grand scheme of a parallel growth axis north and south of Paris which follows the direction of the Seine but safeguards and keeps out of development the river basin itself. The growth axis is supported by a transportation network, including new trains, which is in the process of being built and coordinated with existing routes; parts of it are already in use.

While each new town should be discussed on its own merits, as it has a character entirely of its own and is in a different stage of development, Cergy-Pontoise and Evry are the two towns furthest along in their development. Cergy-Pontoise and Evry carry out the mandate of open-ended, staged, flexible development; they don't follow a fixed plan. Both towns have already completed new "Prefecture" buildings, or regional administrative centers, which attract many people and businesses to the new towns.   The Syndicate, or town development corporation, of Cergy-Pontoise, is in the process of building the first and smaller center of the newly-planned regional development. This center is scheduled to be completed in five years, an incredibly short time.

The second, much larger center, which will be closer to the existing old town of Pontoise, won't be started until the first center is completed. The whole new town, including the existing old town, will have a population of some 300,000 people by the year 2000.

Evry, a short distance beyond the airport of Orly, announced in mid—May 1971 an international competition for seven thousand housing units, including all the infrastructure, schools, and other service facilities. The first stage of the proposal was due in October 1971, the final competition in July 1972. This suggests a magnitude and speed of development and building that is quite unmatched anywhere else.

The new towns of France certainly are different in approach, conception, and design from the first generation of new towns in Great Britain, which mostly are limited to a population of 100,000 or less. Even in Britain, it is felt today that this is too small. The second-generation new towns, for instance Milton-Keynes and the yet unnamed new "area of intense urbanization" planned for Lancashire (near Manchester), will not only have many more people, but they follow a vastly different planning program.

While a British new-town corporation owns the land and most of the buildings in the first-generation new towns (such as Stevenage, Basildon, and numerous others around London, as well as Cumbernauld and other Scottish new towns), the new approach in Milton-Keynes is to bring in private developers from the start. The older new towns, after twenty years, have amortized their investment and are financially solvent and could therefore expand— but they were planned for a maximum size.

The French towns work with private developers from the start. Their syndicate, or town development corporation, has to get its money back in a hurry. The total government loan period in Cergy-Pontoise, for instance, is only six years. As a result, while the French towns will get the capital back rapidly, the long-term profit from land development will go to the private investor and developer instead of to the town or public sector. That is, the vast public investments in terms of roads, infrastructure, and services will never be repaid.

Stockholm's first and now classic metropolitan building program consisted in the city buying, many years ago, the land surrounding the city center and holding it, thus keeping it out of speculative development. Many years later when it was needed, the city built new suburban communities on the land which they had bought at a reasonable price. The two best-known satellite communities, Farsta and Vallingby, have become models for community planning around the world. Similar planned developments have been built around Copenhagen and Oslo, all on government-owned land and with strict controls as to what can be built and how. These towns contain large numbers of inexpensive subsidized apartments and houses were built for economically mixed-income groups.

Tapiola, the delightful privately-developed town outside Helsinki, was planned for only fifteen thousand people and is very much more dispersed than most other new towns. But even here subsidized housing is provided to accomodate different socio-economic groups.

One cannot help but observe that all the new city and town planning and building abroad, in fact all new planned urban development, has taken quite the opposite route from what is happening in the United States. Certainly the U.S. metropolitan areas are growing every bit as fast as any in Europe. But the U.S. metropolitan areas are growing without any planning, without any guidelines, and in many cases not even public investments are coordinated. Furthermore, zoning is used to keep subsidized housing out of the suburbs and, in many cases, also all middle-income housing development, effectively creating racial and economic segregation. By now a noose of white, rich, segregated suburbs surrounds the black, deteriorating U.S. cities. Abroad, middle- and low-income people are encouraged to move into the suburbs and into the new towns, which are all subsidized.

The order of the day in the U.S. metropolitan wilderness is for each developer to get the most for himself. New shopping centers, immensely profitable, are springing up all over, without any environmental or other controls, frequently clogging the roads and highways along which they are built. Despite zoning regulations, when a community needs more tax income, it will accommodate whatever industry comes along.

Any such idea as regional development, let alone national planning, as in France, is still considered "coercive" or "un-American" by a majority of the U.S. public. But the same public, due to the absence of rational planning and public-interest controls, spends countless hours in traffic jams under clouds of car exhaust; and the same people live in the ugliest, most polluted, and most expensive metropolitan areas of the entire industrialized world. While the cities are full of old, speculatively-built housing that is rapidly falling apart, the older suburbs are now beginning to show the same symptoms of deterioration, pollution, and congestion that their inhabitants thought they were leaving behind when they moved. After all, the suburbs were not planned any more than the cities, and the suburban housing certainly was not meant to last much longer than the mortgages.

In the United States, until we face the fact that large public investments are needed to build decent, coordinated, new urban developments, and that *real* planning and controls are required on the local, regional, and national levels, we shall never be able to put up anything that is worthy of the name city or town. The name "Town" also implies openness to all people, and that means that housing must be subsidized or it becomes an exclusive, segregated community.

Finally, it is a fact that racial segregation in cities and suburban development is one of the most pervasive evils in the United States. Though it is illegal to practice racial discrimination, the existing housing patterns, especially new suburban developments, effectively segregate the population. Zoning and economic segregation are not outlawed and are supported by President Nixon, but they accomplish the same discriminating results.

The building of new communities could effectively deal with segregation by a positive commitment to establish from the start an economic and social mixture of new town inhabitants. In the United States this is left to the developer, whose chief goal is to maximize profits and not to offend any potential buyers who come from segregated communities. Columbia is the only new town that has actively sought minority residents, but of course this means upper-middle class and professionals.

The experience in Israel shows that with a positive commitment to achieve racial and economic integration it is possible to reach this goal in less than a generation; and that people of a very different background can live in harmony, side by side, long before that. Israel has successfully settled, in new towns, refugees from backward Arabic villages next door to immigrants from the most sophisticated European urban centers. This was done successfully with the help of a battery of social services, from health care to homemaking, from job training to child care, as well as all kinds of education programs. According to the officials in the respective Israeli government agencies involved, this strategy is essential, no matter what the physical environment. Without the social services and education, the housing and towns could never have succeeded in becoming integrated communities.

New settlement patterns were evolved in Israel to support this integration effort whereby separate villages or neighborhoods are combined with a joint town center. The immigrants are grouped according to background in the residential areas, while in the town centers, the market, in school, and at work they mix. The young people, it was found, soon preferred to mix in the town center, while many of the older generation preferred to stay at home with their own group. Now that the younger generation has reached maturity, the differences in background are disappearing.

Certainly new town building in Israel is one of the most remarkable achievements from the social point of view. New towns also were and are still being built to support regional economic development and to distribute growth which had concentrated on the coast and especially in Tel Aviv—which essentially also is a new planned town. It was imperative to develop the rest of the country, especially the interior. Numerous new communities were developed, in part free standing, by transplanting industrial development, for instance, Carmiel, in the center of the country east of Haifa. Others are built next to existing, often ancient, historic settlements, for instance, near Nazareth. Both patterns proved viable. Social integration, supported by the most comprehensive social service network anywhere, is far more successful than anywhere else in the world.

While the incentives in Israel were very strong in terms of creating stability and, virtually, nation-building, the lessons are obvious and certainly applicable in the United States. The economic benefits that have accrued from both the integrated, national, physical, and economic development, as well as the social integration, are visible in terms of creating the highest standard of living in the Near East, in a country that until quite recently was virtually a neglected desert and has very few natural resources. All this was undertaken, continuously and effectively supported by the Israeli government.

It is the responsibility of the government to plan, design, and create a decent urban environment for all citizens practically everywhere in the world except in the United States. Because it is too important, too big, and too expensive a job for private developers to do alone. It is a continuing responsibility that requires long-range commitments that cannot be subject to day-to-day political pressures and certainly not subject to changing private financial concerns. New towns have to be planned and massively supported if they are to be democratic and open to all people instead of being exclusive, profitable real estate speculations for and by the rich and the few.

Unless we in the United States finally wake up to the truth that there was and is something terribly wrong with our way of approaching city and community building, we shall have more and more trouble, not just in the cities, but throughout the growing metropolitan areas, such as water and electricity shortages, transportation breakdowns, enormous property taxes, poor or no services, and a growing range of social and racial problems, including ever-increasing crime. But it is with air pollution that the crunch will really come. Because in effect hardly anything has been done to significantly improve that situation despite endless talk; only stringent controls and planning can reverse the present trends.

Instead of condemning technology and industry for demeaning life and creating pollution, we should apply technology and industrial methods properly to build a new environment, new towns. Furthermore, the same people who build the new cities should also have the opportunity to live there. Europe's new towns from the start have always been open and available to a majority of people of all income groups. They have been and are experimenting with new environmental ideas, such as traffic separation or creating a pollution-free town such as in Vaudreuil.

Based on a nationally-supported and coordinated plan for new cities and towns, the resulting building program would create millions of unskilled and skilled jobs. This would do much more for employing minorities and blacks in the building trades than all the minority hiring plans combined and would create true upward mobility and economic independence. New towns, supported by the government, can do more to create viable, integrated living patterns than all the school integration and open housing legislation combined. Not that these should be abandoned: but new towns, built on the same scale as in Great Britain or France, could produce viable alternatives to the endless community fights about housing, services, and schools. These fights are over peanuts compared to the need and compared to what new towns could and should do.

Finally, private business has found new town development highly profitable in France and great Britain, where it has received substantial government support. In Scandinavia, a large private building industry constructs all the housing and does not have to worry about sales: because every last housing unit is instantly taken over by the government, which has long waiting lists of people eligible to occupy the housing.

In the United States we can develop our formulas for private business participation. Considering the growing housing shortage, the increasing population, and the failing metropolitan areas, a properly organized new town planning and building program, based on national economic development priorities, is bound to be successful, especially for private enterprise. It also can provide the economy with the badly-needed incentives for job creation and properly-directed growth without pollution.

What is missing then? First, an understanding by the public; next, cooperation by business that has everything to gain, but most of all the unfailing leadership by government which must back the new town building as a profitable public investment in the future of all its citizens.

IV. THE NEW TOWN LEGISLATION AND GOVERNMENT SUPPORT

The Urban Growth and New Community Development Act of 1970, approved December 31, 1970, certainly goes much further than all previous legislation, which has been insufficient as an instrument for creating new communities. That is, the 1970 act goes much further in the wrong direction—which is to help, most of all, private developers to build new towns by underwriting bank loans on a much larger scale than before. This subsidizes first of all the banks; it also subsidizes the profits of land developers, and especially speculators. It does little for the consumer, the future new town inhabitant. But it does nothing at all for those who most urgently need housing, a decent environment, and a job to become self-supporting, contributing citizens.

The new town legislation is designed around the same premises as the housing legislation: to maximize the profits for the investors, developers, and banks. But the housing legislation has utterly failed to provide housing for low- and middle-income people. At present more and more scandals on a nationwide basis are coming to light; for instance, large credit organizations, real estate developers, and public officials have been found to band together to defraud the poor with false credit statements and false appraisals.[8] Defective housing is being sold at enormously inflated prices to low-income people and especially minorities due to collusion between banks, real estate firms, and FHA appraisers and developers. The legislation makes it enormously profitable to make such deals, which often end by the federal government, as mortgage guarantor, becoming the involuntary owner of abandoned housing properties which have been fraudulently sold to low-income people who usually lose all their savings in such a deal. Yet this continues to go on in all U.S. cities involving banks, real estate enterprises, politicians, and public officials, with the help of federal mortage guarantees, while the poor, and especially minorities, are unable to get a decent place to live.

The new town legislation once more supports the private developers, investors, and bankers, and opens the door to enormously profitable land speculation, while the government (read the taxpayer) finances the public investments in urbanization that create the very large profits for the developer.

The new town legislation, as it stands, helps everyone except the new town citizen and consumer, though of course with few exceptions only upper-income people can afford to live in a new town. That is, the whole new town legislation supports segregation and has no social commitment whatever to upgrade the life of the average urban citizen. In fact, he is entirely excluded. Except for a few middle-income housing units in Columbia, almost no housing under $20,000 is built in new towns or for that matter anywhere in suburbia. Nor does the legislation support environmental quality or set building standards of any kind. The main concern of the legislation is to help large developers who are able to control the enormous sums of money needed to buy the land to finance the substantial long-term investments, to hire the considerable managerial and legal talent to produce sales projections that confirm adequate cash flow. That leaves out all but the very largest investors who are willing to take great risks—in return for very large profits, of course.

[8] "Dun & Bradstreet Among 50 Named in Housing Fraud," *New York Times,* March 30, 1972, p. 1 ff. See also John Herbers, "U.S. Now Big Landlord in Decaying Inner City," *New York Times,* January 2, 1972; John Herbers, "Federal Housing Aid Stirs Widening Debate," *New York Times,* January 3, 1972; John Herbers, "Housing and Government: Official Criticism of Subsidy Program is Growing," *New York Times,* February 1, 1972, p. 27; Ken Hartnett, "The U.S. as Slumlord," *The New Republic,* December 11, 1971, p. 11 ff.; Gurney Breckenfeld, "Housing Subsidies are a Grand Delusion," *Fortune,* February 1972, p. 137.

Finally, the present legislation entirely fails to designate or make provision for publicly-sponsored new towns.

New town building on a large scale can create a great many new jobs, no matter who the developer is. But the people who will build the new towns with the help of the 1970 act will not be able to afford to live there: because these private real estate developments will serve upper- and upper-middle-class income groups almost exclusively. HUD's only requirement to broaden the base of new towns is to ask developers to include "some" subsidized housing for middle-income people, but it is not specific and the quantity is left to the developer. Social programming and social services, while mentioned in the legislation, at best will be an exercise in tokenism, in the absence of funding or any specific requirements.

The new towns as projected under the existing legislation are just bigger segregated suburbias, with the addition of planned recreation and shopping facilities and some limited protection for the natural environment. These new communities are subject to all the usual racial and economic segregation that is practiced throughout suburbia. They cannot provide any answers to the growing housing shortage and connected social problems of the cities, as they are in essence profitable investments for the few rather than open communities for the many.

If anything, the Urban Growth and New Community Development Act of 1970 encourages land speculation because the greatest profits can be made by the initial developer of the "raw" land. With the help of federal programs and with federal financing, the developer urbanizes this land, which he can sell at an enormous profit (largely due to public investment for roads, sewers, water supply, etc.) to various subdivision developers. The subdivision developers, of course, stand to take out a second round of large profits. In general, the development of a new town in this way is not very different from the usual suburban pattern except that it follows an overall plan, and the size of the development is much larger and includes commercial and industrial development. The distance from the city center can be greater, as some community facilities and shopping are included. Therefore the land is cheaper to acquire and the profit proportionately higher. The initial investments must be larger over a longer period of time, which makes new town development practically a prerogative of multi-millionaires and the largest financial institutions.

The advantage to the well-to-do consumer or house buyer in such a development, especially for those who come first, is greater in terms of appreciation of his house investment. As the community grows, the initial buyer's investment appreciates more rapidly than a comparable investment in just any suburban house. But the first group of new town inhabitants also pays for it in longer commuting and having to put up with living for years in a half-finished environment, continuously under construction, where many services, including schools, lag behind. The new town citizen will see his taxes increase in due course when it appears that some services are missing that can be procured only after raising taxes when enough people have moved into the new town.

In the publicly-sponsored new towns abroad, the land development profits stay in the town and form the financial base for supplying community services and facilities of all kinds—which are built before the citizens move in and do not depend on raising more local taxes.

A new community under the 1970 Urban Growth and New Community Development Act will certainly have more variety in facilities, more amenities and recreation, and a better balanced environment than the usual suburban development. However, the design and quality of the new community, in fact, most of the decisions, are left entirely to the developer, who will build what is most profitable and that as quickly as possible to recoup his investment. The new communities once more will be economically segregated, and therefore largely racially segregated as well. Rarely, if ever, will anything new be offered in education, in institutional organization, or governmental functions. Because new towns must be integrated into whatever county system or suburban administration exists in the area, even though this may not be viable for the large number of additional people attracted by the new town. The 1970 legislation completely ignores these very important areas.

It seems hard to justify the notion that a private developer should in fact be allowed to make his largest profit on the public investment in infrastructure and with the help of government-guaranteed loans. These guarantees are underwritten by the average taxpayer, who usually cannot even afford to live in a new town. The government in fact underwrites the private profit of the developer, while the public interest and the interest of the future new town inhabitant are not protected at all. What is happening is that taxpayers' money is used to financially guarantee the planning and building of new towns from which most of these same taxpayers are excluded.

Government housing programs have used the same mechanisms of subsidizing interest (via banks), guaranteeing loans, and helping the developer, instead of directly building and financing housing. As a result, there is an enormous housing shortage while housing abandonment is a major problem throughout all U.S. cities. That is, more and more housing in cities, which is no longer profitable due to its poor condition and high tax rate, is abandoned by the owner and eventually reverts to the city because of tax delinquency. The federal government, due to its mortgage guarantees, is becoming a major slum landlord in many U.S. cities. The private investor has made his profit, and it costs too much to maintain the poorly-built housing, so the owner abandons it. But the federal-government-guaranteed mortgage is not yet paid off, so the federal government gets stuck with thousands of deteriorating housing units in cities throughout the United States. All housing is, of course, inspected by the FHA (Federal Housing Administration) inspectors prior to the issuance of mortgage guarantees. Much of this housing is largely built for quick profit by speculative developers and has never been properly planned or constructed to last. Similar financing mechanisms apply for rehabilitation of city housing, largely with the same results of abandonment. It seems utterly irresponsible to legislate once more the same mistakes with new communities.

Furthermore, the New Community Development Act includes no active safeguards against pollution. While the developers' plans must be reviewed by the pertinent public and private anti-pollution agencies, no positive standards are set in the new towns area.

But the greatest mistake of the New Community Development Act is its failure to coordinate new town building with regional and national growth objectives. The National Committee on Urban Growth Policy published its findings and objectives in 1969 in an excellent book, *The New City,* referred to above. It is essential that new communities must be part of a national urban-growth strategy, because new communities must be coordinated with national economic-growth objectives.

Left to the market forces, new town development will take place in the most developed areas of the country that are near the already highly-developed population centers. This is not in the national interest, as it will further contribute to pollution by increasing densities, especially on the eastern and western seaboards and in the Great Lakes area.

Congressman Thomas L. Ashley (Ohio), a member of the Urban Growth Committee, has sponsored legislation to support the formulation of a national urban-growth policy under the 1970 Urban Growth and New Community Development Act. Under this act, the President is given the responsibility of transmitting to Congress a biannual report on urban growth. So far, the Executive has failed to act.

An urban-growth policy should serve as a "guide in making specific decisions at the national level which would affect urban growth" and should coordinate federal programs "so as to encourage desirable patterns of urban growth and stabilization, the prudent use of land resources and the protection of the physical environment." In addition, it should set a "framework for the development of interstate, state and local growth and stabilize policy."[9]

The Office of Management and Budget has impounded more funds for housing, appropriated by Congress, than in any other area. OMB also refused to let the Community Development Corp., created by the 1970 Urban

---

[9] Thomas L. Ashley, speech at the American Institute of Architects New Communities Conference, November 4, 1971.

Growth and New Community Development Act, request adequate funds and supplemental grants (authorized by Congress) to support this legislation, including the urban-growth policy.

It must be clear that an urban-growth policy is essential for new town building. But what is at present included in the New Community Legislation of 1970, especially in terms of supporting any kind of rationally distributed national growth, is only a statement of wishful thinking. It cannot even provide the basis of formulating legislation. For this, both money and an Executive statement and support are needed; then hearings must be held.

To formulate and implement a national policy of this kind takes the strongest kind of national leadership, as shown by the French experience. DeGaulle gave that leadership. It also takes the strongest kind of direct incentives and controls, such as the ones formulated by the French land development office, "Aménagement du Territoire," which functions on the highest level of government. France enacted its national urban-growth legislation over ten years ago, but only now is some of the impact beginning to materialize.

Great Britain has successfully developed more new communities than any other country without any national-growth policy. But Great Britain has regional development policies, especially those concerned with the Greater London area and the South of England. Great Britain always had binding land-use controls, administered by a competent, professionally-trained civil service. In the United States, we have not even begun to develop viable objectives which must precede legislation, while thousands of acres of new land are destroyed every week and growth proceeds in a completed uncoordinated way.

Finally, the most detrimental omission of the Urban Growth and New Community Development Act of 1970 is its failure to support and fund social programming. Under the Act, the development of new communities can be undertaken without any concern for software planning or any innovation of the institutional areas, from education to health care, from counseling to day care. It is left to the developer to use what federal programs are available, but it is obvious that these are simply not enough and frequently don't apply, nor do they support anything new.

The absence of any meaningful social service requirement from the new town development package may well result in the eventual undoing of new communities, much as it has undermined public housing. Though the legislation talks about favoring applications containing social and community features, there is no funding provided. Therefore it is obvious that social services will be included only at a minimal level.

A social programming requirement and funding should be added now, as otherwise some of the new communities may not last the length of the mortgage or the government guarantee. HUD may not only find itself the owner of acres of abandoned inner-city housing, but it will also become the unwilling receiver of all kinds of "new communities." Public-housing projects have become social failures all over the United States, due to the omission of social and community programs.[10] Pruitt-Igoe in St. Louis, which had to be torn down in part recently, is the most notorious example. Certainly a requirement to build middle-income housing without social services is quite unrealistic, especially in a new town.

In the usual suburban subdivision, the developer is "out" in five years or less; whatever happens after that is none of his concern. But in a new town, the developer is on the spot for fifteen or twenty years or more, or long enough to reap a harvest of troubles, from vandalism to drugs to youth gangs and more. It would seem to be in the interest of the developer, first of all, to add to the legislation a viable social programming requirement providing federal funding. It would also seem in the interest of the government to create such legislation since HUD is backing the loans.

Social programming in many countries is an integral part of housing programs, and the following social services are provided: individual family placement, homemaking, job counselling, job training, education of all kinds, child care, health education, family counselling, youth services of all kinds, recreation, nurseries and child care, and more. Added to this are a variety of community facilities and guidance for community groups to formulate their own programs, supervised sports, and recreation. The result is an active, involved community with a potential for healthy growth.

In the end, it also must be clear that many more developers would be served, in terms of becoming profitably involved, if a variety of public corporations would be designated to take on the overall responsibility of new towns. This does not need to eliminate those financial giants that can raise the very large capital requirements for new town development. But it would establish public standards and goals that are in the public interest and that all developers would have to meet. It would also broaden the base for participation of developers, as many more and smaller contractors, including minority enterprises, could participate in pieces of the development, while the public new town development corporation would have the overall planning and financial responsibility.

The present legislation should not be eliminated but changed to include viable software and social service planning and funding. In addition, enabling legislation should be created to form public new-town development corporations which would not only take on major development projects but would also set socially viable development goals in the process. Public new town

---

[10] See Fran P. Hosken, "People, not bricks, make a new town," *Christian Science Monitor,* December 31, 1971, p. 11.

corporations could greatly diversify and broaden the presently one-sided new community development and would enable many more people to participate, both as producers and as consumers in new towns. The new community legislation must also set positive quality standards, not only in terms of preventing pollution, but to achieve high-quality urban design and architectural goals. Visual beauty of the man-made environment cannot be achieved solely by protecting nature; positive design standards must be set from the start. The building of new communities should also support experimentation and should provide for new life styles, new social forms and living patterns to be expressed in innovative design.

A framework of regional and national growth goals must be spelled out and legislation passed to support coordinated physical, social, and economic development, which must guide the location of new towns with continuing long-range government support.

V. A PROPOSAL FOR A COMPREHENSIVE NEW TOWN POLICY

The building of a new urban environment is a challenge to meet long-postponed needs and build the future along more humane and responsive lines; new communities can restructure our institutions and broaden the opportunities for every citizen; they can channel urban growth away from pollution and create an environment of harmony and beauty for all men.

A viable new town policy can be organized into five basic, interrelated components:

1. *National urban-growth planning and development legislation, federally supported and regionally coordinated, supported by tax and other incentives and land-use controls.*

2. *National economic development planning policy, coordinated with national urban-growth planning (1.), authorizing new federally-supported financing mechanisms (National Development Bank) and required to produce four-year comprehensive development plans.*

3. *Software development: government, administrative, institutional, and social services; planning, programming, and management.*

4. *Hardware development: infrastructure, transportation, and building systems; planning, production, and management.*

5. *Citizen participation.*

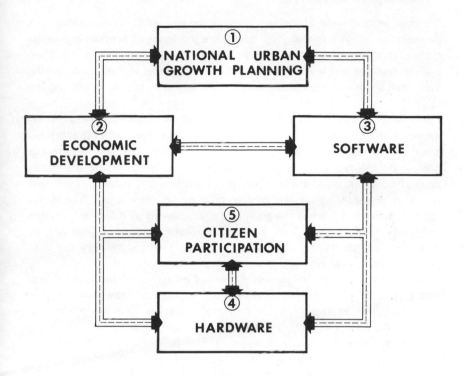

1. National urban-growth planning and development legislation, federally supported and regionally coordinated, supported by tax and other incentives and land-use controls.

National urban-growth planning and development policy is concerned with the location of new towns. New towns are the focus of economic development planned in the national interest to benefit all citizens. New town development must be regionally coordinated and regionally, as well as nationally, supported by tax incentives, transportation, federal installations, and job creation.

It is in the interest of the whole country to redirect growth to areas that are presently left out for many reasons, but mostly because growth attracts more growth in a free market economy. As a result, the eastern and western seaboards and the Great Lakes region have developed more rapidly than other areas of the country and are attracting more business and industry. Therefore, pollution is becoming an ever-greater problem in these areas. It is in the national interest to support the growth of other regions by building new cities and towns supported by fiscal policies, by locating federal installations, by developing transportation, and by creating incentives for industry and business to move into the new towns and create employment.

The location of new towns shall be based on national and regional economic research and surveys that will identify potential growth nodes. The active participation of business and industry will be sought in identifying new growth poles and strengthening the development of new areas.

The work done by the Committee on Urban Growth Policy (published in 1969 in *The New City*)[11] will serve as a base, but much more detailed investigation is needed. A national planning system, coordinating state and/or regional planning organizations shall be established.

Regional and/or state planning organizations shall be created. In some areas where regional interests of states coincide, two or more states shall jointly form such a regional body according to geographic, economic, and demographic concerns. The New York State Urban Development Corp. is one possible model. Where state development agencies exist, their work shall be reviewed and incorporated in the new organization. Such a regional authority shall have the power of eminent domain, the power to float bonds, the power to set development standards and exercise land-use controls.

The regional authority shall set up new town development corporations in specific areas, with the coordination and review by the national planning

[11] The National Committee on Urban Growth Policy, including The National Association of Counties, The National League of Cities, The United States Conference of Mayors, and Urban America, Inc. (Donald Canty, ed.), *The New City* (New York: Frederick A. Praeger, 1969).

agency. Location policies shall be supported by federal tax incentives (see French experience), by local tax concessions, by financial incentives for new job creation and job training programs, the building of new transportation facilities (such as airports or highways), and the coordinated development of planned communities in the area.

2. **National economic development planning policy, coordinated with national urban-growth planning (1.) authorizing new federally-supported financing mechanisms (National Development Bank) and required to produce four-year comprehensive development plans.**

National economic development planning has become a useful tool in many countries all over the world to achieve specific development goals. So far, the United States has only had an annual budget to fulfill this need. However, especially in connection with nationally organized urban growth and development, more long-range plans must be made (and updated annually) on a comprehensive basis: coordinating physical and social development with economic goals. This would greatly strengthen all private economic activity and productiveness and is a *sine qua non* for a rational new town development policy for the public good.

The location and spatial distribution of new industrial development, new business, and new urban development must be organized to fit into the framework of the national-growth plans and national anti-pollution legislation to qualify for federal support. Private business and industry has everything to gain from better spatial coordination between resources and markets and from protection against losses beyond the control of individual enterprise but under the control of regional development agencies. Each new town corporation shall be publicly controlled and funded. Under certain conditions, private new town developers or nonprofit corporations may become sponsors of new communities. Comprehensive, multidisciplinary planning and management teams shall incorporate economic (financial), social (see item 3.), and physical (see item 4.) planning and shall be responsible for the execution of their plans and for the management of the new towns until each permanent new-town administration takes over (see item 5.).

A *National Development Bank* shall be created to directly finance new town corporations on a nonprofit basis, with low-interest (1 to 3 per cent) loans, upon recommendation by the regional development corporation. Regional infrastructure to support new town development shall also be directly financed by the National Development Bank with participation and review by the regional development agency. The National Development Bank shall have the power to grant long-range development loans to private nonprofit sponsors at minimum interest,[12] provided their plans meet specific needs in the area (for instance, building of housing for low-income people) and meet urban design, environmental quality, and other standards, and the sponsors can demonstrate competence in carrying out their plans.

The National Development Bank shall have the power to set up regional branches in specific areas where development activities are concentrated (such as the building of several new towns), with the power to finance infrastructure, housing, and public facilities on a nonprofit basis (rotating loans) in the new towns.

The new town corporations shall be the owners in perpetuity of the land within and around the new towns which they may lease for up to 99 years to private developers subject to periodic renegotiation. Certain areas surrounding the new towns shall be jointly controlled by the regional body and the new towns and kept out of development to provide green space and recreation. The appreciation of land values of the new towns as a result of public investments (transportation, infrastructure, water supply, sewers, etc.) shall accrue to the new-town corporation and after repayment of loans shall be used to finance public facilities, services, and housing on a continuing basis. Long-term leases (for twenty years or more) may be arranged for homes as well as commercial and other facilities.

3. Software development: government, administrative, institutional, and social service; planning, programming, and management.

Software is the invisible part of new town organization, yet the part of the package that determines everything else, including what a new town will look like and how it will work. "Software," or the underlying organizational framework, is the most important component of new town planning that will require a great deal of study and must be flexible to accommodate variety and change. Here it is only possible to outline in general terms the framework of what is needed, as little work has been done in this area, where new ideas and new approaches must be sought.[13]

[12] See IDA (International Development Agency) structure of International Bank of Reconstruction and Development. IDA extends interest-free loans over fifty years under special conditions.

[13] The present approach to new-town building and legislation in the United States completely ignores this all-important area and simply imposes the new physical construction onto a nineteenth-century institutional organization that cannot deal with it. Though some new towns have sought innovations, for instance, in education, very little has been done anywhere to experiment with or initiate something new, especially on the social, governmental, or citizen-participation level. Some new-town plans have attempted to outline innovations in the software area; for instance, the June 1968 New Communities Project by the Graduate School of Design at Harvard and the Minnesota Experi-

Software is the programming of all the administrative, institutional, educational, and social service systems of new towns and their continuous innovation and management. In the software planning, true variety expressing the plurality of our society must be sought. Flexibility is the name of the game. Flexible physical arrangements to house the institutional and service network should support innovation and change (instead of, as now, inhibiting anything new).

New towns offer the possibility to try out new administrative and service systems. Service is the foremost responsibility of modern government, and every effort should be made to allow maximum choice—yet safeguarding the interests of those of limited means. For example, health services which economically depend on participation by many people, should be an integral part of the service package for each new town inhabitant, the same as other services that we take for granted, such as street cleaning or water supply, and not be an option separately financed, as in Columbia, for instance.

New towns most of all are an invitation to launch innovation in education that has often been impossible to implement over the objection of existing immovable bureaucracies. School buildings should take over multiple functions, including community, recreation, and some shopping and cultural facilities: simply to pay for the buildings and keep them open and "alive" every day and the year round.

That is, the activities, the programs, the services, the software contents of a new town will determine the form of the town, the hardware (buildings and infrastructure), and vice versa.

A variety of different "environments" should be planned as part and parcel of each town—allowing future inhabitants to choose. Some real alternative should be considered, especially for young people who prefer different life styles, to give them an opportunity to experiment constructively, for instance, with communal living patterns and cooperatives, instead of being persecuted for expressing their new ideas. Throughout history, a variety of living patterns have been practiced by different population groups. There is no reason to continue to adhere to one-sided, rigid Western nuclear family and community patterns in a plural, industrial society—especially since these traditional living patterns, based on individualism and highly competitive social concepts backed up by competitive economic concepts, are being rejected by many young people now. New forms and new building technologies are available to express different social, including cooperative, concepts and

---

mental City (see Bibliography). New towns in Europe or in other parts of the world have also ignored this opportunity for innovation. The literature, however, is replete with social, economic, and political utopias; none of them has been given physical form by their creators. The new towns in Israel perhaps come closest in combining social, political, and physical innovation.

ideas. The "kibbutzim" in Israel is one recent example of expressing different social organizations in a new physical environment. The building of new towns offers many exciting new possibilities in this area.

Certainly the most important subject is that of social services. Public housing has become an appalling failure in the United States, in terms of providing a stable home as a base for upward mobility, while in other countries it has succeeded. The basic difference is that public housing abroad has always provided multiple social services, including family counselling, homemaking, youth services of every kind, health services and health education, day-care centers and nursery schools, community and recreation services, job counselling and job training, and more. Congress eliminated social services as "unnecessary frills" from the housing legislation shortly after it was passed (in the 1930's). We are seeing the terrible results now.

The current federal new town legislation once more repeats this mistake. While new town development abroad (in literally every country, including some developing countries, for instance, Venezuela and certainly Israel), has taken the software approach—starting with planning of social services for new town inhabitants. This is especially so in free-standing new towns planned away from existing urban centers to initiate and support new regional growth (see item 1.), where an adequate service and community development component is essential to create social stability.

A social and community service component shall be funded by the development bank (see Item 2.). It is the responsibility of each new town corporation or each new town developer (private or nonprofit) to plan such services and facilities into the new town and provide for their operation on a continuing basis. Innovations in software shall be separately funded and special grants shall be available for research and planning—prior to or concomitantly with the funding of the economic and physical planning of the new town.

4. Hardware development: infrastructure, transportation, and building systems; planning, production, and management.

Hardware is concerned with all the physical planning and building: the coordination with the national and regional transportation network (air, highway, railroad), the road system and internal transportation, infrastructure (water, sewers, electricity, gas, etc.), and finally the actual building of houses, apartments, schools, offices, educational, community, and public buildings of all kinds.

A rationalized systems-building approach is the most viable answer in terms of building a new environment in a given time at a reasonable price. A systems approach and innovative new building technologies are available for every type of building. But because of building codes, union regulations, and other restrictions, they often are not used.

Systems building, utilizing industrial methods, means taking advantage of the new technology and management techniques which industry has developed to increase productivity. A systems approach to building means dissecting an actual structure into components and mass producing the components in a plant, on or off the building site, year round under controlled conditions. This saves a great deal of labor on the site and makes building far less dependent on weather, besides offering year-round employment under better conditions.

But the building industry, subject to outmoded regulations, codes, and union rules, has obstructed most innovations. Building new towns and housing on a large scale will increase the demand for building labor so much that it will be necessary to introduce new methods and change. Many more people who need not have the "craft" skills can be employed. There is a great opportunity for much minority employment in the new system-component plants. The pressure to produce faster and more will not only introduce new rational labor practices, but also new building codes, new building materials, and it will change the whole obsolete building industry. In the discussion of Industrialized Building Systems, the technical aspects and the European experience—which are far ahead of the United States—are outlined.

The employment of building systems should provide opportunity in the United States to create a more flexible and varied environment of high quality. Experience has shown that good design and investment in high-quality construction are not only essential in terms of preserving financial investments, but are also the best means to attract people to new towns. The urban design and environmental quality of a new town can be most effective in assuring its success and will become identified with "new." The influence of beauty in our environment has been ignored so long that positive design identification and real innovation in design can become a most effective advocate of new towns. Many different people's needs will be served by the creation of a variety of different environments, instead of adopting the lowest common denominator, as is the case with most suburban developments. Variety without increasing costs is possible when using building systems.

A more rational approach to all hardware development is technically feasible, including mechanical systems and road construction as well as more flexible transportation systems. In the past this has not only been neglected but made impossible to realize by small-scale construction, by obsolete safety and labor practices, and by fractionalized production methods. The demand to build and produce on a large scale will result in innovations in infrastructure and technical systems, transportation, communication, and more. Many possible technical innovations in our everyday urban environment are not made because the resistance to changing existing practices is too great, or the opportunity does not exist. New town building is an opportunity to use the new technology we have for the benefit of many people and to initiate new methods and new policies.

5. Citizen Participation.

A viable framework for citizen participation is most difficult to organize: because new communities and towns are planned and partly built before any of the inhabitants are on the scene.

One possible approach is to arrange for community groups to work as consultants with the developers. Another is to conduct opinion polls among the citizens' groups of roughly the same economic and social composition as those anticipated to move into the new communities. A cross-section of people from all income groups should be questioned by social research organizations experienced in that field. One difficulty with all polls is that most people's opinions are based on what they know from the past, and few are able to visualize anything new, especially concerning their environment.

A framework of participation in the decision-making process, once new town inhabitants are beginning to settle in their new environment, should be organized from the start. Eventually, the experience of the first new town inhabitants can be used for future ones, as well as research from the experience of new town inhabitants abroad. Social research consultants shall be part of the new town planning from the start.

Citizen participation in relation to the innovations of the governmental and institutional framework of new communities is a difficult problem where very little work has been done. Yet an administrative framework, safeguarding the democratic participation of future residents, must be set up first.

In the few new communities that have been built so far in the United States, there has been virtually no innovation. The new town administration is organized within the existing local and county governments, for instance, in Columbia or Reston. The experience around the world has shown that the opportunity to innovate and to create more responsive systems of participatory democracy has been entirely ignored.

The model cities legislation in the United States, for instance, Boston, has resulted in broadly based citizen participation; its methods should be researched and applied in new communities. Local government in the United States in general has been unresponsive to citizens' demands and needs.

> Neither central city nor suburban governments now afford an adequate civic experience. They restrict the meaningful political participation from which such experience is gained, and they are poorly designed to manage conflict. Most local governments were organized for administrative housekeeping. They are based on politically antiseptic assumptions of human behavior and are equipped to deal with routine matters, not major questions of public policy.[14]

New towns, however, in the opinion of many could and should do better:

Participation in all phases of new-town development can be anticipated and provided for from the beginning rather than being grafted onto a possibly hostile system as an afterthought or as a concession to pressures. The objective is to cultivate competent citizenship that identifies with the new town and shares public responsibility for its development both before it is built and after it has been inhabited. Because the development of the town is perceived as being in the public interest and because it affects a large segment of the population, it has a chance of engaging more citizens than do projects which are more limited in scope.

*   *   *

The opportunity for creative political experience is enhanced by the fact that most new towns have no civic history or traditions, no inherited or established power elite, and consequently lack any well-defined rules for the game of civic conduct.[15]

But to date little innovative experimentation exists, though the pragmatic route seems best. Experimentation with citizen participation is generally viewed as being too risky by private developers. Therefore this will have to be publicly supported in the publicly-sponsored new-town corporations.

CONCLUSION

Finally, it must be said that this outline is but an attempt to conceptualize one possible framework of new town organization, with the purpose to safeguard the public interest and to take new towns out of the speculative area, where they clearly don't belong. New town building is too important to allow this to be taken over by a few powerful developers who can control enormous funds and therefore the lives of millions of people.

New towns offer the unique opportunity to physically support and implement social change, and most of all to remedy the mistakes of our present cities, the terrible social burdens of racial discrimination and poverty, by creating new open cities based on social justice and equal opportunity.

There are many possibilities for organizing the building of new towns. In essence it means devising and initiating new processes of continuous change. The failures of our cities and our man-made environment in no small part derive from the rigidity of our institutions and physical arrangements and

---

[14] *New Towns: Laboratories for Democracy* (Report of the Twentieth Century Fund, Task Force on Governance of New Towns) (New York: The Twentieth Century Fund, 1971). Quote is from Background Paper by Royce Hanson, p. 57.

[15] *Ibid.,* pp. 60, 66.

their inability to deal with change. The framework outlined here hopefully is a flexible process that is open-ended and can change continuously with pragmatic experience.

After this chapter was written, the Report of the Commission on Population Growth and the American Future[16] was published. The findings and conclusions of this important report support in every way the suggestions made here, which are a logical outcome of how to deal with population growth. However, as the Commission also points out, population control is a *sine qua non* in order to achieve a better quality of life and environment—quite aside from effectively dealing with pollution. The report also urges that objectives and criteria for national growth distribution policies should be established and ties in directly with the recommendations of the National Commmittee on Urban Growth Policy, and with Title VII of the Housing and Urban Development Act of 1970.[17]

Finally, the building of a new environment offers an opportunity to express new values, new social forms, and new behavioral patterns and a variety of new ways of life which are especially desired by the young. Indeed, a new environment offers much constructive opportunity to experiment and to abandon some of the outdated social practices that are "built-in" and that do a great deal of harm. B.F. Skinner in *Beyond Freedom and Dignity*[18] points out that science and technology have developed a truly scientific approach of dealing with the physical environment, but we are lacking a comparable technology of behavior, which has not progressed much beyond the old Greeks. New concepts of science were attacked unmercifully as "heresy" when they threatened the tenets of the established view of the world in the Renaissance and later. Much in the same way, Professor Skinner's suggestions that we should develop a scientific approach to behavioral problems and that we must learn an effective behavioral technology are attacked by people of all established political and scientific views. Yet it is clear that our behavior is seriously threatening our survival on earth.

From an economic point of view, the building of new towns offers many very profitable investment opportunities to business, as well as a whole range of creative ways to channel economic growth in non-polluting yet productive ways. While large investment opportunities have been shrinking overseas and have become more and more hazardous politically and economically, the opportunities for major and creative innovation here at home in the neglected fields of housing and environment have so far been overlooked by business. Also, business has lacked consistent positive government support in the environmental field.

[16] Donald Canty, ed., *The New City.*
[17] The 1970 Urban Growth and New Community Development Act.
[18] B.F. Skinner, *Beyond Freedom and Dignity* (New York: Alfred Knopf, 1971).

The demands and needs in this area have built up for many years in all income groups. The investments in a house and in transportation—that is, a car—or shelter and related needs—are still the largest investments of any one family. To build new towns or many new towns and "environments for living" could have a major impact on the economy of the United States if properly structured and supported.

Experience has shown that valorization, the increase in land values due to urbanization, can finance all the necessary investments as outlined in the discussion "Urbanization and Economic Growth in Developing Countries," as well as here under "III. The Experience: United States and International." That is, in the long range valorization can amply support all the physical building and infrastructure, as well as the software planning and programming, management, and maintenance. What remains to be done is to organize more specific methods and mechanisms, especially as far as financing is concerned. The excuse, "We cannot afford it," no longer exists. Specific economic models which should be devised for given areas will prove the viability of this approach. One such program for the eastern seaboard was outlined in a paper prepared for the 2020 Conference of the American Institute of Planners (A.I.P.) by Dr. David Wallace.[19]

In the context of restructuring the U.S. economy to successfully compete with other industrial nations in the world market, the building of a supportive, well-functioning physical and social environment, including decent housing—that is, new towns—should be given priority. Productivity in the United States has recently seriously lagged behind other nations, while industrial wages continue to increase. In 1971, the United States incurred the largest balance of payments deficit in its financial history. The largest part of each family's income goes to pay for shelter, but the cost of shelter has recently increased all out of proportion. By reducing the cost of shelter, industrial wages can be brought into line, and U.S. production would again be able to compete successfully in the world market. Besides, a more efficiently planned physical environment would enhance profits as well as wages by reducing waste, such as excessive transportation and commuting costs.

Therefore, the building of a new environment on a large enough scale will not only create a great economic upturn and millions of new jobs but it will also subsidize the entire industrial production of the country, change the deteriorating position of the United States in the world market, and make

[19] David Wallace, "A Practical Utopia for the Region." Paper delivered at the 2020 Conference, Waldorf-Astoria Hotel, January 30-31, 1969. A comprehensive regional urbanization study for the Eastern Seaboard. One of the most imaginative, yet practical, proposals to achieve quality and urbanization, including an economic feasibility study. To obtain this paper, write to A.I.P., Mr. William Ewald, Jr., Program Chairman, 1555 Connecticut Avenue, N.W., Washington, D.C. 20036.

U.S. exports once more competitive. Many other industrialized countries, by supporting housing for the majority of their workers, are in fact doing this. By building a whole new urban environment, the United States, with much greater resources, can do this on a much larger and more effective scale.

The building of new towns is the greatest challenge that faces the United States in the last quarter of the twentieth century, because it is the one area where our society has so far completely failed, though success is entirely within our grasp. To adapt our immensely successful technology to the basic human needs of creating a decent, life-supporting environment of quality and beauty for all citizens is not only possible, but it is one way to implement a new creative process of change, and assure economic success and a better life for all.

BIBLIOGRAPHY

University of Minnesota Experimental City Project, School of Architecture, University of Minnesota, Minneapolis, Minnesota. Bibliography of new towns prepared in 1969.
This is the most complete bibliography on new towns.
Write to HUD, Washington, D.C. 20410, for information on the new communities that they have underwritten.

BOOKS

Benevolo, Leonard. *The Origins of Modern Town Planning.* Cambridge, Mass.: The MIT Press, 1971. Paperback.
A historic survey of town planning.
Berler, Alexander. *New Towns in Israel.* Jerusalem: Israel Universities Press, 1970.
A technical study of new towns in Israel.
Canty, Donald, ed. *The New City.* New York: Frederick A. Praeger, 1969. (Report of The National Committee on Urban Growth Policy, including The National Association of Counties, The National League of Cities, The U.S. Conference of Mayors, and Urban America, Inc.)
A summary of the findings of the above organizations and an evaluation of the British new-town experience.
Clapp, James A. *New Towns and Urban Policy.* New York: Dunellen Publishing Company, 1971.
An academic study of new town development with emphasis on the United States.
Doxiadis, Constantinos A. *Ekistics.* New York: Oxford University Press, 1968.
A far-reaching, comprehensive study of a completely new scientific approach to town planning done by a multidisciplinary team under the leadership and inspiration of Doxiadis.

Entwistle, Clive. *Holopolis, Systemic Sketches of a New Whole World.* New York: The Macmillan Company, to be published in 1973.
An ingenious, far-reaching proposal of a complete reorganization of our physical environment.

Fuller, Richard Buckminster. *I Seem to be a Verb.* New York: Bantam Books, 1970. Paperback.
A most imaginative evaluation of the fractured urban life. Fuller has published and continues to publish many books outlining the many new ideas of his fertile mind.

———. *Operating Manual for Spaceship Earth.* Carbondale and Edwardsville, Ill.: Southern Illinois University Press, 1969.
A most important summary of Fuller's philosophy.

Geddes, Patrick. *Cities in Evolution.* London: Williams and Norgate Ltd., 1949.
A classic by one of the foremost proponents of town planning, originally published in 1915.

Goodman, Paul and Percival. *Communitas. Means and Livelihood and Ways of Life.* New York: Vintage Books, a Division of Random House, 1960. Paperback.
A most imaginative proposal of alternative new communities seen by one of the foremost social critics of our time and his brother, an architect.

Hilberseimer, L. *The New City: Principles of Planning.* Chicago: Paul Theobald, 1944.
The forward-looking ideas of a former member of the Bauhaus who worked with Mies van der Rohe.

Howard, Ebenezer. *Garden Cities of Tomorrow.* Cambridge Mass.: The MIT Press, 1965. Paperback.
The classic book of all times on new towns, first published in 1898.

Isaacs, Reginald. *Gropius and the City* (tentative title. New York: New York Graphic Society, first volume to be published in 1973.

Kettaneh, Anthony, ed. *Project Romulus: An Adaptable High Density Urban Prototype.* Cambridge, Mass.: The MIT Press, 1968. (M.I.T. Report # 12.)
An excellent study of a new-town proposal by a multidisciplinary team from M.I.T., including engineers and economists.

Le Corbusier. *The Radiant City.* New York: The Orion Press, 1967.
A summary of Le Corbusier's city and town planning ideas, using specific cities worldwide. Le Corbusier's visionary genius in the area of city planning is still far ahead of our time.

McHale, John R. *Buckminster Fuller.* New York: George Braziller, 1962.

Newman, Oscar. *CIAM '59 in Otterlo. Group for the Research of Social and Visual Inter-Relationships.* London: Alec Tiranti Ltd., 1961.
The summary of the CIAM (Congres Internationaux d'Architecture Moderne) work and ideas on city planning.

Safdie, Moshe. *Beyond Habitat.* (John Kettle, ed.). Cambridge, Mass.: The MIT Press, 1970.
The creator of Habitat looks into the future and explains his far-reaching ideas.

Sert, J.S. *Can Our Cities Survive? An ABC of Urban Problems,* Their Analysis, Their Solutions. Cambridge, Mass.: The Harvard University Press, 1942.

A classic study based on the proposals formulated by the CIAM (Congrès Internationaux d'Architecture Moderne). This is a study of cities and urban development that has become most influential and has much to offer even now.

Skinner, B.F. *Walden Two.* New York: The Macmillan Co., 1967. Paperback.

–––. *Beyond Freedom and Dignity.* New York: Alfred Knopf, 1971.

Spiegel, Erika. *New Towns in Israel.* Stuttgart/Bern: Karl Krämer, 1966.

An excellent bilingual study of the new towns in Israel. Republished in English in the United States by Praeger.

Stein, C.S. *Towards New Towns for America.* Cambridge, Mass.: The MIT Press, 1966. Paperback.

A classic reprint of one of the original new-town designers.

Tyrwhitt, J., Sert, J.A., and Rogers, E.N., eds. *The Heart of the City: Toward the Humanization of Urban Life.*

PERIODICALS

AIP Journal, 917 15th Street, N.W., Washington, D.C. 20005. Write for articles on new towns which appear from time to time.

The Architectural Forum, 130 East 59th Street, New York, N.Y. 10022. See especially January-February 1972, "The World of Buckminster Fuller," pp. 49 ff.

City. Published bimonthly by the National Urban Coalition, 2100 M Street, Washington, D.C. 20037.

Ekistics. Published by the Athens Center of Ekistics, Box 471, Athens, Greece. Write for information on the annual Ekistics meetings in July and new reading material from the Ekistics Library.

Journal of the Royal Planning Institute. Published by the Royal Town Planning Institute, 26 Portland Place, London W1N 4BE, England.

Progressive Architecture, 600 Summer Street, Stamford, Conn. 06904.

Town and Country Planning. The Journal of the Town and Country Planning Association, 17 Carlton House Terrace, London SW1Y 5AS, England.

ARTICLES

Breckenfeld, Gurney. "Housing Subsidies: A Grand Delusion. *Fortune,* February 1972, pp. 136 ff.

"Dun and Bradstreet Among 50 Named in Housing Fraud." *New York Times,* March 30, 1972, pp. 1 ff.

Hartnett, Ken. "The U.S. as Slumlord." *The New Republic,* December 11, 1971, pp. 11-13.

Herbers, John. "Federal Housing Aid Stirs Widening Debate." *New York Times,* January 3, 1972.

———. "Housing and Government: Official Criticism of Subsidy Program is Growing." *New York Times,* February 1, 1972, p. 27.

———. "U.S. Now Big Landlord in Decaying Inner City." *New York Times,* January 2, 1972.

Hosken, Fran P. "Are new towns a cure for our urban ills?" *Christian Science Monitor,* September 17, 1971.

———. "New Cities for People." *Christian Science Monitor,* January 25-27, 1969.

———. "A New Town Within London." *St. Louis Post-Dispatch,* March 1, 1970.

———. "New Towns in U.S. and Europe." *Architecture Canada,* November 1969, pp. 44-50.

———. "Our Cities of Tomorrow." *Boston Herald-Traveler,* January 7, 1968, pp. 7-18.

———. "Paris Points the Way in Planning." *Boston Herald-Traveler,* February 23, 1970, p. 24.

———. "People, not bricks, make a new town." *Christian Science Monitor.* December 31, 1971, p. 11.

———. "Suburbs Have an Obligation." *Boston Herald Traveler,* February 8, 1969, p. 4.

———. "Tomorrow's Cities Today." *Boston Herald Traveler,* February 23, 1969.

McQuade, Walter. "An Assembly-Line Answer to the Housing Crisis." *Fortune Magazine,* May 1, 1969, pp. 99-104.

"New Towns of the Paris Region" (in French). *Techniques et Architecture,* November 1970. 25 av. de l'Europe, 92-Sevres, France.

"Systems Building: What it Really Means." *Architectural Record,* January 1969, pp. 147-154.

"Villes Nouvelles" (in French). *L'Architecture d'aujourd'hui.* # 146. October-November 1969. 5, rue Bartholdi, 92-Boulogne, France.

van Eckhardt, Wolf. "Building Crisis." Eight articles from the *Washington Post,* October 27-November 4, 1968.

PAPERS AND REPORTS

American Institute of Architects Conference on New Communities, November 3-6, 1971. Papers available from: American Institute of Architects, 1785 Massachusetts Avenue, N.W., Washington, D.C. 20036.

Write also for other literature, especially their pamphlets on the National Policy Task Force.

"New Communities: One Alternative. A Harvard Study of a New City." June 1968. A New Communities Project by the Graduate School of Design, Harvard University, Cambridge, Mass., financed by HUD.

This is a comprehensive new-town study for an actual site south of Boston.

New Towns: Laboratories for Democracy. Report of the Twentieth Century Fund Task Force on Governance of New Towns. New York: Twentieth Century Fund, 1971.

A fund-supported study to formulate new administrative software approaches.

Report from the International Systems Building Round Table Conference. Held at Boston Architectural Center, November 17-19, 1971. To be published in 1972. Write to: Mr. Duncan Wilson, Boston Architectural Center, 320 Newbury Street, Boston, Mass. 02115.

Report: *Commission on Population Growth and the American Future.* Superintendent of Documents, Government Printing Office, Washington, D.C., 1972.

"Triton City: A Prototype Floating Community." Triton Foundation, Inc., Cambridge, Mass., 1968. Distributed by Clearinghouse for Federal Scientific and Technical Information, Springfield, Va. 22151.

"Urban and Rural America: Policies for Future Growth." A report by the Advisory Commission on Intergovernmental Relations, Washington, D.C. Report # A-32, U.S. Government Printing Office, 1968.
This contains a list of all new towns in the United States and a history of the new-town development to 1968, aside from other most useful information.

"Urban Growth and New Communities Development Act of 1970." Approved 12-31-70, Public Law 91-609. For a copy write: HUD, Washington, D.C. 20410.

Wallace, David. "A Practical Utopia for the Region." Paper delivered at the 2020 Conference, Waldorf-Astoria Hotel, January 30-31, 1969.
A comprehensive regional urbanization study for the eastern seaboard. One of the most imaginative, yet practical, proposals to achieve quality and urbanization, including an economic feasibility study.

Weissbourd, Bernard, and Channick, Herbert. "An Urban Strategy." Santa Barbara, Calif., Center for the Study of Democratic Institutions (Box 4068). From *The Center Magazine* I, 6, September, 1968.
This "Strategy" report suggests a method to achieve integration by building new communities.

For more information on recent publication of new-town articles consult any professional architectural library of a university or architecture school. This bibliography is not comprehensive but only can mention some of the foremost literature that has been used specifically as a resource for this new-town proposal.